T0383133

Developing a Poly-Chronic Care Network

An Engineered, Community-Wide Approach to Disease Management

Pierce Story, MPHM

CRC Press
Taylor & Francis Group
Boca Raton London New York

CRC Press is an imprint of the
Taylor & Francis Group, an **informa** business

A PRODUCTIVITY PRESS BOOK

CRC Press
Taylor & Francis Group
6000 Broken Sound Parkway NW, Suite 300
Boca Raton, FL 33487-2742

Printed in the United States of America on acid-free paper
Version Date: 2012924

International Standard Book Number: 978-1-4665-5474-0 (Hardback)

Library of Congress Cataloging-in-Publication Data

Story, Pierce.
    Developing a poly-chronic care network : an engineered, community-wide approach to disease management / Pierce Story.
        p. ; cm.
    Includes bibliographical references and index.
    ISBN 978-1-4665-5474-0 (hardback : alk. paper)
    I. Title.
    [DNLM: 1. Chronic Disease--therapy. 2. Community Networks. 3. Delivery of Health Care, Integrated. 4. Patient Care Management. 5. Program Development. WT 500]

    616'.0478--dc23   2012035128

Visit the Taylor & Francis Web site at
http://www.taylorandfrancis.com

and the CRC Press Web site at
http://www.crcpress.com

Contents

Preface

Kenji's Dilemma

Kenji was frustrated. It should have been so much easier, so much faster. The changes he expected to see weren't there. He found himself trying more and more often to prove to his boss that his efforts were, or perhaps would, have an impact on the bottom line. Though he could see, even sense, the change that had taken place, the CFO couldn't count it, so it might as well not be happening.

It had been almost three years since the dream he had while sleeping in a metal chair in an emergency department (ED) waiting room rattled his cage. That dream, that nightmare, had stirred something deep inside him that made him leave the world he'd known since college, his manufacturing comfort zone, and step out into a whole new world of healthcare. The work was different, very different, from anything he'd seen in a factory. The intense work of analysis, the preaching, teaching, begging, and arguing for every minor incremental improvement, all seemed worth it when he started. But now he was beginning to wonder.

His son, the reason for his late-night visit to the crowded ED on that fateful rainy night, was so proud of him when he announced that he was leaving the Toyota plant that had been so good to him and his family. Toyota treated its employees well, and there was never any real threat of unionization in this traditional Southern town with its ingrained work ethic.

It was therefore a tough choice—one that would see a cut in his pay, benefits, and career progress—but one he never questioned.

Though healthcare was new and very different, what he'd seen made him initially believe that it was a world he could fix. Change was to have come easily and swiftly, given how broken the system seemed to be. He'd suspected that even small improvements should show up as huge benefits. His long history of change management in manufacturing assured him that he could lead his new employer to a higher level of sophistication and productivity.

His new job at the local hospital, secured by interviews set up through well-connected neighbors in his subdivision, was to "fix it." "It," as it turns out, was just about everything. The emergency department was "broken," which was apparently hospital lingo for "completely and totally dysfunctional." The operating room (OR) was mostly run, or rather lorded over, by a small cadre of politically powerful surgeons who seemed to hold the chief executive officer (CEO) in the palms of their hands. What they asked for they generally received. What they didn't like generally did not happen. And they didn't like Kenji's ideas.

In his manufacturing days, if the paint line was slowed down, it impacted everything upstream. This was both intolerable and quickly fixed. Kaizen teams would descend on the problem area like gulls to a clam, picking at it until the problem was solved. The upstream work cells would be as demanding as the downstream bottleneck cell, since everyone's compensation and/or bonus was, in some way, tied to the productivity of the whole plant, not just their particular cell. All worked together as a unified army, bent on the absolute annihilation of any and all waste and inefficiency, no matter where the root cause lay.

Kenji sat at his desk in his stark, windowless basement office, just down the hall from his hospital's purchasing department and linen services. Here, surrounded by whiteboard covered with scatterings of ideas and process maps, he thought about his "good old days." He smiled wryly as he thought back to the project one of his teams had undertaken at Toyota to ensure that the men's room near section 45 was cleaned more regularly. Within a few hours of working with the janitorial staff, they had literally value-stream mapped the entire bathroom cleaning process, 5S'd the cleaning carts, and scheduled the workload to allow the janitors to clean the bathrooms when it would do the most good. Quick work, quick solution, even if to a very minor problem. The janitors were, at first, too shell-shocked to argue, and frankly didn't care much about it until they realized how much easier their work actually had become. They walked less, accomplished more in the same amount of time, and were even given the incentive of an extra thirty minutes of break time at lunch if "customer satisfaction" (i.e., men's room users) scores remained high. Ironic, he thought, that similar results on a similar project at the hospital might take months to come to fruition. And, as Kenji thought back, he was pretty darned sure that his old boss never challenged the financial significance of *that* project. It was never about the finances. It was about the workers—his friends, neighbors, and fellow citizens—at the plant.

He snapped back out of his stroll down memory lane to look around his office. Value-stream maps of the ED. A Kaizen event that planned for discharge processing. A 5S in the cardiac care unit (CCU). It struck him again, as it had months before—that both the problem and the solution lay in these many projects. It wasn't the projects themselves that were the problem. Had this been his factory, these would lead to improvements, to some degree. They had potential to do the same at his hospital, too. Here, though, the projects were all *individual, isolated* projects that would likely not lead to the massive, systemic improvements his boss wanted. Rather, they would lead to siloed impacts that often created more problems than they solved, assuming they actually solved anything substantial. Oh sure, he could fix ED triage, as long as there was physician capacity to see more patients when the boluses arrived into the main ED from the triage area. Those were the simple projects. But the downstream, external department silos—well, that's another story.

The silos. Hah! More like fortresses! They were fortresses armed with archers and cannons and boiling oil to ward off any change agents who might try to enter from another, equally hardened fortress. Worse, each silo had its own internal issues that made changing one risk negatively impacting another. This made the second throw up its defenses against any changes within *and* without. Even if he could penetrate them all at once, as he'd been trying to do for the past three years, he wasn't sure that he could piece together the entire system into a coherent picture and a systemic, quantifiable goal. It changed so much from day to day, week to week, month to seasonal month. This constant change and the constant battles between fortresses made him feel like a man in a huge field chasing rabbits. The minute he got close to one, it would dive into a hole and pop up somewhere else in the field. He could never catch up. All his Lean training did not prepare him for such a crazy, chaotic world.

Not that he wasn't trying everything he knew to try. To help with grasping and analyzing the complexity of the system he was trying to fix, he'd put in a purchase request for a simulation tool that he'd seen at a healthcare conference. He'd seen a presentation by another management engineer who'd used a simulation software package called Arena to replicate the flow of a patient through the entire hospital. Wouldn't *that* be cool, he'd thought. He researched the simulation vendors, and chose the most popular one on the market, in part because they were so supportive of the industrial engineering schools and societies, and in part because it was used by the presenter's team. Alas, however, his Arena software purchase request was buried somewhere on his boss' desk awaiting next year's budget cycle. Maybe he'd see a license in eleven or so months. Like a carpenter without a good hammer, he'd have to find a way to make progress without the right tools. He scoffed, maybe if one of the orthopedists would make the request, it would be on his desk by Friday!

He shook his head and vowed, as he did every day, to march on. Just as he was about to leave for a 10.30 a.m. meeting with the nursing director on 4-west, the phone rang. It was his wife. A shiver went up his spine, just like every other time she called now that her mother was back at home instead of in the nursing home. Was today the day he'd get "the call?" The thought itself turned his stomach queasy as he reached for the phone. "Hi, baby. How are you? Can't chat but a minute or I'll be late for a meeting with Janet Savage. What's up?" he asked, hoping for a good answer.

"It's mom, honey. She's taken another turn for the worse. And I cannot get Dr. Goodall on the phone. He's off today or something. The answering service picks up every time."

"What's the problem?" he asked, while simultaneously looking at his watch and feeling guilty for doing so.

"Her weight is up another few pounds since last week. Her breathing seems more labored. At least I think, I can't remember. She says it's not, but I think it is. She doesn't look well, and she says her chest is still 'cramping,' whatever that means. I might have to take her back to the emergency department if Dr. Goodall cannot see her right away. I'll bet that's what he tells me to do anyway, if he calls back today. I think he's off. I certainly cannot figure out what's going on, and I'm no doctor."

Great, he thought. Just what his ED and Nana (as the family called her) don't need—yet another trip the ED for her chronic obstructive pulmonary disease (COPD). Or was it her asthma, or her two bum knees, or the chest pains that put her there last time? It's not like we don't know what she has! Yeah, he recalled, she was just admitted to the hospital, what, a few weeks ago for her COPD. And now she might have to go back? Is there a revolving door on this place?

Kenji knew Dr. Goodall. He was a caring physician with a soul of gold. He was very near retirement (assuming, he routinely joked, the government lets him and his portfolio doesn't hit zero). But he was still seeing a full load of patients. He worked "the old fashioned way," the way a lot of docs still do—a lot of hours, a lot of rounding and phone calls after hours, a lot of early mornings and long weekends. He was one of those who had medicine in his blood since he was a kid. And, good or bad, he was still a believer that medicine was 70 percent art and 30 percent science. In other words, this was not a doc who would be using a computer-based algorithm to help create a care plan.

Yet, for all his commitment, the system wasn't supporting him well. His small office staff was a dedicated group that worked hard to take care of his patients. But they too struggled. Both their antiquated computer systems and the latest software gave them regular fits. Dr. Goodall chased specialists for opinions, while the specialists chased down results of someone else's last lab orders. Kenji's mother-in-law was not well, so she saw a lot of doctors in the community, and was a classic example of the complexities of disjointed care delivery. None of them seemed to communicate with each other, at least not readily or easily. It seemed such a struggle just to get a coherent set of instructions for one of her conditions, let alone all of them. Worst of all, he thought, they always seem to take time off when Nana gets sick.

Of course, his mother-in-law was often her own worst enemy. Compliance was a foreign word, one that meant little or nothing. Inconsistency and stubbornness were more characteristic than following directions. She was just not a good patient. She cancelled as many appointments as she kept, which meant her care was sporadic at best. Small wonder her conditions were so hard to treat, or that one of her specialists had threatened to stop seeing her.

And talk about fortresses! There were so many it was hard to count them all—the specialists, the offices, the hospital, the clinics, Medicaid. How many phone calls had his wife made from her office, during breaks or her lunch hour, to try to get answers that should be readily available?

Perhaps most concerning about Dr. Goodall was his imminent retirement. It was a mystery where his patients, especially Nana, would go when he left his practice at year's end. None of the other docs in the area were taking new Medicaid patients, which meant his wife's beloved mother might not have a primary care physician (PCP). Without Dr. Goodall's tender and forgiving spirit, who would put up with Nana and her crazy attitude?

"Should I just go ahead and take her in, honey? She's not going to get better sitting at home alone. And I can't take off work tomorrow because I have a board meeting to attend. Today is the only day I have to wait in the ED. She's got no one else, and nowhere else to go." And wait she would, he thought. If only his employee status could jump her to the front of the ED line, like a Platinum Club membership on an airline. She was, after all, a frequent user! "I dunno. What's she like?"

"Alone. Confused. Stubborn. Just like every other day. Baby, I just don't see that I have a choice. How bad is the wait today?"

He wished he could tell her, and he should be able to, but he didn't have the first clue. "What else *can* you do, baby? Take her in, I guess. I just wish the doc would see her first."

Kenji left for his meeting with the unit manager, knowing where Nana would be within the next eight hours—probably on Janet's unit. Then, back out of the hospital to cycle back through again. There had to be a better way, he thought.

As he walked the long hallways and climbed the stairs to the fourth floor of the aging facility, he passed a window that looked out onto the center of his small town. He paused there and thought about his Nana, who was only one of many elderly in the area. She was blessed to have him and his wife to help tend to her needs. Many were not so fortunate, yet he had a suspicion that there was more that could be done.

As he walked on after his short pause at the window, he thought of the folks in this community. The entrenched organizations, like the local Elks, the Lions club, and the small YMCA that had just been renovated. Seems there was a church for every ten residents around here. And a lot of health problems occurred every hour of every day that his hospital would never see or know about, probably because his hospital was its own fortress. Certainly, new ideas could not penetrate its hardened walls. He knew that, with his siloed focus on the individual fortresses within this hospital he'd never even begin to understand all the complexities that lay just outside the doors in the surrounding medical community. He wondered, is it as chaotic and inefficient there as it is here? Surely it's better out there. Yet, based on Nana's experience, he knew otherwise.

He began to consider the problems his community faced. People like Nana, with nowhere to turn but his ED and hospital, maybe a PCP if they were lucky. The problems he was facing in his hospital seemed to pale when he thought about his hospital as only a piece of the larger puzzle. An important piece, mind you, but a seemingly small piece when he considered all the care that was delivered outside these walls. Probably a thousand office visits and consults for every ED arrival. There, he thought, is a much bigger conundrum.

He began to wonder how much his hospital might actually contribute to the problem, and whether or not the hospital leadership even realized how they interact with the rest of the community. Suddenly, the problem with ED triage wait times and discharge processing began to take on a whole new meaning, one with a broader implication than just the ever-precious Press-Ganey scores. His departmental problems spilled out into the community, to Nana and everyone else in his little town. It was like a dead canary in a coal mine— a warning of the cause and effect of the issues around him that he could not yet see or impact.

As he leaned against the pale yellow concrete walls of the old hallway outside Janet's office, he realized that this was going to be far harder, and infinitely larger, than he'd ever suspected. What on earth had he gotten himself into? Was there any way to heal Nana from a hospital bed when she couldn't, or wouldn't, see her PCP when she gets back out? Suddenly, the hospital felt very small and insignificant to him.

Acknowledgments

As was stated in the first book of this series, I do not profess to have solved the world's healthcare problems. I can only humbly use the gifts with which God has seen fit to bless me to give what I can to a country and a people I care deeply about. To Him always goes the greatest gratitude, and so I thank Him for this small accomplishment.

It is also appropriate to thank the parents and family who raised and nurtured me; the friends, both near and far, who supported me; the many acquaintances who shaped my thoughts and ideas; and the enemies who curse me. From my mother, father, and brother to my good friends Phil, David, and Andrew, I have a supportive group that offers both encouragement and brutal honesty when either is required. Special thanks go out to my dearest of friends, Heather, who has been nothing short of a true blessing in my life. Through their love and support, they give me the strength and passion to carry on, just as scoffers and detractors offer me constant motivation to achieve new heights and bolder visions.

Introduction

Taming the Tail: A Focus on the Few to Benefit the Many

This is the second book in a series of publications designed to dramatically change the healthcare system in the United States and perhaps across the globe. The first, *Dynamic Capacity Management for Healthcare: Advanced Methods and Tools for Optimization* (CRC Press, 2010), was focused on developing new ways to increase, optimize, and sustain hospital capacity. In that book, the capacity of a hospital to see patients and serve its community was seen in the context of the dynamism, patterns, and outliers of communal demand. The text challenged readers to change their thinking about everything from patient flow to staffing to cost and quality, and to think *dynamically* about the systems in which they work. The premise is that, by doing so, we can more dynamically manage the capacity required to meet the ever-changing, dynamic demand from the communities we serve. This is the basis of DCAMM, or dynamic capacity analysis, matching, and management.

The first book was positively accepted by thought leaders in the industry. According to some who have read it, it is a "breath of fresh air in a room made stagnant with 'industrial' methodologies like Lean and Six Sigma." As executives and consultants realize that traditional industrial methodologies lack the necessary components to optimize complex healthcare systems, readers have seen DCAMM as an additional and powerful "tool in the bag."

Indeed, the DCAMM concepts are slowly making their way into the thinking of hospital executives and consultants who see the need for tremendous leaps in performance. More and more hospitals are beginning to adopt a dynamic view of their demand and capacity, helping them to better understand how to optimize the latter for the service of the former. Consultants, using different terminology but similar tools and concepts, are beginning to push the DCAMM concepts through their offerings. This process is indeed slow, moving only as fast as the most advanced healthcare systems can move the entire industry. But the turn is visible.

However, as powerful as the DCAMM concepts are, there is a large piece of the puzzle still missing. This was recognized and pointed out in the first book and is the reason for the need for this treatise. While DCAMM can apply to any highly variable and interdependent system, it is necessarily narrowly focused on what is, in reality, only one element in a much larger healthcare system: the hospital. But simply optimizing the performance of the hospital is, in the grander scheme of things, like optimizing the performance of the emergency department while neglecting the rest of the intrahospital system, such as inpatient bed flow. Therefore, the missing element, and the key to solving the larger and more complex issues of healthcare delivery, actually lies outside the four walls of the hospital.

Seeing the Future

Though the concepts for this current effort were initiated before 2008, even as the first book took shape, the knowledge of the need for such solutions was not new. The knowledge of the problem of systemic failure of capacity for chronic disease management certainly precedes this text. But while much has been written on the subject of chronic disease management, I have not yet encountered a specific "how to" guide for implementing a system such as the one described herein, nor have I seen a methodology quite as explicitly expressed.

For instance, in 2010, some two years after this text was initiated, the U.S. Department of Health and Human Services published its *Multiple Chronic Conditions: A Strategic Framework*,[1] which outlines concepts similar to those described herein. Indeed, when I finally ran across this publication after having completed this text, I was both amused and enthused by its direction. Though, like other such efforts, it still lacks the specifics and detailed vision of this publication, it makes clear the notion that there were and are similar thoughts in the marketplace. In fact, much of what is described in the *Strategic Framework* was already more thoroughly and specifically designed here and in the first DCAMM book. Therefore, it is with this tacit approval for the concepts described that I offer this publication as a means to advance the general discussion via a more detailed and visionary description of the future state of care delivery.

A Broken Model

The U.S. healthcare system is facing some very grim numbers, many of which have come to the forefront as the healthcare reform debate has raged on. These numbers range from the percentage of the population soon to be tapping into government-run healthcare payment systems; the percentage of Americans who are or soon will be obese; the shrinking percentage of taxpayers who will shoulder the burden of the government's massively expanding healthcare responsibility; the shrinking numbers of critical healthcare professionals, such as nurses, primary care physicians (PCPs), and other physicians; the growing costs of these same resources; the increasing demands for quality and access; and the growing percentage of patients with chronic diseases, many of which are brought on by decades of bad living, bad habits, complacency, dependency, and entitlement.

There is much wrong with the current U.S. healthcare system. Our insurance and reimbursement systems push patients into expensive care settings, hide the true costs of care and delivery, and encourage the overuse of resources. The government-instilled fee-for-service model creates perverse incentives and has been the cause of much of the system's excesses. Insurance now completely shields the ultimate user (the patient) from the true costs of the delivery of care (if it is even known, which most often is not the case), leaving patients with a false sense of a "money tree" from which all payments will flow. Government intrusion into the insurance markets has also created an environment wherein "insurance" against unexpected high costs now involves more *cost spreading* for even the most predictable of personal health choices (e.g., birth control). This in turn yields *cost shifting* from those who cannot pay or pay little to those who are forced to pay much more. Also, the legal environment adds to cost as it promotes excessive utilization and the overuse of testing, procedures, and utilization (aka "defensive medicine," which is said to use up billions each year in unnecessary costs).[2]

Furthermore, our resource costs are much higher than the rest of the world's (which makes international comparisons to our "excessive" healthcare costs somewhat of a folly). U.S. nursing salaries are the highest in the world, even without accounting for overtime pay, benefit packages, and artificial cost escalation through union-demanded nurse–patient ratios and unionized workforces. The average U.S. nurse salary is 40 percent higher than in Germany, 50 percent higher than in France, and 10 times higher than in Thailand.[3] These dramatic differences are reflected in the costs/salaries of other healthcare resources, such as technicians and pharmacists.

Likewise, our physicians (the best in the world, mind you) are the best paid in the world. Using the general practitioner as a proxy, U.S. salaries are almost 300 percent higher than in France, and again, some 10 times higher than Southeast Asia.[4]

Additionally, the traditional models of care are constructed in a sort of triangular relationship among physicians, hospitals and clinics, and the patient (assuming that the patient is even considered part of the system). This is perhaps the most expensive way to deliver care, since the bulk of the care is dependent upon the most expensive resources in the system: the hospital (with its own high resource costs) and the physician. Of course, there are outpatient settings wherein patients can receive some care. Yet these too remain largely dependent on expensive resources, and thus only change the venue of the care delivery but not the constraint or much of the cost. Perhaps the closest thing we've seen to altering this construct is the doc-in-a-box concept, in which a PCP, nurse practitioner, or similar resource sees patients in a retail setting. I've seen these in airports and large retail stores, as a quicker and less expensive alternative to the traditional physician office visit. Clever in concept, these are the beginning of the realities of the changes necessary for the future sustainability of the system. However, even these creative solutions don't deal with the most costly patients in the system, thus providing more convenience than significant cost reduction. Certainly they don't begin to tap into the vast pools of resources often readily available in the community. And it is here, within the unnoticed and untapped potential, that we will find solutions.

Importantly for this text, there is a tremendous disparity in the way healthcare funds are spent. The top ten chronic disease patients use roughly 70 percent of the healthcare spending. Indeed, the reasons that the optimization of the health system writ large is so important have much to do with the trends, costs, and financial constraints facing the U.S. and world economies vis-a-vis chronic diseases. Chronic diseases are not only painful and terrible ailments; they are stunningly expensive to treat. Cures are often simply unavailable, so patients are not expected to actually recover. One doesn't just "get over" chronic obstructive pulmonary disease (COPD). Often, the best one can hope for is to live (and die) less painfully, in better condition, and less expensively. At worst, these patients will continue to tap the system for extraordinary and rapidly growing costs and resource consumption.

It's bad enough that the U.S. baby boomers, who gave us the productivity and economic expansion of the last several decades, will soon stop working and become "wards of the state." But too many of these Americans will enter the tax-payer's care in poor and worsening health. Obesity, smoking, sedentary lifestyles, and generally poor care of the bodies they were given have led to a generally unhealthy populace. These retirees will tax the system as never before, as they are pre-dicted to generate far greater demands for care and costs than have previously been estimated.

Furthermore, our young people are also in dangerously bad health. Childhood obesity is at an all-time high[5] and continues an ugly trend toward future unnecessary health demands. The percentage of Americans smoking seems stubbornly stuck at the 20–22 percent level, despite the billions spent on cessa-tion and education. Look around and you'll see that the young smoke more than we'd like. This means that our youth are not going to slow the pace of care demand as they age since the likelihood of long-term chronic disease is increasing rather than decreasing. Unfortunately, genetics aren't helping, espe-cially with minority communities.[6]

As citizens, we face the growing costs with a deep-seated, if unspoken, knowledge that we might not be able to pay for it all. Literally trillions of dollars of healthcare-related financial commitments await us in the next 10 to 40 years, even with the rosiest of projections. Those who established Medicare and Medicaid (and the National Health Service [NHS] and other similar systems) might not have seen the crisis coming 50 to 60 years in advance, but recent generations of analysts know and speak the numbers regularly enough. At the risk of getting political, decades of national leaders have kicked

many a can down the proverbial road, refusing to reform
the system while it was still only mildly painful. Votes and
power seemed more important than doing what was right,
as if being elected and powerful gave our leaders the right
to pass the buck to the next generation rather than take the
responsibility to fix a vexing issue. Those brave yet isolated
souls who tried to change the system, even nominally, were
either voted into submission by their legislative colleagues or
voted out of office by their self-serving constituents. Thus,
we have brought the nation to the financial brink through an
unwillingness to stomach the changes necessary or to elect
those who would.

Perhaps no other piece of legislation has done more to
shine a light on the realities of the issues facing us than
the Patient Protection and Affordable Care Act (PPACA) of
2010 (aka ObamaCare). If it does nothing else, it has yet
again revealed what we should have already known: (1) the
government-run healthcare systems, Medicare and Medicaid,
are financially unfeasible in their current forms; and (2) the
government is likely no place to find a solution, due to the
politically incorrect and unpalatable decisions that must now
be made. Like teens without the assistance of parental control, neither the legislative nor the executive branches show
the willingness to make tough, yet very rational, choices. Even
now, our elected officials dabble in minor tweaks to a broken
system, constantly kicking at the can to see how much farther
down the road it can be pushed.

Ironically, perhaps fortunately, the solutions proposed in
this book are truly bipartisan (if there is such a thing). Since
I began developing the concept some four years ago, I have
been struck by the way it mingles common right-wing themes
like personal responsibility, integrity, concern for the least
among us, and faith-based resources with common left-wing
themes such as communal responsibility, equality, centralized
control systems, and concern for the least among us (yes, both
share this latter attribute but with different approaches).

Thus, it is my hope that the concept can be spared the usual political wrangling and become at least part of the solution discussion.

Furthermore, as with the first text, this book seeks to "blow up" traditional business and delivery models, re-creating some of them entirely from the ground up. It will not be enough to simply nip at the edges of the current system constructs. Our traditional models must be literally ripped apart and reconstructed in order to meet an entirely new demand paradigm. And this will require a reconstruction of not just the hospital's systems (as the first book depicted) but the creation of an entirely new care system focused on the most challenging patients in our populations. This broad, deep, and intense revamp will create what is actually only a subsystem within a broader healthcare delivery system. Like the body of a patient who receives a new heart, the entire system will benefit. Thus, the new model will take the traditional healthcare delivery model, tear open a gaping hole, and place the functionality that will save the entire system within that hole.

I cannot address the legal system, nor propose a way to whack nursing and physician salaries to reduce the cost of care. But I can propose a solution that focuses on a broader application of dynamic capacity management, taking it from the hospital into an entire *community of care*. The community of care and all the sundry resources therein make up a much larger number of patient "touches," and offer us tremendous value if knitted together and used appropriately. Indeed, if properly developed and managed, DCAMM applied to the broader community could hold the key to simultaneously solving the main issues facing healthcare today: cost, quality, resource constraints, access, and capacity.

Thus, this book will look beyond the four walls of the hospital and reach well outside the traditional healthcare business models to develop an entirely new and very different care model from which can flow the solutions to the "healthcare crisis."

A Caveat to the Contents of This Text

The poly-chronic care network (PCCN) is meant to be a very flexible business and care model. Your iteration may be small or large, sweeping or narrowly focused. You might start with one iteration and develop an entirely different one later on. Your technology and governance structures may differ dramatically from that of other PCCNs. However, in order to offer as broad a view and as deep an understanding as possible, all the major components of a PCCN are described in this text. You might need a few, or only one or two of these components. Therefore, when reading this text, don't be alarmed if you anticipate that your community would not support a massive technology and governance implementation. It need not. Likewise, you should not expect to have to deploy the entire infrastructure at once, nor will your participating population go from zero to 100 percent overnight.

Take what you read here, and if you feel it is valid, apply the necessary components to your specific community and its needs and capabilities. As your PCCN grows, expands, or even contracts over time, amend the blend to account for the size, scale, scope, and population of the community and patients you wish to serve. Take what you need from what is listed, but don't think you have to have it all.

Conclusion

It is my humble opinion that if a solution is to be found, it will be the private sector that will innovate our way to it. The powers that be in our state and national capitals will not amass the vision to develop the solution. Neither Washington nor our state capitals are truly innovative places. If anything, the innovations that will be developed by the private sector (including and especially this one) might be killed by the bureaucracies, politics, and power trappings of government.

It is, therefore, highly unlikely that government will save the system even though taxpayers will foot the bill for failure. The one government entity that holds out potential for innovation, the Center for Medicare and Medicaid Innovation (CMI), may have a chance if the "bureaucratic antibodies" don't kill off the ideas before they have a chance to live and breathe. Fortunately, they have the vision to tap into the private marketplace and seek solutions. Thus, the industry must challenge itself to innovate beyond our current models and thinking, and develop an entirely new construct that the taxpayers, patients, and caregivers can accept.

Endnotes

1. U.S. Department of Health and Human Services, *Multiple Chronic Conditions: A Strategic Framework: Optimum Health and Quality of Life for Individuals with Multiple Chronic Conditions* (Washington, DC: U.S. Department of Health and Human Services, December 2010), http://www.hhs.gov/ash/ initiatives/mcc/mcc_framework.pdf (accessed June 4, 2012).
2. Jackson Healthcare, http://www.jacksonhealthcare.com/ media/8968/defensivemedicine_ebook_final.pdf (accessed September 2010).
3. Taken from International Average Salary Income Database, 2005 data, http://www.worldsalaries.org (accessed August 2010).
4. International Average Salary Income Database, 2005 data.
5. Centers for Disease Control and Prevention, "Childhood Obesity Facts," http://www.cdc.gov/healthyyouth/obesity/facts.htm (accessed May 2010).
6. L. K. Brennan Ramirez, E. A. Baker, and M. Metzler, *Promoting Health Equity: A Resource to Help Communities Address Social Determinants of Health* (Atlanta: U.S. Department of Health and Human Services, Centers for Disease Control and Prevention, 2008), http://www.cdc.gov/nccdphp/dach/chhep/ pdf/SDOHworkbook.pdf (accessed May 2009).

Chapter 1

The PCCN Concept: An Overview

This chapter will offer a brief overview of the *poly-chronic care network* (PCCN) concept and its goals, some of the nomenclature, and the general requirements for implementation. As you read the later chapters in this text, these topics and more will be discussed in greater detail.

The PCCN in a Tweet: engineered, connected, community-wide care networks, concurrently addressing quality, capacity, cost, and access for chronic disease patients.

PCCN Description

A poly-chronic care network (PCCN) is an engineered, interconnected, community-engaging care subsystem that simultaneously addresses cost, quality, access, system capacity, and gratification for the most problematic patients in the population—those with multiple chronic diseases or a single chronic disease with multiple comorbidities (aka *poly-chronics*).

PCCNs align patients, clinicians, and broad arrays of precisely coordinated communal resources to support physicians' care strategies for poly-chronic patients. PCCNs go beyond *care managers* and *patient navigators* by directly integrating myriad communal resources, such as churches, families, Federally Qualified Health Centers (FQHCs), YMCAs, friends, pharmacies, community groups, students, volunteers, and so on, into organized *care circles* that provide ongoing assistance and personalized care to their patients. Care activities are coordinated and delegated with the guidance and oversight of physicians, while patient status and care activity updates are communicated back "upstream" to clinicians via a social–clinical networking (SCN) platform, which could be thought of as a "Facebook for chronic disease management." Via the SCN, care circle resources can coordinate their activities, collaborate on patient needs, exchange ideas to improve care, interact with patients, and engage in an ongoing dialogue with their patient's clinicians. This extends physician reach into the lives of patients, expands their capacity to care to more patients, increases the number and quality of patient "touches," and promotes and improves ongoing monitoring, compliance, and lifestyle management. Patients thus receive the right assistance and care at the right time via the most cost-effective, convenient, and familiar local resources.

This holistic communal approach enables physicians to focus on what they do best—outcomes management—while improving patient contact, compliance, and overall disease management, especially for the poor, frail elderly, and rural populations, through a more proper allocation of care tasks. The PCCN expands the total clinical capacity of the system without taxing scarce current and future clinical resources, yielding a simultaneous impact on cost, quality, access, gratification, and capacity, and encouraging business and payment model innovation.

PCCN as a Visual

Take a look at Figure 1.1, and keep it in mind as you read the remainder of this text. Visually, it represents the extent

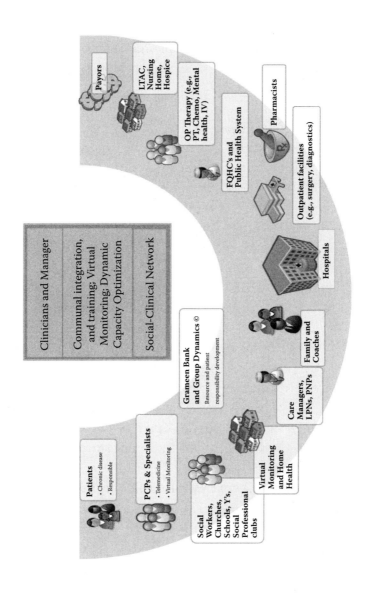

Figure 1.1   A visual representation of a single iteration of the PCCN infrastructure.

of the resource pool and technologies suggested for a typical PCCN. This text by no means excludes other resource types, nor does it preclude the use of new technologies, infrastructure, and approaches as they arise. Though the PCCN is by far the most integrated and sophisticated approach to be published thus far, I hope it is only the beginning of the discussion on dramatically new care model development.

Application Overview

As we already know, our healthcare system is broken and in desperate need of repair. Furthermore, the old system is clearly incapable of managing the coming "grey wave" of an aging population. With its high resource costs and capacity limitations, the old care models do not offer the ability to solve for society's growing healthcare needs in a cost-effective way, especially for those with complex chronic diseases. Yet we already know chronic disease patients are the locus of the real cost, quality, access, and capacity issues in healthcare. Their cost (some 70–90 percent of total cost expended on only 10–20 percent of the total population) is reflected in both actual care delivery costs as well as the costs of lost productivity and absenteeism. Furthermore, accessibility, capacity, quality, and provider and patient gratification must be simultaneously addressed for our poly-chronics if we are to truly and permanently fix the system.

One of the core principles of the PCCN is quite simple: patients with chronic diseases require a dramatically different care system because they themselves are very different. They need entirely different care streams and resources providing different services in different quantities. Tweaking the existing infrastructure is fine for the 80+ percent of the population who are relatively healthy. The 80+ percent doesn't commonly need ongoing, coordinated care from multiple disparate physicians and providers in order to try to maintain or improve health.

Their care is simply not that complex (though, as we'll discuss later, we cannot quickly dismiss the needs of this 80 percent). But for the poly-chronics, better care means developing an entirely new model of care delivery—one that literally blows up the existing systems and replaces, or at least augments, it with an entirely new look, feel, and functionality.

This new way of thinking takes patients out of the old *cure* system in which episodic, longitudinally bounded care is the norm, and places them into *care strategies* and resource pools specifically designed to address their complex care needs. Customized and resourced at the local level, the PCCN is essentially a conceptual foundation upon which is built a customized care infrastructure, designed for the community in which it is placed.

To be accepted, the PCCN model must at least meet the same standards of quality, access, and resource accountability as existing systems. It must not only expand the capacity of the entire system via new resources, but assimilate all resources into a new care culture such that their individual capacities to support patients are greatly increased.

Furthermore the PCCN, in part due to its greater complexity and the complex clinical needs of the patients served, requires not just care coordination but the "engineering" of these resources and their work in support of unifying care strategies. This broader approach moves from a linear and disaggregated series of treatments, procedures, and care steps to an integrated, community wide strategy for the general and long-term wellness of the sickest of the population, from home to hospice.

The success of this unique approach to care delivery depends on a holistic implementation plan that includes some limited supporting technology; precise resource organization, utilization, and assimilation; training and ongoing mentoring; and patient and resource accountability. In order to achieve these high aims, the PCCN requires specific but relatively low-cost technologies and perhaps a few specialized, full-time support staff. Without its underlying infrastructure, the PCCN could fall prey to the same systemic constraints, silos, and inefficiencies that plague the current models. However, there are a number of ways and speeds with which the PCCN might be implemented, depending on the existing technology infrastructure, community resources, physician engagement, and patient willingness. Commonly, there will be engagement with large physician groups and collaborative hospitals to develop mutually beneficial synergies for addressing populations that create unnecessary costs and burdens for clinicians, facilities, patients, and their communities. However, don't be surprised if your PCCN has its roots in a church congregation or community service organization.

Though radical, the PCCN has been universally praised. Recent efforts across the country show that community resources, such as pharmacies, YMCAs, and volunteers, are anxious to help save the system. Yet they are stymied by lack of integration and clinical guidance. Coordinating these disparate and siloed resources into a functional, efficient, cohesive care continuum will allow dramatic change to take place at a low cost while improving outcomes, capacity, and quality.

An Engineered Approach

The PCCN does not haphazardly throw resources, time, and materials at a problem. Indeed, one of the major issues I have with some of the initial efforts at care redesign is the seemingly careless use of expensive resources. Many of the current strategies are resource intensive, making sustainability and dramatic cost savings difficult to attain without grants and stipends and ancillary payments.

Instead, nurses, techs, or any other expensive resources should only be used as they are appropriate to a given task. Furthermore, their utilization should be optimized within the context of the larger system, so as to prevent the misallocation of workload and the invariable constraints that come with it.

Cost overruns, overtaxed or underutilized resources, long waits for service, and frustrated customers are a direct result of the failure to properly utilize the available resource pool. Just as a pilot of a commercial airline doesn't serve drinks mid-flight, a physician or nurse should not be required to do nonclinical tasks that might be better handled by another, more appropriately skilled and/or proximate resource. Indeed, misallocation of resources is quite common in nonengineered approaches to resource provision. We readily see the impact of inflexible and inefficient approaches to resource allocations in healthcare. You don't have to look much further than mandated patient–nurse ratios to see the negative impact of a bad approach to resource, task, and workforce management on efficiencies, cost, and capacity. These siloed and rigid work breakdown structures have always led to periodic over- and underutilization, higher costs, terrible inefficiencies, and increased risks to quality wherever they've been tried.

The only way to solve for a resource-constrained environment is to engineer the task allocations effectively, such that all work is done by suitably trained and qualified resources at the appropriate time in the correct manner, maximizing the utilization of the resources and thereby sustainability of the model. The best way to do that is to use traditional *industrial engineering* principles, tools, and concepts. These have been used by industry for decades to squeeze out the kind of productivity that has made American business as great as it is and our economy strong. Data analytics and tools (such as simulation, as we'll discuss later), and structured deployment are all hallmarks of proper and effective work breakdown structures. Using these principles heavily in the planning and deployment phases of the PCCN implementation almost guarantees a more optimal outcome. And by engineering a resource pool customized for the community to be served, the PCCN helps guarantee that there will be no constraints in service or resources, or lapses in care, access, capacity, and/or quality.

It should be noted that this engineering approach goes well beyond Lean. Indeed, what is called Lean in healthcare is often referred to as industrial engineering lite among the more sophisticated industrial engineers (IEs). Lean, though used widely by IEs and companies around the world, is not as sophisticated as IEs would normally be. Indeed, in many companies, especially healthcare organizations, Lean is no longer Lean. It has morphed into something more robust, complex, and useful. But because Lean is not a *dynamic* analytical system (as I described in my previous text[1]) it is largely incapable of the detailed and complete analysis of complex and dynamic systems. Though useful as a *process* improvement methodology, it is ineffective as a *systems* improvement methodology. Thus, we use DCAMM (dynamic capacity analysis, matching, and management) as our methodology of choice, since it is much more appropriate to the highly variable, interdependent, and ever-changing world of care provision.

PCCN Components

As we go through the subsequent chapters, we will delve more deeply into the following attributes of the PCCN, and how they will be developed, implemented, and managed. For now, let's take a high-level pass at the concepts, principles, and requirements of the PCCN model. (*Note:* Chapters 6 and 8 contain greater detail on the specific resource definitions, roles, and functions within the PCCN structure.)

Resource Pool

Obviously, as seen in Figure 1.1, the pool of resources in a PCCN can be quite broad and deep. It encompasses many of the existing resources that are common to communities, such as YMCAs, churches, and community colleges. It may include resources that are not as common and that might be listed in general categories like "volunteers," which might include parish nurses and pharmacy school residents. It may encompass existing communal resources such as Meals on Wheels, or largely untapped resources such as retired healthcare workers, emergency medical technicians (EMTs), school nurses, and premed university students. This pool, however constructed and populated, should encompass as many dedicated resources as are required to accomplish the tasks at hand. There is little doubt that a given resource pool will evolve and morph over time, as the circumstances, patient population, and resource availability changes over time. Thus this resource pool may need to be augmented periodically as specific individuals or groups move in and out of availability. Recruitment and ongoing training will be required, as will monitoring and the occasional "weeding out."

That said, within every resource pool for every PCCN currently imagined there must be a *core*. This would include dedicated physicians, nurses, and other clinicians who will, of course, be augmented by the rest of the resource pool members. Without clinical oversight and direct clinician participation, the optimization of the PCCN and the proper guidance of nonclinical resources are impossible. Likewise, without an expanded resource pool, even if small and limited, the PCCN loses its value to the patients, the community, and the healthcare system as capacity and access continue to be more constrained. The PCCN thus requires an expanded resource pool to include core groups of clinicians as well as myriad nonclinical resources.

Fortunately, expanded resource allocations are becoming more and more common, as seen in the work of the state of Vermont, Cambridge Health Alliance, Gunderson Lutheran Medical Center, and others around the country. Care coordinators, patient navigators, and other similar titles are popping up in physician offices and hospitals across the country as more and more see the advantages of the distribution of tasks, especially for the chronically ill. This demonstrates a growing sensitivity to capacity constraints and the special needs of specific patient types. But, while laudable, these models risk continued cost and capacity constraints, since the resource expansion is typically limited to highly compensated and often specialized clinicians. These, of course, can be further augmented by the resources of the PCCN model, which will advance their goals, expand their care capacity, and improve their reach into the lives and health of their sickest patients.

Key to the PCCN resource pools are several specific roles we'll discuss in greater detail later:

- **Primes:** A *prime* is the patient's choice as primary care partner, and serves as the go-to resource for all other nonclinical issues for all other resources in the patient's care circle (see next bullet). The prime is the point person, and is normally designated by the patient as their advocate and the person responsible for ensuring communications and care strategy implementation are ongoing. (Primes may be assigned by the PCCN rather than selected by the patient in situations of the lonely elderly, cognitively impaired, etc.)
- **Care circle:** Previously mentioned, this is the group of communal and clinical resources aligned around an individual patient's care provision. These may be large or small, but will always be directed by a physician, with day-to-day operational oversight offered by care managers, PCCN managers, and primes. Care circles will commonly use the SCN to communicate, coordinate, exchange, update, and support as they intervene in the lives of the patients they touch.
- **PCCN managers:** This role, whether housed in a local hospital, a community agency, or a physician office, will manage the communal resources and care circles, ensure task completion, handle issues and questions, promote new and current participation, and generally support the program.

■ **PCCN trainers:** Resources, physician office staff, and others will need training on everything from the essentials of chronic disease management to the basics of the technologies to be used. Some or all of this training may require a specific resource to ensure continuity, ongoing mentoring and training, and the maintenance of information quality. So important is this role that it is one of only two possible full-time resources in a PCCN implementation.

Communal resources, even if passionate and enthusiastic, need to be properly coordinated and managed. Otherwise, they will remain as they are: caring but disjointed and siloed. Therefore, the PCCN is clinically directed by either specialized clinicians whose interest and expertise lies in the management of chronic diseases (which I call *chronicists*), and/or primary care physicians (PCPs). (See Chapters 8 for a more detailed description of these and other PCCN clinical and management roles). The chronicist may be an internist, geriatrician, PCP, or other specialist. However, the chronicist must have a passion for chronic diseases, since his/her career would now be dedicated solely to the care of the most complex of patients. Alternatively, as we'll see, PCPs are able to serve these same functions if their expertise is sufficient and their patient population warrants such focus. Indeed, the two terms are nearly completely interchangeable in this text.

The chronicist or PCP sits at the top of the pyramid, working with PCCN managers, trainers, office care managers, and the communal resources to direct and manage the care of the patients under their supervision. This pyramid structure is important for clinical, legal, logistical, and efficiency reasons, so it is unlikely to be altered unless there is a significant alteration in the structure of the PCCN itself.

These clinical leaders will, of course, need help from other clinical specialists, such as orthopedists, neurologists, and nephrologists. If the PCCN is set up with the right technologies and infrastructure, help can also come from outside via ties to national and even international specialists in chronic disease management. This network of remote experts would be available (for a fee, no doubt) to assist in diagnostics, care strategy development, and general clinical advisement. Indeed, Mayo and other famed or highly specialized health systems already use remote conferencing and monitoring to aid disparate health systems in better managing patient care. This helps build a body of knowledge of best practices for these conditions, spreads the information throughout the country, and allows for communication of results and outcomes to specific care strategy regimens.

Operationally, the resources are coordinated and supported by a PCCN manager, as described previously and later in the text. This resource will be the go-to person in most iterations of the PCCN concept, which will prevent structural and program breakdown and promote ongoing activity and accountability.

Resource Training

You might be jumping ahead and asking, "But how can communal resources care for patients without clinical expertise?" Fear not! This will be covered later in this text. But consider this: you needn't be fluent in a foreign language to get around, order a meal, or find a restroom in a foreign country. You need only to know the basics of the language, culture, and people to enjoy a visit and interact with the locals. Likewise, the myriad communal resources needn't become nurses or licensed practical nurses (LPNs) or physicians to assist in the care of patients.

Suffice it to say, for now, that communal resources will indeed require training and ongoing education in their roles, the patients they care for, and the diseases they encounter. While they will not be expected to become clinical experts, communal resources will have the right knowledge to work with, engage, and assist in the clinical management of the patients in their care circle. Depending on the resource, their desired and expected role, and the needs of the patient, appropriately trained and vetted resources will be assigned so as to ensure high quality and patient gratification.

Technology Infrastructure (TI)

Note: Chapter 9 contains a detailed description of the various technologies mentioned in this section.

One of the main reasons that the PCCN is even possible is the technology that will lie "under the hood." In fact, such a concept would have been difficult, if not impossible, before the advent of web-based communication tools. There are several potential technologies that could be involved in the development, implementation, and sustenance of the PCCN, though only a minimal amount is actually required. These technologies and a limited number of full-time staff support the resource utilization optimization, clinical information exchange, compliance monitoring, and patient engagement required to allow physicians to care for more patients at a lower cost while promoting more patient contact, better compliance, higher metrics, and optimal outcomes. The good news is that these are not exclusive or patented technologies. Even more significant, you may need only one or a few of those listed, depending on your particular situation. And, since this text is meant to give guidance on the necessary systems and implementation plans to develop your own PCCN, any applicable technology, whether purchased or home-grown, could suffice if it achieves your particular PCCN-related goals. Indeed, there is only one technology vendor specifically mentioned in this text, so as to maintain the objectivity of the concept.

The following technologies may be part of a PCCN program. Some are more necessary than others, and at least one is critical to success.

1. **Social–clinical network (SCN):** The SCN is the only "required" technology of a PCCN. Think of this as a private "Facebook for poly-chronics." The SCN provides patients, caregivers, and their specific communal resources with a means by which to communicate, share, exchange, and learn. The SCN (as currently developed) is a web-based networking tool that allows for ongoing communication among the members of patient care circles and clinicians while ensuring the patient's privacy, personalization, and sharing preferences. The SCN can be used as a(n):

    i. Communication platform for private and open inter-actions among physicians, patients, and clinical and communal resources in and among the care circles

    ii. Private social networking among patients with similar disease states and clinical conditions and among communal resources within and outside their specific care circle(s)

    iii. Extension of Group Dynamics™² through which patients can communicate with and support each other

    iv. Information dispersion system through which patients and resources can be kept informed on PCCN news, relevant clinical research and treatment options, policy issues, and other important communal information

    v. Means for scheduling patient interactions, visits, prescription refills, appointments, and other events among care circle members

    vi. General PCCN information source, wherein PCCNs from across the country can collect and disseminate information relevant to patients and providers

   The SCN will give a personal and communal touch to the caregivers and their tasks; allow sharing of ideas, thoughts, comments, and suggestions among clinical and nonclinical care circle resources; empower the enthusiastic to share their successes; help patients better communicate with those with like clinical conditions; and support collaborative care by integrating clinical, nonclinical, communal, and familial resources in a single online community environment.

2. **Process simulation:** Because process simulation (hereinafter simply *simulation*) is capable of the analysis and optimization of complex, variable, and interdependent systems like these, it can be a critical tool in the development, implementation, and ongoing improvement and optimization efforts of large PCCNs. Depending upon how many tasks, resources, patients, and disease states there are in your PCCN, simulation may be a useful analytical and implementation assistance tool. Small implementations may not need the power of simulation, as the implementation logistics can more easily be worked out.

3. **Virtual monitoring (VM):** Technologies now exist, and more will be developed, that will aid the PCCN in the ongoing and immediate monitoring of patient compliance and medical conditions. PCCNs are in fact great support structures for the use of VM tools, since they can provide in-home assistance for elderly or "technology impaired" patients. Patients with VM systems can work with the care circle resource to ensure proper data collection and transmission, and even be onsite for virtual appointments with physicians to promote understanding and compliance with care directives.

4. **Population modeling and prediction:** Population modeling and prediction (PP) helps you anticipate the health outcomes of future changes in the demographics and health characteristics of a community. Used commonly by actuarials and insurers, PP allows for the prediction of population trends, down to the individual patient. By predicting the health outcomes of current and future health trends, PP can aid the PCCN in better predicting

the future need for space, resources, and even medical equipment and VM systems.

5. **Health information exchange (HIE):** HIEs are becoming more and more common in the marketplace, as health systems try to tie together disparate electronic information sources into a single, coherent, and useful source. An HIE will allow for all the parties to communicate, receive and send information, create accountability, develop schedules and care alerts, and serve generally as the clinical information exchange system. More robust and sophisticated than the SCN, the HIE will also allow disparate parties to access patient clinical histories and care strategies across large communities, promoting care collaboration, reducing waste and redundancy, and ensuring seamless care provision. Though an HIE can be part of the PCCN if it is already available, it would likely be too expensive and complex to purchase and install just for this purpose. Additionally, since HIEs do not have the social networking capabilities of the SCN, the latter would remain a requirement.

These technologies, however cleverly combined and utilized, will allow the kind of care transformation the PCCN promises. Regardless of how yours is assembled, the goals of linking resources, clinical information, and patients together to form an efficient, truly integrated, and sustainable network is important to the longevity and functionality of the program. If properly implemented, the technology infrastructure can morph as the PCCN evolves, patient needs change, and the technologies develop.

Palliative and End-of-Life Care

If we are to create a truly holistic approach to the care of poly-chronics, palliative care and end-of-life care and planning must be a part. This is not, as some might suspect, strictly a cost and utilization issue. Yes, those are both impacted by

these programs. But more importantly, so are patient gratification and family comfort and compassion. As we'll see later,
palliative and end-of-life care can and should be integral
components of a patient's overall care strategy, and should be
part of a holistic engagement in a patient's spiritual, mental,
and physical well-being.

Of course, these programs require unique and specially
trained resources. However, these resources can be used as,
and when, needed to add their small but important part to the
care strategy, thus needn't be part of the individual care circles
of all PCCN patients.

Assimilation and Passion

Resources must be passionate about the care they give. And
in order to best channel that passion, resources will need to
be properly assimilated into the PCCN framework. This means
more than just signing up for a few tasks. Assimilation is a status
of engagement at a much higher level and intensity. Assimilated
resources are therefore fully committed to the cause, the way
some are committed to their politics, favorite sports teams, and
hobbies. This is important because this will not be easy work.
There will be setbacks and frustrations. And if your resources
are merely "unpaid volunteers," the tendency might be to take
a self-serving and easy way out: leave. Thus, it is important to
work with your communal resources using techniques of volunteer management and deploy resources that are knowledgeable
of their communities, patients, and fellow resources such that a
high degree of loyalty, passion, and commitment exists.

Capacity as Strategy

If the PCCN concept is based on a single issue, it is the capacity constraints that continue to face our healthcare systems.
Too many very sick patients, with fewer and fewer financial

resources, vie for too few care providers. As we saw in the Foreword, the dearth of physicians, nurses, and other expertise will continue to grow worse over time, even with current increases in the number of enrollees of training programs. The capacity of the current model will be unable to meet the demand of the coming generation of retirees.

Furthermore, we face increasing financial constraints as the population ages with fewer and fewer taxpayers to foot the bill. As demographics take their toll, and fewer and fewer taxpayers support the full load of the system, the healthcare system will continue to feel the pains of financial constraints. This is not expected to lessen in the foreseeable future, leaving us with harsh alternatives from massive taxation that will stifle the economy to the direct rationing of care.

Thus, either we dramatically ration care or we develop an entirely new delivery system that will expand the capacity of the scarcest of resources without expanding their workload. Thus a *capacity strategy* that accounts for the entire system is required.

The PCCN encompasses all aspects of the patient's care, inclusive of their personal circumstances, community bonds, friends, self-respect, and self-worth. This is an important aspect of the expansion of capacity. Since the PCCN uses multiple resources in the community, including specialists, mental health workers, social workers, volunteers, and so on, the workload is spread yet the care is ultimately coordinated and effectively guided. This allows the mission-critical resources, physicians and other caregivers, to do what they do best, what they are trained to do, and are paid to do—manage and direct care provision. This capacity expansion helps the system to meet an ever-growing demand without demanding more resources at less pay or greater workloads.

Thus capacity becomes the ultimate strategy in the work to achieve a sustainable, effective, and efficient system.

Other Important Attributes of the PCCN

The PCCN should also include:

1. An *outcomes* focus rather than a financial, activity, patient, or resource focus. By focusing on outcomes, the patient is automatically part of the equation.
2. Patient accountability and personal responsibility. (If healthcare is a right, it is also a responsibility!)
3. An "It's not about me!" mentality among all resources.
4. Community learning and focus on chronic disease prevention and management.

The latter should not be discounted. As the PCCN takes hold in the community, and more and more communal resources become engaged in the care of complex patients, the understanding of and respect for chronic diseases will grow organically. This will be reflected in the way communal resources understand their own healthcare and that of those around them. Thus, through "osmotic learning," communities will become more and more self-aware of the need for lifestyle choices and preventative care that can reduce the likelihood of chronic disease onset.

An Additive Solution

Is the PCCN a better model? Based on the nearly unanimous accolades from experts I admire, I'd have to say "Yes!" Our current healthcare/"sick-care" system is not designed for the efficient, effective, and holistic treatment of poly-chronics. Just look at the state Medicaid programs and how they struggle with the cost of care provision for this group. And even while new concepts such as care coordinators and navigators are being developed, and government agencies and private insurers tinker with the base business model, there has not been the kind of wholesale upheaval that will be required to truly save the system.

The PCCN may be such a model. As a more holistic approach to care delivery, the PCCN takes into account the sheer complexity of the poly-chronic's care requirements, and develops a more appropriate and broader resource pool with which to provide less costly, higher-quality, and more accessible care. Furthermore, by engineering those resources into a truly integrated delivery system, optimized for the community served, the PCCN helps ensure that the right care is always available and that the "bottlenecked" or constrained resources are always given as much capacity as possible. Lastly, by using technology appropriately, the PCCN ensures its own longevity and sustainability for the long haul toward better care at a lower cost.

Yet, I've described the PCCN as a care subsystem. Meaning, the PCCN doesn't require the current advancements in patient-centered medical homes (PCMHs), care navigators and care managers, and so on, to be replaced. Rather, the PCCN can and should be added to these important efforts, augmenting these care models with new care capacity and "reach" into the lives of poly-chronics. If implemented properly into even the most advanced of PCMHs, the PCCN should offer its same benefits and help these advanced models do even more.

PCCNs and ACOs

As they stand now, accountable care organization (ACO) models are collections of patients under one roof. Of course, regardless of the overarching business model, a small population of those patients does and will continue to drive most of the cost of any care system. Yet the ACO does little, if anything, to help redesign the delivery of care of these patients other than to coordinate their care under the auspices of the same constrained resources we have now. The newer business models, like ACOs, will need some sort of PCCN-type model within them to ultimately be successful in sustaining healthcare throughout the coming demographic changes and financial crises. Thus a PCCN should be part of *any new larger business model if that model is to hit its targets of cost, quality, access, and gratification without breaking the bank or overloading clinical resources.* I am not suggesting that we blow up ACOs. Rather, if an ACO is your business model of choice, the PCCN can and should fit within it as a care subsystem capable of aiding in the reduction of risk, cost, and resource consumption among poly-chronics. Thus, integration of the PCCN as a subsystem is expected and should be welcomed. (Indeed, full integration is required; else a health system might become a *poly-chronic patient centered accountable medical home care network!*)

A Caveat to the Contents of This Text

It is worth repeating (in case you skipped the Foreword) that the PCCN is meant to be a very flexible business and care model. Yours may be small or large, or broad or narrowly focused. You might start with a single iteration and develop an entirely new model later on. Your technology and governance structures may differ dramatically from that of another PCCN across town. However, in order to offer as broad a view and as deep an understanding as possible, all the components of a PCCN are described herein. You might need only a few, or only one of these components. Therefore, when reading this text, don't be alarmed if the need of your community would not support a massive technology and governance implementation. Likewise, you should not expect to have to deploy the entire infrastructure at once, nor will your participating population go from zero to 100 percent overnight.

Take what you read here, and if you feel it is valid, apply the necessary components, small or large, to your program.

As your PCCN grows, expands, or contracts over time, *amend the blend* to account for the size, scale, scope, and population of your community and patients as they change over time.

Take what you need from what is offered, but don't think you have to have it all.

Two Missing Elements

If you know this business well, you will quickly pick up on two missing elements in the discussions in this text.

Mental Health

One significant issue with the care of poly-chronics is the prevalence of mental health issues. I understand and appreciate this conundrum, as it inherently makes the care of these patients more difficult. Indeed, additional work is now being done to configure the PCCN with a mental health patient focus. This will be published in the coming years as these unique models are tested and vetted for effectiveness.

That said, while I recognize the importance of both this issue and the need for a holistic approach to patient care, this text will intentionally leave out deep references to this subpopulation of patients. This is true for several reasons:

1. Though mental health is significant among poly-chronics, a large majority of poly-chronics do not exhibit mental health issues. Thus, there is an opportunity to treat these latter patients using *standard* and *common* communal resources without additional mental health expertise in place.
2. Volunteer communal resources would need more significant training if they were to deal with patients with depression, bipolar disorder, and so on. While not impossible or improbable, this training adds a level of

complexity to poly-chronic care that some PCCNs may be unwilling to take on. Indeed, some may feel that is it entirely inappropriate to use communal resources until a patient's mental health issues are under control and well managed. Furthermore, it generally adds to the complexity of the care required, which may put some patients out of the scope of a nonclinical resource mix.

3. Mental health patients may require specialized infrastructures, care tasks, and other elements that will not fit well with a generalized PCCN model. Instead, you should seek to add mental health resources to the clinical resources, and use communal resources only insofar as they can aid in the care and management of these special patients.

Indeed, though not explicitly mentioned in this text, mental health expertise and care can be added to a PCCN, or perhaps more appropriately a *sub-PCCN* that focuses specifically on patients with these mental health issues. The structure, volumes, capacity, and resource requirements of such a specialized PCCN might be very different from others, but the overall model and its goals and objectives can still be attained. Certainly, then, if there is a desire and willingness, and if proper training can be achieved such that these patients receive appropriate and truly holistic care, the PCCN is an appropriate model to which to add poly-chronic mental health patients. And of course you, the reader, can and will configure your PCCN to your needs and desires, inclusive of mental health patients or not.

Therefore, do not read into this missing element a disregard for, or lack of interest in, poly-chronics with mental health issues. To the contrary, these patients are as important as any to the solutions for the healthcare system writ large. In this text we will cover the non-mental health patients in the poly-chronic population, knowing well that mental health issues are important and all-too prevalent. We'll save the mental health poly-chronics for future, more specific publications.

The Bottom 50

The other missing element is "the rest of us." That is, the 80 percent of the population that only use a small portion of the total healthcare expenditures. Indeed, the statistics in this text will show that the bottom 50 percent of users account for only about 3.5 percent of total spending. That is, of course, why this book is focused on the small percentage that uses so much.

But it would be unwise to ignore the *bottom 50 percent.* Though they cost little now, they will surely cost more later in life. In other words, some of the bottom 50 percent will eventually become the high-utilizing 20 percent of tomorrow. This is one of the ancillary reasons why the PCCN's community engagement is important.

As communal resources engage in the care of the PCCN's poly-chronics, the general public awareness of the issues, complexities, and costs of care is bound to grow. As more and more are involved and hear about the PCCN and its patients and resources, more information will be shared about chronic diseases and their causes. And this will bring opportunities to educate entire communities on the vagaries of chronic diseases such that goals of personal responsibility, personal health awareness, and self-management will become more readily attainable.

Thus, as you move forward with your PCCN implementation, consider its potential to impact both the top 20 percent of utilizers as well as the future 20 percent who currently cost so little. Take any and all opportunities to educate both ends of the utilization curve.

A Word on U.S. Privacy Regulations and the PCCN Concept

Hopefully you are excited about the prospect of implementing a PCCN (or some form of a "Care Circle Network") structure in your community. Soon you will find yourself envisioning the benefits this program offers to your patients and their families and caregivers. Naturally, as you read this text, you will no doubt come up with your own questions about implementation and the "witches behind the trees" (aka the "devils in the details"). Thus as you begin to think about the use of some of the technologies described herein, you will likely ask the question, "What about the government and its many privacy regulations? How does this work in the real and libelous world of HIPAA?!" This is a very legitimate question. Indeed, HIPAA and other privacy regulations could be the bane of this concept were it not for the ingenuity of technology providers. (Since I am no expert on the privacy regulations of other countries, I will only write to the needs of U.S. healthcare providers. Naturally, you should apply these same precautions to your local implementations, wherever they may be).

First, let me say that while they could make implementation more challenging and costly, I fully understand and respect the need for privacy regulations. Simply put, there are just too many evil people out there who would use a patient's private medical information for nefarious purposes. This could include everything from denying employment to denying insurance coverage to blackmail and extortion. Even with the advent of new insurance regulations through which coverage cannot be denied and all U.S. citizens are covered, there still lies a risk of the misuse and abuse of private medical information by dishonest people.

Regardless of whether you or I believe that these regulations, like many governmental efforts to do the right thing, go too far and do as much harm as they do good, they are law and must be dealt with. Even if patients opt in, sign off on all communal resources, and all communal resources agree to tightly and judiciously respect and protect patient privacy, we must protect patient information from those who would do evil with any ill-gotten information. Thus, unless and until some government waiver is granted for the implementation of this and similar care models, laws must be precisely obeyed.

Second, it might go without saying that without the proper structure of the collaborative technologies (e.g. the SCN) and the requisite privacy protections, the Care Circle Network and PCCN concepts would likely die on the hill of U.S. government regulations. While the exchange of patient information can occur between communal resources using current technologies (e.g. email) and online communities (e.g. CaringBridge), the inclusion of any medical professional in many communications platforms would be precluded by the strict provisions of current law if precautions are not put in place. This, of course, would dramatically limit the value of the concept for patient care, efficiency, and care capacity expansion.

For instance, take this example: an elderly patient is being seen in her home by Nancy, a local church congregation member. Nancy learns during a bi-weekly visit that the patient cut her hand while slicing fruit, giving herself a nasty-looking wound that has only been treated with a simple Band-Aid. Were Nancy to take a picture of the wound and send it through an unencrypted and unsecured email to the physician for advice, the physician would likely do nothing with the information and only advise that the patient be seen, regardless of the extent of the wound. U.S. Federal and State regulations would preclude anything else. Indeed, the transmission and use of such information, even if well-intentioned and wildly efficient, could place both the resource and the physician at significant risk of serious financial and legal penalties. This, of course, saves nothing and negates the efforts and advantages of the Care Circle.

Thus in order for the Care Circle Network concept and its collaborative technologies to become reality, the technologies used must account for any and all regulations protecting private patient information.

This has been and can be achieved, of course, thanks to the ingenuity of technology innovators and good legal advice. Thus, for the purpose of the Technology chapter (Chapter 9) and this text, it will be assumed that you have sought out and found technology providers that can abide by the requirements of government regulations. Furthermore, I will assume that you have sought out and obtained the specific, necessary legal agreements, etc., allowing you to implement the program and its technology in your state. If this has not been done, you should begin the process of consulting with your legal department or counsel to ensure that you fully abide by any and all State, Federal, and local regulations. While doing so might seem onerous at first, the long-term benefits of a properly built infrastructure will ensure that you impact your community to the extent you desire.

Summary

The PCCN is a new and exciting concept. Though not rocket science, it elegantly combines resources, technologies, and operational models as has never been done before to develop a powerful solution to the most difficult problems healthcare faces today. By using some combination of its attributes and some blend of its technologies, health systems can begin to close the enormous gap between cost and budgets while maintaining and improving quality, accessibility, gratification, and capacity for the sickest of our patients.

Endnotes

1. P. Story, *Dynamic Capacity Management for Healthcare: Advanced Methods and Tools for Optimization* (Boca Raton, FL: CRC Press/Taylor & Francis, 2010).
2. "Group Dynamics™" is a concept borrowed mostly from the work of Grameen Bank and its use of group interactions to promote responsible behavior on the part of microloan recipients. Grameen Bank was started in Indonesia by Nobel Laureate Professor Muhammad Yunus to support the start of small businesses by poor women. Grameen's work

demonstrates the importance of guided and facilitated group accountability in promoting the motivation, accountability, and responsibility of microloan recipients. Grameen Research, the dissemination arm of the Grameen Bank, has agreed to support the implementation of Care Circle Networks and Poly-Chronic Care Networks in the U.S. and abroad with its own concepts, educational materials, and other assistance.

Chapter 2

A Brief History of Previous and Current Healthcare Reforms

Been Here, Done This?

See if you can guess who said the following (there will be a quiz at the bottom of the quote):

> We need legislation which reorganizes the system to guarantee a sufficient volume of high quality medical care, distributed equitably across the country and available at reasonable cost to every American. It is going to take a drastic overhaul of our entire way of doing business in the health-care field in order to solve the financing and organizational aspects of our health crisis. One aspect of that solution is the creation of comprehensive systems of health-care delivery. I have strongly advocated passage of legislation ... as a viable and competitive alternative to fee-for-service practice. ... I believe that [this reform] is the best idea

put forth so far for containing costs and improving the organization and the delivery of health-care services.

Was it

- U.S. President Barack Obama?
- Sir David Nicholson, Chief Executive, National Health Service (NHS) of the United Kingdom?
- Donald Berwick, former head of the U.S. Center for Medicare/Medicaid Services?

Well, you might have been correct on any of the above. It sure sounds like the comments any or all of the three of the choices might have made. However, in truth, it was none of these three. In fact, it was *Senator Kennedy, (D-MA), and Rep. Harry Staggers, (D-WV), from speeches to Congress in 1973, speaking on the value of health maintenance organizations (HMOs).*

Whence Innovation?

Yes, it seems some have been saying since the 1970s that government could fix the problems it essentially created. Even back then, less than a decade after the introduction of Medicare and Medicaid to the U.S. healthcare landscape, proposals for "fixing" them were already in the works. Needless to say, based on the quote, we still use the same language as we did nearly forty years ago to describe the "innovations" being proposed for fixing the healthcare system.

Today, the need for innovation is even more urgent. Decades of a broken system have left financial troubles in its wake, and the current and future economic landscape begs for a new and dramatic solution. For instance, the National Health Service of the United Kingdom has announced that it needs to reduce spending by some £20 billion. And here in the United States, where we spend far more per capita on healthcare than any other industrialized nation, we likely need far more than that to make the system sustainable at a reasonable economic cost.

Yet, the political willpower simply isn't available, on either side of the aisle, to accommodate bold steps and dramatic change. While the newly formed Center for Medicare and Medicaid Innovation (CMI) has shown great speed and the willingness to introduce new concepts, they rely partly on the private sector for the innovative ideas and concepts that might solve this nation's largest problems (in addition to the committed personnel resources they have managed to pull in from the private sector). Indeed, within CMI's mantra is a professed desire to seek out and advance innovative ideas from healthcare providers across the country and the globe, in "incubator" fashion. (Perhaps someone at CMI will read this text on the poly-chronic care network [PCCN], like it, and begin to push it!)

Therefore, if innovation is to come to the United States (and other struggling industrialized nations) in a grand and bold way, it will need to come from the private sector and into the government's payor systems, not the other way around. This is certainly the case with the PCCN, as it has within it many elements that might trip up even CMI's aggressive efforts to innovate. These would include the use of possibly politically incorrect communal resources, such as churches and YMCAs, or the high demand for additional personal responsibility and the sensed loss of choice and freedom that might come with an insistence on virtual monitoring and communal responsibility for patient management.

Accountable Care

One such innovation is the ACO, or accountable care organization. Introduced back in the mid-2000s, and seemingly built upon the failings of previous policy experiments, the ACO is the latest, perhaps more highly evolved concept to hit healthcare's marketplace of ideas. The ACO has gained momentum throughout the current U.S. debate on healthcare "reform," and now dominates the discussion of new healthcare business models. The current enthusiasm for it is based in part on its origins, as it was first noticed in works and publications of the infamous Dartmouth School of Health Policy (Elliott Fisher) and Mark McClelland, a former Centers for Medicare and Medicaid Services (CMS) director. Others have had a hand in the concept's development, including the current CMS leadership under Dr. Don Berwick (until December 2011, at least), and the many lessons available from experiments and models within the European single-payor markets. However, it might have remained an obscure management concept were it not thrust into the public limelight via four pages in the Patient Protection and Affordable Care Act (PPACA) legislation, which called specifically for its trial and implementation. Like the HMO, it was developed outside government and embraced and thrust onto the scene by government. Thus the ACO achieved a momentum not seen in a healthcare business model concept since the HMO that had Senator Kennedy so excited.

The ACO is an organization, currently loosely defined and open to interpretation, that is accountable for the healthcare of a given population of patients (hence the name). Part of the result of an ACO, if not a specific goal, is to shift risk from payors to providers, thereby changing the locus and intensity of provider attention to cost, quality, and outcomes. Since the definitions and parameters of the system are works in progress, there is no one single model. This is, of course, by intent, because CMS would prefer to see the innovations within the ACO framework occur within the broader context of experimentation throughout the country. This is now happening through the ACO application and tweaking process, in which provider groups from across the nation make their pitches to CMS as to how and by how much they can impact the three aims in their communities. Therefore, while many legal challenges and issues remain to be worked out, and the actual

look and feel of the ACO has yet to be solidified into a rep-
licable model, continued enthusiasm for its implementation
will drive some degree of innovation within those willing to
attempt it.

Without getting into gory details about the ACO and its
benefits and flaws (many a book and journal article has already
been written on the subject), it is worthwhile to analyze it in
the context of a possible government-imposed business model,
since the PCCN may well need to fit within such a framework.

In many ways, the ACO steps us toward what may be
inevitable—capitated payments for a given population of
citizens. In this sense, it is much like the HMOs about which
Senator Kennedy sung such high praise. Indeed, since the
current fee-for-service (FFS) business model (which was first
deployed by Medicare/Medicaid and then by the entire payor
industry) is no longer viable, the alternatives are limited.
Though capitation brings back bad memories of HMOs and
doomsday predictions of rationing from opponents, it is one of
the simplest and most effective business models available—*if* it
can be made to work.

The key to ensuring that the new business and risk models
work for both payor and provider is to broaden the insured
base to the maximum, such that the cost of those who need
care are covered. This is especially true of covering the costs
of the outliers (i.e., our poly-chronics), who drive much of
the cost of the system. As any self-insured American business
will profess, it only takes a small number of high-utilizers in
a small pool of patients to drive the insurance costs for everyone through the roof. Thus, the ACO needs a certain depth
and breadth to the population under its management to spread
the risk such that enterprise viability can be ensured. This is
why the much-damned individual mandate, first tried in the
United States in Massachusetts, is a critical component of the
ACO model. It is also why Europe's more "socialist" healthcare
systems are already far down the path of this business model,
while the United States is just beginning experimentation.

Precursors to ACOs in Europe

The ACO concept seemingly, was not created from whole cloth. Indeed, the single-payor systems of Europe have created and implemented similar concepts over the past decade. One such concept is the managed clinical network (MCN), which was created in Scotland and has been used for many clinical applications, including cancer, cleft palate, and sexually transmitted diseases.

As an example, one of the first managed clinical network projects was established in 1999 to integrate all cancer treatment settings across western Scotland and provide complete coordination of care for all cancer patients. The goal was to have the patient at the core of the system, to implement care pathway protocols in conjunction with national datasets, and to incorporate multidisciplinary team (MDT) meetings within the care pathway. The MCN now covers 50 percent of the population of Scotland—2.5 million people—and connects 5 regions and 10 hospitals (in a small, rural nation like Scotland, that's a lot).

The objectives of the MCN include cost reduction, care innovation, outcomes measurement, monitoring, and improvement, and general care coordination. The MCN established clinical discussion protocols and technologies, such as video conferencing, to prevent excess patient and provider travel in rural areas. The MCN provided a secure clinical information system to record the patient history and store clinical information and medical images, so as to allow exchange while maintaining patient confidentiality. The MCN also provided a means of informing primary, secondary, and tertiary care teams of ongoing cancer care, to encourage collaboration and proper intervention.

Similar programs and concepts have been popping up all over Europe, due in part to the same issues we have here in the United States. Learning from these trials and experiments will be important, even if the U.S. maintains its current private–public payor and provider systems.

ACOs and HMOs

When many hear of an ACO and its general concepts, they immediately think of the "bad old days" of the HMO. Indeed, HMOs seemed to fall into two categories: they either worked very well or were abysmal failures. Fortunately, there are myriad reasons why the ACO is not like the HMO of old, even though many of the remaining HMO-style providers (mainly in California) are already claiming to be ACOs. The reasons for the differences lend great credence to the PCCN model, so it is worthwhile to explore them here to help you understand the critical business implications.

On one front, HMOs were meant to be a way to control costs, though they didn't necessarily succeed. They quickly became known as a means for insurance providers to reduce care provision so as to hold down per-patient utilization, which in turn allowed them to make more of a profit. The less medical utilization there was, the more per-patient revenue the providers/insurers were able to keep in their pockets. (This is why the same congressmen and senators who once lauded the approach later came to demonize it.) This ran counter to the "freedom" patients had come to expect in the unconstrained provision of their care. In time, holding down utilization was seen as an indicator of poor quality, as it might have created lapses in care and put the physician at odds with the needs of the patients.

Furthermore, HMOs were seen as bureaucratic entities that controlled both access and care provision, as well as pay to the actual care providers. With a layer between the patient and the provider, voters and patients quickly became frustrated and stayed away in droves. Some worked and worked well; others did not. Thus, HMOs and similar managed care plans still exist, but have been modified greatly from their original designs.

In contrast, ACOs have a lot going for them that HMOs did not. While both are designed to lower the cost of provision of care, ACOs do it in a more elegant and patient-centered way (at least that's the claim). For instance, they achieve savings through care coordination within a group of providers via technologies and collaboration rather than the explicit control and restriction of access to specialists and procedures. This collaboration will, it is said, reduce waste and ensure better clinical outcomes than the disjointed FFS and HMO models of the past.

Yet even if the concept of *coordinated care* had been as developed in the early days of the HMO as it is today, the technology to make it happen was not. Today, we have web-based systems that were only dreams at the time of the HMOs. We have communication technologies, home/virtual monitoring systems, electronic data systems including PACS, and so on, that might have made the HMO a more viable enterprise. Indeed, much of the streamlining of care, the reduction of care redundancies, optimization of resource utilization, and overall cost controls that are the talking points of ACO advocates were largely unavailable in the early days of the HMO due to system and technology limitations. Without the lifting of these limitations, it is doubtful that ACOs could be as successful.

Additionally, ACOs are *open systems* rather than *closed networks* of providers. This means that, at least initially, patients within ACO systems can select which facilities and physicians they want to use without the restriction of access common to managed care plans such as HMOs. For instance, managed care networks and HMOs would commonly restrict access to specialists via the primary care physician (PCP) gatekeeper role, and furthermore restrict which PCPs and specialists could be used (i.e., those that are in the network, and have financial and contractual obligations to the HMO). This prevented (theoretically) unnecessary visits, procedures, and costs from being incurred, as might be the case in a more open access system.

Lastly, HMOs began to be maligned by providers for an increasing amount of regulation and restrictions and a decreasing amount of per-patient reimbursement. (This could readily happen with the ACO concept if FFS is replaced, as it likely will be, by a capitated payment model, and costs continue to be squeezed.)

Thus ACOs and managed care plans are in many ways dissimilar, though the end results could well be the same if the same issues of care rationing, payment squeezing, and cost over patient care erupt.

It should be pointed out that in both systems, "someone's ox is going to be gored." Regardless of what we call it, whether it is reduction in redundancies, streamlining of care delivery, home/virtual monitoring, and so on, someone in the health-care system loses something—mostly revenue. All the redundancy, waste, and excess, while definitely in need of removal, is actually income to someone's pocketbook. If the business models are to change, especially to the point that the cost of the delivery of care is reduced, someone in the system makes less. Therefore, as we consider the new business models, we must be cognizant of the protectiveness some will feel for their incomes and revenues, as they try to keep their oxen whole.

Can ACOs Save the System?

Even CMS has questions about the actual implementation of the ACO model, despite their insistence that it is a plausible and reasonable solution. In an interview with *CQ Healthbeat*, a Commonwealth Fund online journal, Dr. Don Berwick (CMS director, 2010–2011) is quoted as saying, "There are many variables, like how much shared savings? How do you attribute a patient to an ACO given that they have full choice? How will we watch quality carefully enough to make sure skimping doesn't occur? What about collusion? We're now going to have cooperation between doctors and hospitals and when does that deteriorate into distorting markets? And on and on—there's probably 20 or 30 questions that arise from this rather interesting idea of merging coordination with fee for service care."[1]

And, as has been shown, there is room for many critics. Those who question the concept claim it's an overly bureaucratic approach with too many regulations and operational requirements to assure that quality of care is expanded and maintained. The ACO, they say, is a burden rather than a salvation, due in part to the onerous nature of the regulations, requirements, legalities, and reporting.

Yet, despite this, ACOs are currently all the rage since they are seen as a business model capable of salvaging the broken system. How? In part, through several key attributes and contributions.

The reduction in the cost of provision of care is expected to come largely from care coordination. That is, physicians, hospitals, care managers, and so on, collaborate and cooperate to streamline patient care, reduce and remove redundancies in care, reduce and remove communications errors that lead to excess cost (via medical error), and better patient engagement and self-management. As Dr. Berwick states, "The doctor who's seeing the patient in her office doesn't get paid to make sure that the cardiologist and the pulmonologist know everything that's happening with the patient. The payment system is chopped up. So the ACO rule is a clever idea."[2] As with the MCNs of Scotland and similar models across Europe, ACOs stand a chance to allow such collaborative care to take place, thus achieving the dramatic cost savings and other goals promised. As its proponents point out, most patients go to the same hospitals and physicians for long periods of time, and regardless of external incentives, patients are likely to stay within their assigned ACO assuming their local residency is maintained. Thus, patients can be followed over longer periods of time using electronic record keeping and sharing, and thus can be cared for more effectively and efficiently.

Second, the collaboration and connectivity of the ACO lends itself to new payment models. Initially, these will be models such as *bundled payments*, in which an entire procedural episode of care is paid for in a single, lump sum by the payor, and distributed to the various parties within the care episode based on some preset agreement. The bundling of payments is thought to eventually reduce paperwork, eliminate multiple billings and payments, force the coordination of care and the control of costs, and allow for a streamlined and clinically effective longitudinal care of the patient throughout a given episode. Since quality, cost, and efficiency metrics can be tied directly to the care episodes and their associated bundles, there is incentive for all parties involved in the episode to monitor the metrics and address any quality or cost issues.

Third, it is anticipated that the mere act of coordinating the delivery of care across a larger set of educated, committed, and compassionate providers will inevitably lead to better quality and outcomes. If fingers can no longer be pointed, and patients can no longer be passed off to the next care provider so as to avoid excess cost or hassles, the natural coordination of care among accountable providers will ensure that clinical behavior matches the objectives of the healthcare system: better population health and outcomes of disease interventions.

To achieve the goals of the ACO, several process-related issues must be addressed in the early and later stages of the development of the business model.

■ Reduce variation and disparities in care delivery among practices and individual providers, i.e., standardizing care, or at least obtaining provider agreement on the best practices to be followed. (Standardized care sounds to many like "cookbook medicine," whereas practices that are directionally correct allow for tailoring and study of care nuances within a set framework of best practices.)

■ Identify the most effective care delivery processes to drive the organization's strategic goals. This is, in part, the engineering of healthcare processes, something I have touted for years as a solution to cost overruns. (This engineering shows up in the PCCN concepts as well.)

- Then, identify and implement effective interventions to standardize care around the desired processes matching outcomes and processes to ensure they are mutually supportive.
- Develop a culture of learning and innovation that fosters ongoing improvement, and the consumption, distillation, and dissemination of best practices. (This thinking is matched in the PCCN networking concept, wherein PCCN providers from across the country and around the world exchange ideas, data, results, and outcomes to expand and discern the best practices for any given patient population.)
- Center care on patients and engage them, to the extent possible, in the management of their own health.

Many of these process-related concepts will lead to the need for supporting technologies, some of which are not even being considered, such as, simulation (covered in detail in Chapter 9). And by optimizing care processes to reduce cost and impact outcomes, this new process infrastructure supports the inevitable changes in risk and payment models, such that the population health of entire communities is managed under an ACO umbrella, complete with financial risks associated with payor metrics and requirements.

ACOs and PCCNs

Some of the ACO management concepts and requirements are obviously well matched with the design and implementation of the PCCN. However, the PCCN remains a very different and uniquely powerful business model. As a potential subsystem within a larger business model, the elegance of the PCCN structure is in its focus on small groups of patients within existing, trusted networks of communal resources. Thus when comparing the ACO and other managed care models to the PCCN model, a number of significant differences arise.

The ACO, like other similar business models and concepts, retains the current base business model and merely pivots off these central themes. The basic *care triangle*, made up of the patient, the physician, and associated resources (e.g., in-practice care managers), and the local hospitals and clinics, is thereby preserved. Albeit flawed, it remains at the core of the ACO model. Yet, as we all know, one size does not fit all, especially as it relates to the management and improvement of chronic disease populations. Caring for chronic disease patients in the same care systems and models as the rest of the healthier population can seem nonsensical if there is another, better way. The PCCN, by contrast, creates an entirely new care subsystem. An integrated group of physicians (chronicists, PCPs, and clinical subspecialists) works with a much broader array of community resources to manage the care of a specific and relatively small group of high-utilizing patients, or the poly-chronics, from within a given community or geography. This new system is created solely for the poly-chronic patients, and therefore does not rely on the constraints of the previous care models.

Furthermore, the PCCN leaves open the possibility of innovation within the subsystem, such that changes to the care streams, patterns, resources, and systems impact a small group of patients and providers rather than the entire population or community. Such speedy innovation is much more difficult within a community population setting, but will be critical as patient populations, technologies, and resource pools evolve within and external to the PCCN. This innovative agility will allow for the kind of patient care specificity and care strategy development that will inevitably be necessary for this high-risk, high-cost, high-utilizing population. Furthermore, it prevents the inevitable issues raised by attempting to innovate within the care models for entire populations of patients, since large-scale change requires much greater coordination and cost.

Thus, since the PCCN creates an entirely new business model, it is much like a boutique firm elsewhere in the marketplace. Just as a local, hometown business here in Oakhurst,

Georgia, specializes in organic, home-baked treats for dogs, or a local sporting goods store caters only to high-mileage runners, this boutique system will cater to the needs of patients who otherwise would be tossed into the "big-box retailer" of the healthcare system—patient pools that include entire communities, which neither cater to needs of the poly-chronic patient or fulfills those needs effectively.

Furthermore, the ACO will ultimately manage risk differently. ACOs will, at some point, shift the financial and health risk of an entire population of patients onto the provider groups. This is expected to evolve over time, of course, as the payment models within concepts such as bundled payments force risk and capitation onto the providers. The PCCN may indeed share in a similar payment model for the core networks of providers. However, by focusing on such a relatively small group of patients, for whom risk and cost are already very high, the PCCN takes risk *out* of the general population and places it within a smaller group of providers where it can be more effectively managed. These providers, inclusive of chronicists and specialists, will have a better view of the total risk of their smaller patient group, since there will be no *hidden* risk as there would be in the larger population of an entire community. By putting risk boundaries around the highest risk populations, and by managing the care for that group, the PCCN takes much of the risk out of the broader population and allows for a very different risk and payment model for both populations. Thus, by creating both a business and a risk subsystem, the PCCN allows for two (or more) very different business models upon which risk, resources, and population health can be built. And while capitation is a good payment model for the PCCN, the risk is contained and thus not spread excessively to the general population of patients, preventing cost escalations and premium risk spread for everyone.

The good news is that the PCCN can live easily within a larger ACO business model. Indeed, if you examine the literature on the ACO model itself, you will find that much of the focus is on chronic disease management. Unfortunately, the ACO model simply fails to create a unique and wholly different infrastructure for those high-risk, high-cost patients, and merely tries to account for them within the general and current business and risk framework. Indeed, the individual mandate currently being so heavily debated in the United States is simply a means by which to force the young and healthy to pay for the care of the very sick, rather than addressing the cost of the very sick. The ACO locks in enough patients (minimum 50,000) to spread risk far and wide enough to allow for an ACO to be financially viable, even with a capitated model. Thus, the PCCN serves to help the ACO better manage this population by focusing the risk and care management within a smaller group of specialized and dedicated resources.

PCCNs and Other Business Models

By creating and knitting together a specialized resource pool, and offloading the most complex patients in the population into their own, specially constructed care network, the PCCN works well within any larger business model, whether the current FFS model of the United States or an MCN in Scotland. Thus, the PCCN can be constructed anywhere, under a variety of circumstances, as the population's health and risk stratification requires. Indeed, there are a number of business models that are currently evolving toward the PCCN, though its organization structure has yet to be truly honed and tested. Most notable are the following examples of some of the health systems that have tried to develop some of the elements of the PCCN in their models (though none have gone all the way):

■ **Maine's PHO:** The physician–hospital organization (PHO) of Maine Medical Center is currently applying for ACO status, and has already begun to build a small, integrated network of resources. These currently include care managers and mental health specialists who are employed by the PHO and serve the associated physicians with specific services for high-cost, high-risk patients. While not fully integrated electronically, the PHO and Maine Med have made a unique commitment to reaching a PCCN-esque concept.

■ **AtlantiCare:** Made famous through a magazine[3] article by Atul Gawande, MD, in *The New Yorker,* AtlantiCare uses a variety of resources, all focused on the care of high-cost patients. While it is not engineered and optimized for full effectiveness, and doesn't deal with all varieties of chronic disease (as of this publication), the model nonetheless takes a solid step toward the kind of coordinated care delivery that will be part of the PCCN.

■ **Ambulatory ICUs:** The use of ambulatory intensive care units (ICUs) is a new concept in the dissemination of resources throughout a community. These are separated from the larger hospital, and can more readily flex to care for high-risk patients in a lower cost setting. This sort of thinking is critical to the spread of care and risk through-out a given community, and may be especially important for rural or semirural populations.

■ **Ascension and other ACO applicants:** There are a few cutting-edge systems around the United States whose efforts to transcend the current, broken FFS business models should be applauded. To varying degrees and in several ways, these systems have shown courage and creativity in developing new systems of care, resources (e.g., care managers within the physician practice), business models (bundled payments), and payment models (e.g., financial risk sharing and shared savings). Many of these are precursors to the massive changes that will need to take place within the structures of the current U.S. healthcare system in order to make it finan-cially and structurally viable for the next generation.

Summary

Both the European and U.S. healthcare markets undergo constant revision. In Europe, more centralized systems yield different business models, each with pluses and minuses, than we have seen here in the United States. The current debates over PPACA and the pending financial tidal wave facing American taxpayers make change—dramatic change—the requirement in the coming decade. Without a new business model for chronic disease patients like the PCCN, the three aims of the Institute for Healthcare Improvement (IHI) and CMS will remain elusive. That a few health systems and some European innovators are inching toward similar solutions lends credence to the concept, and should allow it to leap to relevance as it becomes more widely known.

Endnotes

1. John Reichard, "Washington Health Policy Week in Review: Berwick Not Blue About ACOs Despite Beat Down of Proposed Reg, Commonwealth Fund," October 11, 2011, http://www.commonwealthfund.org/Newsletters/Washington-Health-Policy-in-Review/2011/Oct/October-17-2011/Berwick-Not-Blue.aspx.
2. John Reichard, "Washington Health Policy Week."
3. Atul Gawande, "The Hot Spotters: Can We Lower Medical Costs by Giving the Neediest Patients Better Care?" January 24, 2011, http://www.newyorker.com/reporting/2011/01/24/110124fa_fact_gawande.

Chapter 3

The Five Pillars of Healthcare for the PCCN

Common to the discussion of healthcare change is the Institute for Healthcare Improvement (IHI)'s well-known and often quoted Triple Aim. These aims are:

- Improve the health of the population.
- Enhance the patient experience of care (including quality, access, and reliability).
- Reduce, or at least control, the per capita cost of care.[1]

This is also reflected in the new three aims of the Centers for Medicare and Medicaid Services (CMS), which Dr. Don Berwick brought with him when he moved over from IHI to lead CMS. These aims lit a fire in healthcare that has yet to be extinguished, and should forever be remembered as a "tipping point" (to quote Maxwell) in the history of the evolution of healthcare delivery. By bringing the Triple Aim to CMS, Dr. Berwick made the famed work of the IHI national in scope and fundamental to the future of healthcare delivery in the United States and elsewhere.

Yet, I firmly believe that the Triple Aim encompasses much more than just the three commonly listed aims (since they are most often listed without proper definition and footnoting). Indeed, the detailed description of the three adds many ancillary aims to the short list of objectives. However, those additional or ancillary aims and benefits are not called out specifically. And while these three are certainly laudable and important goals, I believe there are other, equally important, considerations for the system that deserve explicit mention. In fact, by influencing a few additional factors simultaneously, and implementing new care systems such as the poly-chronic care network (PCCN), we can optimize the impact of all of the elements and ancillaries of the Triple Aim.

This is particularly important as it relates to the PCCN and its community-wide, community-engaging approach. The elements that I have considered when developing the PCCN relate directly to the healthcare needs of the patient, community, resources, and the entire system. Simply put, since ours is a broader approach, we need a larger set of elements if we are to adequately set goals and monitor our performance. These include the obviously important and succinctly stated elements of the Triple Aim, such as cost, as well as the unspoken ancillaries such as access and quality. Indeed, the five elements of the PCCN, if achieved together, will result in the attainment of the first and perhaps most important of the aims, *population health*. Thus, at risk of adding yet more confusing nomenclature to the many healthcare discussions, I will add the Five Pillars of the PCCN concept. I will speak of these throughout the text.

Understand that, in the end, the goals of all those trying to improve the delivery of healthcare are likely very similar if not identical. Therefore, it would not be surprising if the concept of the Five Pillars only lasted you until the end of the reading of this text. As long as you, the reader, understand how the PCCN concept and implementation tools and methodologies impact the pillars, the Triple Aim, and similar groups of optimization metrics, you will have received the correct message.

The Five Pillars are the optimization of the following:

- Quality and outcomes
- Access
- Capacity
- Cost reduction
- Participant gratification

Let's describe these in greater detail as they relate to the broader, community-wide approach of the PCCN.

Quality and Outcomes

This is at the top of the list, though not because it is a more important goal than the others. All are equally important, as failure to achieve one will inevitably and negatively impact the others. Quality is included in the IHI Triple Aim, but only as part of the second aim, patient experience. I feel that it is important enough to warrant its own category, as the patients of the PCCN will need the highest possible quality of care in order to see positive results in the remains of the three pillar metrics. Furthermore, quality, as an increasingly important focal area for payors and providers alike, should warrant its own special category, considered on equal footing with cost reduction.

Quality is commonly and generically known as a degree of excellence, or some superiority in kind. Quality can be both an outcome and an indicator of measures like organizational effectiveness.[2] The latter indicators are most commonly relative measures, as quality can be either subjective or quantitative, but is often determined through comparative standards to other, lesser samples. Quality in healthcare can mean everything from the patient experience (how good did the patient feel after the procedure?) to lack of adverse results (zero surgical infections during a given timeframe), to clinical measurements (diastolic function, or percentage of patients receiving tissue plasminogen activator [t-PA] within three hours of the onset of a nonhemorrhagic stroke). Quality can also refer to a measurement of the functions and processes that support clinical operations, such as cleanliness of operating theaters.

Quality related to clinical outcomes is a sort of a combination of the above. The term *quality outcome* often reflects a combination of patient experience, clinical indicators, and standards of care. When discussing quality and outcomes, it is therefore important to settle on those clinical measures for which standards will be set, such as degree of post-rehab knee flexure for nonrevision total knee replacement surgeries, while employing flexibility in the measurement of nonclinical indicators such as patient satisfaction. The measurement of outcomes can thereby be amended as needed to reflect the patient's experience and desires ("I can at least walk now even though I can't bend my knee as much as the doctor would like"), while using stricter clinical guidelines among caregivers (e.g., zero tolerance for central line infections). This can make quality outcomes a "squishy" measurement, for which a completely rigid set of standards cannot be made. Care must be taken to quantitatively account for the variances, so as to effectively study and compare quality outcomes within and outside a given care system.

Yet, high-quality care is an obvious goal, as the alternatives (poor to moderate quality) will mean negative impacts on our other metrics, including patient satisfaction, cost (e.g., readmissions for the same procedure), and capacity (rework reduces total community capacity). Without attention to and desire for the highest possible quality and outcomes, the other metrics of the pillars will not be fully optimized.

Access

Access, mentioned as an ancillary to the second aim, will be critical in the coming years as an aging and increasingly chronic population requires more and more resources, which in turn are increasingly financially constrained and relatively fewer in number. Yet access will have many more meanings in the future. Access will be access to information, such as care processes and interventions; care resources, whether they are physicians or emergency departments; and access to physical space, such as a hospital bed or clinic. All forms of access must be optimized in order to maximize the effectiveness of the entire care system. Since access can occur in an increasing number of ways and locations, e.g., the Internet, direct care provider contact, minute clinics, virtual monitoring, and so on, the possibilities for increasing access will multiply, assuming that patients have the ability to take advantage of the many new access points. Access points may and should expand from the traditional access points, such as the hospital and physician office, to include the Internet, community resources such as YMCAs and churches, and virtual monitoring systems that both transmit clinical data and accept educational materials and clinical advice. Therefore, when we consider access in any new care system design, we should consider the availability of multiple potential points of access within a broader and more complex care network.

Capacity

This is perhaps the most important but most overlooked of the pillars. Indeed, it is neither directly nor indirectly referenced within the Triple Aim, yet it encompasses all the key elements required for care provision, such as labor, space, and processing capability, some of which are in short supply. Capacity refers to the general and total capability of the system to provide care, as well as that of the capabilities of individual components and resources within the system. Capacity is, then, the sum total of the capacities of all the components of the entire care system. Capacity will encompass clinical resources and their ability to care for/manage a certain number of patients or citizens within a population. Capacity will also refer to space, such as the number of ED beds within a given geographic region.

Capacity is critical since, as we saw in previous chapters, certain clinical resources will be in increasingly short supply as their numbers dwindle relative to the increasing demand. The supply of these clinical resources will simply not be able to keep up with the growing demand of retirees and the elderly. Therefore the system's total care capacity may be relatively reduced. (This is, of course, a relative measurement. Since the actual number of physicians, nurses, and so on, is due to increase, the actual numerical capacity of the system will go up. However, since the demand will outstrip this new capacity, the relative capability to care for the population will decrease.)

Capacity is also reflected in processing capability. If there are not enough spaces in the hospital or clinic, additional clinical resources will not help. Likewise, if we create a system in which the processing of patients and information is difficult, tedious, or onerous, then the care capacity of the system is inevitably reduced. Thus, capacity can and should include reference to the processing capability and technology infrastructure required to effectively treat and manage patients. Without the right infrastructure and processes in place, the capacity of the system might be greatly reduced.

Thus, when I refer to *capacity* you should think holistically about its meaning and how the various forms of capacity are included in its definition.

Cost

The PCCN is specifically focused on cost reduction. Indeed, the original impetus of the PCCN and dynamic capacity management work was dramatic cost reduction to save the system. As we discussed in the previous chapter, cost is an obvious and necessary consideration for any healthcare reform proposal. Without dramatically reducing total provision cost, any healthcare reform will fail to support our national economy since sustainable economic growth and high employment will be hampered as healthcare consumes too many financial resources, draining important capital away from the rest of the economy. Thus, like the Triple Aim and similar objectives, the Five Pillars includes a distinct cost reduction element. Fortunately, cost reduction is a key attribute for the PCCN and the care systems proposed in this text.

Participant Gratification

While patient satisfaction is important, it is not enough in the PCCN. In order for the PCCN to function properly, all participants must receive something of an emotional and psychological benefit. And I believe that the *something* should be more than simple satisfaction. There needs to be a sense of *participant gratification* that can only come from doing something significantly good, either for you or someone else. Gratification, at least by my definition, is a deeper and more significant sensation than mere satisfaction, and more appropriately applies to an environment that promotes personal responsibility, community engagement, and long-term system change. That's why I replace the overused term *satisfaction* score with a term that implies a higher level and more broadly applied sensation.

Indeed, the concept of patient satisfaction, in and of itself, and by definition, is too limited for me. First off, though patients matter, so do the healthcare workers in whom we invest and in whom our patients trust. More importantly, it has even been suggested that the focus of patient satisfaction is wrong. According to some, the focus should instead be on physician satisfaction, because with physician satisfaction comes the best in patient care and outcomes focus, and patient satisfaction as a byproduct. However, even physician satisfaction has the following shortcomings:

- It leaves out the other clinical resources commonly associated with care provision. Think of the fussy radiology technician who grumbles impatiently through an exam.
- It fails to account for myriad other nonclinical resources that can add to or take away from a patient's satisfaction. Think of that billing clerk with that nasty, "I'm entitled" attitude.
- It fails to account for the satisfaction of parents, friends, and certainly the host of communal resources engaged by the PCCN.

Alternatively, *participant gratification* can and should be felt by the patient but should also be felt by all others in the system, from communal resources to physicians to office and hospital staff. Furthermore, the sense of gratification should come to all participants from the "higher good" that is being achieved through the PCCN, the benefits developed for patients and the community, and the patients' sense of accomplishment though self-help and communal support.

The Five Pillars and New Approach

Perhaps if there is a distinct difference between the Triple Aim (and other similar objectives) and the Five Pillars of the PCCN, it is that the former is simply a list of objectives, while the latter is an actual workable system for care delivery that supports the goals defined in the pillars. The former tends to leave open the question of how aims should be attained, while the specific system of the PCCN is designed to achieve the Five Pillars. Thus, we can see how to achieve the pillars (and the aims) through the system that derived them.

Because it builds a new a system of care delivery for a specific population of patients, the PCCN is designed from the ground up to deliver on the objectives of the Five Pillars. While the pillars guide the program like a beacon in the night, the vehicle that gets us to the destination is the care delivery system set forth as the PCCN. Thus the PCCN (or some even grander and bolder version thereof) should be the actual goal, as its proper implementation will inevitably lead to the realization of both the pillars and the three aims.

Summary

If for no other reason than distinction of the scope of the solutions, the Five Pillars are herein set apart from other healthcare nomenclature. Since the scope, scale, and foci seem to be much broader and holistic than those of other solutions, the PCCN needs its own goals and objectives that align with its potential. The Five Pillars support and are supported by concepts like the infamous Triple Aim, and thus the latter is in no way meant to be downplayed or made any less significant. But for the PCCN, the Five Pillars better speak to its full capability to forever change the delivery system.

Endnotes

1. Details on the Triple Aim initiative(s) can be found at http://www.ihi.org.
2. B. Winn and K. Cameron, "Organizational Quality: An Examination of the Malcolm Baldrige National Quality Framework," *Research in Higher Education* 39, no. 5 (1998): 491–512.

Chapter 4

Assessing the Community and the Patient Population

As we look to create a new care subsystem for our poly-chronics, we must first select a population of patients to care for, understand their care needs, and develop care strategies to be implemented to achieve the Five Pillars. This will lead us to the proper selection and allocation of the community resource pool, which will provide both the care and the necessary physical plant and technologies. We will then dynamically match the demand from the patients we intend to serve with the capacity we create.

Selecting Patients

Chronic conditions are, of course, closely linked to high expenditure levels. More than 75 percent of high-cost beneficiaries (the 25 percent of Medicare beneficiaries with the highest costs) had one or more of seven major chronic conditions, according to the Congressional Budget Office.[1] "The elderly and disabled, who constituted around 25 percent of the Medicaid population, accounted for about 70 percent of Medicaid spending on services in 2003. People with disabilities accounted for 43 percent of Medicaid spending and the elderly for 26 percent. The remaining 75 percent of the Medicaid population, who were not elderly or disabled, accounted for only 30 percent of spending."[2,3] This may be due to several socioeconomic factors and the patients typically enrolled in Medicaid programs.

The patients in your poly-chronic population will likely come from private payors and from Medicare, Medicaid, and dual eligibles. It might be surprising to find that the majority of poly-chronics are currently insured in the private market (65 percent)[4] and not through purely government programs (31 percent)[5]. Poly-chronics are typically 45 years old and older, and may or may not end up in government insurance programs later in life, depending on contractual agreements with unions and employers that currently sponsor their care.

Of course, the sponsors of Medicare/Medicaid (i.e., taxpayers) are quite interested in the reduction of costs for the poly-chronics as so many are cared for via these programs. Of the three groups (privately insured, Medicare, and Medicaid), Medicaid patients are by far the most costly. This is why you might find your payors (state, federal, and private) to be ready partners in your cost-reduction efforts, as the state of Vermont has seen with its care management programs.

In an ideal scenario, we would simultaneously determine the patients to be served as we determine the available and willing resource pool. This would save total implementation time and allow for an ongoing match between demand (patients) and capacity (resources). It would also avoid a complete or partial rework of the applicable patient population if severe limitations in the resource pool are discovered, and vice versa. For the sake of this discussion, however, I will not make the assumption that this is possible, as you may encounter resource, focus, and/or time constraints in your implementation team.

If you perform these two tasks serially (that is, one after the other), it is recommended that you perform the patient population assessment first. Assessing the resource pool won't mean much without first determining the patients to be served. On the other hand, knowing the population to be cared for within the poly-chronic care networks (PCCNs) of your community will allow you seek out the most appropriate resources rather than trying to garner support from all possible participants in hopes of finding patients to which to assign them. This eliminates work and prevents the chaos and frustration of the *narrowing down* process. It also allows you to tap only those resources that are immediately needed, saving others for future expansion of the PCCN framework into a larger population.

It is worth noting that, for this exercise, you can assume that at least a certain percentage of patients will opt in to the program. This analysis is meant to determine the population of patients you can and want to serve, and not necessarily the exact number. The precise numbers or percentages of participating patients is less important at this stage than determining which patients could achieve the largest health impact and the largest possible return on your investments. So, while you should not assume 100 percent opt-in, you should go forward with your analysis under the assumption that some or most patients will agree to be part of the program, especially as it matures over time.

Selecting the patients in the community to be served by the PCCN could be based on several criteria, including (but not limited to):

■ Underserved populations such as rural communities or poor urban areas
■ Highly chronic and complex patients who are not receiving the kind of care that is required to improve their health
■ Specific disease states such as chronic obstructive pulmonary disease (COPD) or diabetes

- Highest-cost patients or those using the most expensive resources; e.g., "frequent fliers" in local emergency departments (EDs)
- Disease states with the highest prevalence
- Communities known for low health scores, regardless of the disease states, and populations within those communities (in other words, a small-scale population health effort)
- Patients known to impact local healthcare finances, e.g., ED "frequent fliers"

I do not recommend any of these as being a better choice than the others. However, I would suggest that the bolder and grander your vision for the population you'll serve, the better. Starting small may seem to have its advantages. However, there are significant disadvantages to starting too small, as we'll discuss shortly.

Keep in mind that you may have a number of smaller sub-PCCNs within a larger community or PCCN infrastructure. This might occur due to the following:

- Ethnic population or language mix
- Neighborhood or community ties
- Religious or congregational bonds and commitments
- Location and proximity to services and other PCCN patients
- Physician or group service areas
- Location and proximity of resources

In some iterations, a large PCCN infrastructure (meaning, the management team and structure, total resource pool, technologies, etc.) might serve several small PCCNs within small subpopulations. Each smaller PCCN might be different in focus and need than its brethren, depending on the population and disease(s) each one serves. For instance, one congregation-based PCCN might service shut-ins and highly chronic patients within their church family, while an employer-based PCCN might only service the diabetics in its employed ranks and their families. Both might fall under the care of a single, large physician group practice and PCCN infrastructure, which would serve as the locus of care management and clinical guidance. Management of the PCCN would likely come under the physician group practice, as would the clinical responsibility and oversight. While this adds some complexity, it is important to remember that the PCCN concept is designed to accommodate just such a scenario, as it is flexible and dynamic enough to allow for this degree of customization.

Size, Scope, and Scale of Your PCCN

Important to the short- and long-term successful operation of the PCCN is its size. How many patients should, can, and will it serve? Will its focus be broad or narrow, and thus its size either relatively large or small? While this is a critical question to be answered, we can only address it as an estimate for the moment since we don't yet know how large and complete the resource pool will be or how many patients will opt in over time. The available resource pool may only have the capacity to serve a small percentage of the desired population. However, it is important to estimate the size, or at least the desired size, of the population to be served at this stage so as to allow for a more targeted resource assessment later. This will also help you develop your financial justifications, investment requirements, implementation timeframes, and potential clinical and financial outcomes. As the resource pool is further defined (after or during this community assessment phase), you can use simulation to test for care gaps between the demand and the capacity, and dynamically match the two.

The size of the population to be served will depend on more than just the number of chronically ill patients. There are a number of other factors that will influence the size of the PCCNs you'll want to establish and manage within your area. In addition to those listed in the following text, we'll see in the next chapters how the resource pool itself might limit or expand the PCCN's capacity.

Proximity of Space and Resources

This is especially true of rural communities, where there may be limited available clinical space. The rural PCCN may rely more heavily on in-home technologies and "remote visitation" for distant patient contact (assuming connectivity is not an issue), and churches and community centers for space. Space is important not only for clinical care but also for Group Dynamics meetings, clinical coaching and instructions, and periodic wellness and health clinics. Space, like communal resources, should be openly considered for its possibilities such that local churches, schools, and even large private residences would be considered for clinical and meeting locations.

Of course, the proximity of resources is important as well. Taking the care to the patient, rather than the other way around, becomes more difficult and time-consuming in rural and dispersed populations. If applicable resources remain distant, the PCCN will need to reflect this in its capacity and resource utilization assumptions.

Physician Participation

Not all physicians within a given community need to participate. Only a few offices, either solo or within a large group practice are needed support a PCCN infrastructure with expertise and connectivity rather than demanding that all physicians adopt the required technologies. This means that the strategic selection of physicians and offices may improve the chances of successful impacts on your population. (We'll cover physician selection in much greater detail in Chapter 6.)

Technology Constraints

The availability of technology will have an obvious impact on the size and scale of the PCCN and its capacity to care for patients. For instance, the lack of Internet, broadband, and/or wireless communications might make home monitoring more difficult and tedious and electronic personal health records more difficult to manage and maintain. Lack of technology will not only inhibit the patient in their home, but could limit access of communal resources to care strategies and clinical updates from physicians and other clinicians. This lack of electronic access may make the cost of delivery of care higher, as resources will need more face-to-face time to achieve the same goals, driving up cost of transportation and driving down utilization. Thus, the capacity of the system may be constrained by the technology infrastructure available.

Additionally, the relative effective use of various electronic medical records (EMRs) and paper records in both urban and rural areas may hinder the use of the PCCN's recommended technologies. Many practices still use paper records and are only grudgingly entering the twenty-first century of medical management. (My former primary care physician [PCP] some-how manages to simultaneously use both electronic records and paper. Yet, a specialist I recently visited swore that EMRs were pure evil.) For these practices, the addition of new technologies might be an unwelcomed strain.

In urban areas, it is not uncommon to see multiple EMRs in use in a single geographic area. While the typical health information exchange (HIE) can help manage these differences by gathering data from one and all, some EMR providers are harder to work with than others. (Surprisingly, the largest and most popular of the larger providers is also said to be the hardest to work with on data extraction, and most reluctant to participate in HIE implementations). However, the PCCN is fortunately flexible enough to manage even this, since the social–clinical networking (SCN) platform can help manage connectivity even in the face of the worst or most limited EMR implementation. As we will see in Chapter 9 on technology, PCCNs can be implemented with only an SCN in place.

Patient Population Chosen

Depending on the patient population you've decided to impact, there may be inherent resource and capacity limitations due to their specific care needs. Some disease states may require more or less intense care or assistance. The higher the degree of acuity, the more intense the care requirements, and therefore the more intense the resource requirements will be. More or fewer clinical resources may be required for a given PCCN population. Thus, it would not be uncommon to see the PCCN's goals and affected populations altered if stubborn resource constraints emerge.

Furthermore, choosing several disease states or a larger population of true poly-chronics from the population will mean more intense care and resource requirements than would a single-disease-state PCCN. While this will not be understood until the care strategies are devised and resources assessed and aligned, it is worthwhile to consider the disease states the PCCN is to attack as you consider the scale and scope of the effort since this will drive your population health results.

There are, of course, several tacks the PCCN could take from here. The PCCN might focus on a single chronic disease rather than the full spectrum. For instance, it might only focus on diabetes, or all chronic diseases except cancer. A limited scale and scope might be wise in the initial stages of development, when resources and managers are unsure of the ground upon which they are about to walk, or if the resource pool is just developing and needs to "test the waters." The PCCN might also take on a small group of test patients, such as the members of a single church congregation or current poly-chronic members of the local YMCA.

However, limiting the scale and scope of the initial system has potential downsides, as well. While a limited scope prevents overloaded resources, it also prevents the kind of dramatic improvements that the PCCN might expect to see. So, cost savings and population health impacts might not be as great as hoped or worthy of investment of time and resources. Also, several of the technologies required would not make financial sense in a limited engagement as implementation costs might prove prohibitive for the financial and clinical returns expected. Even the lightest implementation plan (assuming only a few full-time resources and limited supportive technologies) would require an annual budget of between $225,000 and $450,000 (see Chapter 10 for more detailed financial considerations). Finally, limiting the scope may slow the full implementation if managers await results before expanding. Significant improvements may be years away for some disease states. Thus it may be some time before a next phase could be justified and started, thereby limiting the potential impact of the programs.

As you scale your effort, keep the short- and long-term risks, costs, and opportunities in mind.

Community Acceptance

While this might seem an odd metric, one that cannot be effectively measured if even grasped, it is nonetheless important to the capacity of the PCCN. Some communities and community members may be more or less inclined to accept the assistance from a PCCN and its resources. There may be some reticence to accept the assistance of nonclinical resources, or even use nonclinical facilities as part of the PCCN engagement. Shoving the PCCN concept into the lives of the impacted patients would more than likely fail. Thus the acceptance of the PCCN concept within a given community or subpopulation is vital to its short- and long-term viability and sustainability because, in order for the PCCN to work optimally, patients and resources must be fully engaged and committed. This commitment should go beyond mere willingness to be part of the PCCN to being truly assimilated into the PCCN concepts and culture of care. It is not enough for patients to merely go along for the ride, or accept care while not themselves engaging in their own health and well-being. They must instead fully accept the ideas of Group Dynamics, the resource pool's goals and aspirations, and the requirements for the improvement of their health and the health of the other PCCN patients.

Assimilation, as we'll see later in this chapter, should therefore be defined as a much stronger alignment than participation or engagement; a far more intense commitment to the PCCN care processes and strategies, goals and outcomes, and population health of the patients served. Without true assimilation, patients will see the PCCN much like a person who believes in God but never worships, goes to church, or reads the scriptures. He will not, in the end, commit to the requirements and will drop out at the first sign of hassle, failure, or frustration. Assimilation is therefore a requirement for all patients in the PCCN. (For those patients mentally incapable of understanding and making such commitments, to understand or make such commitments, the caregivers and resources must have a similar level of commitment such that they will take responsibility for those unable to truly grasp the concepts.)

Assimilation Propensity

In my years of working with communities and population health, I have come to realize that some communities are far more interested than others in promoting health and wellness. Some of this depends on the resources in the community, often notably a local hospital or widely used clinic. It may also depend on other social factors, not the least of which are community attitudes toward the environment, pollution, smoking, and other potentially causal attributes of healthy living; religious fervency; and the strength of communal ties. The willingness of both resources and patients to participate in the PCCN is what I call its *assimilation propensity.*

As you look to the willingness of the patients and community resources to assimilate, there are several factors you'll want to consider:

- How readily is technology already used, both for patient care and generally?
  - Is there solid accessibility to and use of broadband, wireless, and the Internet?
  - To what degree are local schools "wired" and computerized?
  - To what extent do local physicians use EMRs? Does the local hospital use an HIE or large-scale EMR within its physician network (assuming there is one)?
- Is the community known for its "greenness," recycling programs, and antismoking ordinances?
- How strong are churches in the community? Is it known as a solidly Christian or religious community, or do congregations struggle to fill the pews?
- How prevalent is the Christian and religious outreach to the poor and indigent?
- How well or poorly and where are the homeless and indigent cared for?
- How strong are any ethnic ties? Is there a subpopulation of specific ethnic, religious, or language groups that are strongly bound together? Is language an obstacle to the dissemination of healthcare provision for this group(s)?
- Are local employers engaged in the wellness and health of employees?
  - How do employers engage with employees?
  - What programs are currently in place to encourage exercise, good diets, healthy lifestyles, smoking cessation, and so on?

- Do large local employers have any degree of local social commitment, such as sponsorship of health and wellness for employees and local populations?
■ To what extent have local schools promoted wellness?
■ What are the local communal organizations, and how does their participation in the local area take shape? Are they merely private social or politically focused clubs or do they have a true community service mission (e.g., the Rotary, Lions, and Crusaders)?
■ What public facilities exist? Is there a Y or other public health facility readily accessible to the public? To what degree are chronic disease management programs available?
■ What is the degree of participation of local hospitals and clinics in wellness programs and healthy living? Do the local healthcare providers participate, or do they sit idly by?
  - One way to tell this is to examine the calendar of events coming from the local hospital and healthcare providers. If there is no calendar of wellness events, or if there is little or no wellness outreach or passion, you may find it more difficult to use them to unify participation.
■ How prevalent is dependency versus independence in the mindset of the population?
■ How strong are ties to extended families? Do the elderly in your area become wards of the state or are they more likely to be cared for by local and familial resources?

Answers to these and other questions will help you determine the likelihood that your community, or at least critical parts of it, will assimilate into the PCCN framework. If you are developing multiple PCCNs within a larger geographic area or population, I would suggest you develop a scoring mechanism, by which you can gauge your various subcommunities according to the factors that most influence their assimilation propensity. This might be as simple as a spreadsheet with rankings of the variables, giving you a relative scoring and a means to gauge the relative ease of the various implementations.

Cultural Barriers

For some patients, simply preparing the foundations for participation will result in newfound motivation and willpower to join in. As care circles are formed and assimilation is promoted, communal resources will become intimately involved in all factors of a patient's life. Thus, the PCCN's holistic approach to care provision can and should include a focus on those factors that often inhibit patients from self-management, whether housing or tendencies toward depression.

Therefore, in many ways, the PCCN's communal resources must take up the slack for at least some of the patients in the population and promote and support their assimilation. This must be accounted for in the resource planning phases of the implementation, since those patients who are least likely to engage may be the population most in need of care improvements.

On the other hand, employers will likely find that assimilation is a bit easier, since employees will have more of a vested interest in care enhancements, if for no other reason than employer pressure. After all, the cost of healthcare increasingly impacts workers' wages and benefits. For this reason, employers may have the best chance to start a localized and focused PCCN and gain assimilation. Importantly, if the employer's PCCN goes well, and aids in helping to improve the Five Pillars for the affected employees, it is likely that the PCCN concept will spread further into your community. In fact, it may behoove the employer to encourage the dissemination of a successful implementation, since the productivity and absenteeism of employees are often impacted by relatives (parents, husbands and wives, etc.) who are poly-chronics.

Barriers to Assimilation

Keep in mind that patients and resources may need to break barriers in order to participate and assimilate. In some of the PCCN implementations, technology aptitude may inhibit participation if the technology is too far advanced of capabilities or understanding. The sickest patients are often the least likely to be engaged in their own care or willing to use an elaborate new technology. This is true of virtual monitoring and will be equally true of any PCCN technology. This, however, is another justification for both the use of local, familiar, communal resources to support patient care and a simple yet powerful connecting technology like the SCN. By using the local resources in support of patients, more enabling technologies can be brought forth without fear of misuse or errors. Furthermore, augmenting patient care with these resources will aid in the use of communication technologies that can better enable ongoing physician oversight of the patient's condition.

Social constraints or inhibitions may also prevent full participation, must less assimilation for some patients. These can include lack of local family members, lack of transportation, availability of consistent access to food, medication, and treatments, safe living conditions, and proper housing and utilities.

Furthermore, patients whose mental health has impacted or will impact their physical health may be less likely to voluntarily engage the network. These patients may require additional and specialized mental health and social workers who can help in breaking down participation barriers. As we've already discussed, a specific Care Circle Network may be required for these less-able populations.

Summary

Assessing the community and selecting the patient population is a critical part of the short- and long-term strategic planning of your program. Carefully consider at least the elements related earlier, and wisely lay out a detailed plan for the initiation and rollout of your PCCN. Without careful consideration of all facets and attributes of the community and the patients to be served, your PCCN may fail to achieve expectations and disappoint both sponsors and patients.

Endnotes

1. "High-Cost Medicare Beneficiaries. A CBO Paper," Congressional Budget Office, Washington, DC, May 2005, http://www.cbo.gov/showdoc.cfm?index=6332&sequence=0 (accessed February 2010).
2. "Medicaid: A Primer," The Kaiser Foundation, Kaiser Commission on Medicaid and the Uninsured, Washington, DC, July 2005, http://www.kff.org/medicaid/upload/7334%20 Medicaid%20Primer_Final%20for%20posting-3.pdf (accessed February 2010).
3. It is worth noting that these percentages vary among studies and publications. Generally, a sort of "80/20" rule applies to the analysis of the percentage of expenditures used by a specific segment of the population.
4. "The Concentration and Persistence in the Level of Health Expenditures over Time: Estimates for the U.S. Population, 2008–2009," Agency for Healthcare Research and Quality, January 2010, http://meps.ahrq.gov/mepsweb/data_files/ publications/st354/stat354.pdf.
5. "Concentration and Persistence."

Chapter 5

Care Strategies and Task Analysis

Once you have determined the current status of your target population and their assimilation propensity, you'll then need to plan for the care of each patient type.

To help create a new way to think about the care of complex chronic disease patients, and since we are developing an entirely new care system for them, we should use an appropriately holistic term to describe our disease management approach. The term *care strategy* will be used to describe a holistic, complete, and both short- and long-term approach to the care of poly-chronics. While a *care plan* tends to invoke an image of physician's prescriptions for drugs, tests, and treatments, a care strategy goes beyond that. It includes all of these elements plus self-directed long-term care goals, self-management of habits and personal responsibility, diet management and medication control, Group Dynamics™, palliative care, end-of-life (EOL) care and preparation, spirituality and spiritual well-being, safe housing and living conditions, proper utilities, dependency treatments, as well as other concepts that advocates will no doubt add in the future. A care strategy (CS) is therefore an approach that encompasses the strategic alignment of the full spectrum of available communal resources and complete wellness in the optimization of care provision, outcomes, and subpopulation health.

Care strategies will initially be crafted from scratch, customized specifically for each individual patient. As your poly-chronic care network (PCCN) grows and the participating patient base expands, you will find that you can create templates for many of the disease states, from which you can then customize a CS based on a patient's individual needs and care requirements. Furthermore, as physicians learn more about the interactions of communal resources and how they can add to care provision, the CS templates will evolve over time and become integrated into the local PCCN's infrastructure and culture. Of course, as the PCCN concept grows and more are created, these CSs can be shared locally and nationwide among PCCNs, promoting learning and cross-pollination of care methods and approaches.

In order to develop a solid CS for any given patient or population, we must first determine what both local clinicians and general clinical consensus say are the best demonstrated practices (BDPs) before moving into the addition of nonclinical elements such as spiritual well-being.

Establishing BDPs and Patient Involvement

The use of the participating chronicists, primary care physicians (PCPs), specialists, and other clinical resources is vital to the establishment of PCCN protocols and practices, especially if they deviate in any way from what some consider as being *best practice*. Consensus and full agreement must be obtained on each of the clinically significant steps in the care process such that the clinicians are satisfied with the process, its location, the potential resources used, and the frequency of task provision. This will prevent undue variance in process and care provision, and future discrepancies over outcomes and root causes of success or failure. It will also ensure that the communal resources receive consistent and singular task messaging and instruction, which will also prevent task and possible outcome variation.

Advice on BDPs can be sought from myriad sources, from external clinical experts such as those at university research programs, to AHRQ and other federally funded research centers, to renowned clinicians. A vast amount of information is now available on diseases such as diabetes, including standardized treatment protocols. Some disease treatments, however, are less concrete and thus will require consensus building among the participating clinicians. However you attain it, it is important to settle on care processes and treatment protocols, as variation can have significant negative impacts on operations and clinical outcomes.

BDP consensus should include the resource requirements of each task and subtask, and any constraints (clinical, location, etc.) that must be considered in the allocation and completion of any given task. Variances that may negatively impact performance can be built into the care process maps, analyzed for potential impact, and discussed for possible elimination or mitigation to the extent possible. Variances that occur but that may not necessarily impact performance or outcomes may also need to be replaced for the sake of consistency, implementation ease, and future risk reduction.

There is an important patient role here, as well. Patients know their preferences and from whom, how, and where they would like to receive care. Therefore, it is imperative that the PCCN managers and clinicians involve PCCN patients in the planning of the PCCN infrastructure and care strategies, to the degree possible. This will prevent the use of BDPs and CSs that do not match the true communal needs. (For instance, a BDP might prescribe a clinic environment for a Coumadin International Normalization Ratio [INR] check, whereas patients may prefer to avoid an office visit.) This will also prevent the appearance of cramming the PCCN down the throats of the community, since the patients will have a hand in its creation and implementation.

Patient input might come from a small group of sample patients if there is to be a large-scale PCCN, or individual patients from a specific subgroup such as a church congregation or a specific PCP's practice. These patients should be regionally and clinically relevant and representative of the broader PCCN population.

Keep in mind that certain ethnic or religious populations may cause specific deviations from BDPs due to faith-based requirements and constraints. Depending on the specificity of care requirements and degree of deviance, a small PCCN may need to be created to ensure both care consistency and respect for the individual's preferences. This, of course, would have its own mapping process with the subpopulation patients included.

Swimlane Mapping

These processes, resource allocations, and requirements should be mapped in a longitudinal format, following the ideal path of patient treatments, visits, and so on over the course of a given span of time, and aligning the communal resources with the tasks to be performed in the continuum of care. Perhaps the best way to achieve this (though certainly not the only way) is through a *swimlane style process map*, as shown in Figure 5.1. The swimlane map breaks down tasks longi-tudinally by resource type, helping the user to visualize the progression of tasks, overlaps and redundancies, and potential efficiencies of the system as a patient moves through the care process. The key is to understand the *root causes* of the best possible outcomes for a given patient, then align resources and their tasks to ensure that those impacts are made using whatever means necessary.

Ms. Jones' weekly Care Strategy for Care Circle

Prime	
Church member	Visit each Sunday. Check week's food supply and expected diet. Monitor previous week's diet. Shop as needed.	Comm. w/ Care Manager as needed for instructions	Monitor Care Circle activities; Relay changes in instructions to others	Communicate with Care Manager once per week
EMT	Visit each Tuesday and Thursday afternoons after work. Check blood pressure and weight	Comm. w/ Care Manager as needed	Visit each Tuesday and Thursday afternoons after work. Check blood pressure and weight
Volunteer			Drop by each Saturday to take Ms. Jones to the YMCA for her Group Class
Care Manager	Check Care Circle comm weekly, or as necessary	Update EMR and Physician; relay new instructions to Care Circle

Figure 5.1 Sample swimlane map depicting the breakdown of work, flow, and patient interactions.

We will commonly want to start by mapping the *current state* care processes and resources to offer a starting point for gap analysis and for determining future state improvement opportunities. This can be quite effective in determining where you are and how far you need to go to implement a PCCN framework, or in determining a potential return on investment (ROI) on the investment required. The ROI could be seen as the reduction in cost, creation of additional care capacity, and/or the quality and access improvement available through the PCCN. Also be constantly vigilant for the root causes of wellness, gratification, and clinical outcomes as you develop and implement your new care strategies.

However, mapping the current state might also be seen as an ineffective use of time and resources if the existing systems look nothing like a PCCN and therefore would not offer a reasonable comparison, or if the current state is known to be in dire need of complete revamping. You can bypass the current state maps and move directly to the future state mapping using BDPs, capturing the future state system using the same swimlane tools and methodologies. Regardless of which you choose, keep in mind that your starting point, whether current or future state, will be important for future investment and strategic decisions and direction.

Because of the scope and scale of the care provision of some of our poly-chronic patients, your swimlane maps can get quite large and even cumbersome. Therefore, it is always wise to use programs specifically designed to create these maps rather than Excel or Word or other generic solutions. The full version of Microsoft's Visio is a good tool to use here. Though swimlane maps can be created in live working sessions involving PCCN clinical participants, much like process or value stream mapping sessions, these will inevitably need to be captured electronically to be useful. Therefore, even if you choose the "paper-on-walls" approach to the map creation process, it will be critical to transpose the swimlane into something more readily transmitted and altered.

Task Classifications

Task identification and classification should not be so general as to miss important resource requirements. Depth and detail are important. Depending on the system being analyzed, these maps should often be broken down into the components of the major portions of the care continuum to obtain the right level of process detail and task specificity. This will allow for a much more detailed study of the tasks and associated resources over time, and prevent future confusion. So, rather than use *home visit,* which is far too generic a term to use for our analytical purposes, we need to analyze the subtasks of the home visit to ensure that the right resource is deployed for a given visit type, and that our objectives can be achieved. A home visit might therefore be broken down into clinical and nonclinical tasks, or tasks related to a specific intervention, visit, or need, using one or more swimlane maps. This will help you not only understand the tasks and subtasks involved, but the resource, time, and technology requirements of each. However you decide to conduct the *work breakdown structure* analysis, do so in a manner that helps you to decipher the root causes within the system and the related tasks and resource requirements.

Another consideration is task grouping. A given task might be performed by a variety of possible resources. Yet, other related tasks may not have the same resource flexibility. For instance, a standard blood pressure check can be performed by a number of trained clinical and nonclinical resources, if need be. However, if that task is often grouped with other tasks in a clinical assessment, some of which require the expertise of a nurse or other clinical resource, then the option of a nonclinical resource is reduced or eliminated. Grouping tasks may preclude the use of certain resources, or require distinct processes built around certain resource requirements. Therefore a single home visit might be broken into two or three separate visits to accomplish the full and necessary spectrum of care requirements. Normally, this might be seen as wasteful.

However, remember that in the PCCN, some of our resources will not be classified as a *cost* as they would under the normal fee-for-service (FFS) care system. Therefore, multiple visits do not necessarily yield waste and inefficiency, and may instead indicate greater efficiency and proper resource utilization. Also, shorter clinical interactions augmented by nonclinical tasks will enhance total system capacity. Thus you'll want to keep your mind open as you create these swimlane and other process maps, since it is all too easy to fall into the trap of re-creating the old system using the terminology of the new.

Indeed, if at the end of your mapping exercises your swimlane maps look strikingly similar to the current state of patient care, you likely have not challenged the current thinking enough to fundamentally change it. Unless your systems are so advanced and dynamic as to have already achieved the PCCN concept and implementation (and some have), you should most likely go back and reassess how you have developed the work breakdown structure and anticipated resource deployments.

Task and Resource Considerations

As you consider the swimlane maps you create and the related resourcing options, you should also examine the frequency, intensity, risk, processing time requirements, potential variability, and interdependencies of each task and assigned (and poten-tially assigned) resource. Risk, process variance, and process-ing time can be influenced by resource expertise and skill set. Resource requirements may also morph as frequency and time requirements change, since, for instance, resource constraints may lead to the splitting of task groupings. Let's quickly examine a few of the aspects you'll want to consider.

Note: Depending on the size and scale of your PCCN program, the following may appear to be overwhelming or overkill. Indeed, much of the following would only apply to those attempting to truly optimize a large-scale operation. Even if yours is not, it will behoove you to understand the topics and concepts that follow, as they will aid you in developing a solid, functional, and operationally sustainable program, no matter what its size. If it seems intimidating, however, remember that none of it is as involved or complex as it may first sound. So, don't be intimidated by it. Rather, evaluate the needs of your community and its patients and make plans and analyze your program accordingly.

Risk

Risk is not only the best board game ever invented, it is the inherent potential failure and harm associated with the performance of any medical process. Risks include the potential for errors, incorrect information, communication errors and gaps, and incorrect clinical diagnoses, instructions, and guidance. The potential for these risks goes up or down depending on the expertise and knowledge of the person performing the task, and should be considered when mapping your swimlanes. As you lay out your tasks throughout the care continuum, and consider the resource options, you should always consider the acceptability of an extraneous risk taken by a given resource assignment.

Variation

Variation eats capacity for lunch. Actually, variation eats a lot of things, like throughput, length of stay, number of tasks completed in a given amount of time, resource utilization, number of resources required, and so on. Variation is perhaps the most confounding constraint on optimal performance.

If you read the previous book, you'll recall that I discussed variability in depth. I won't repeat that here, but it is nonetheless important for the reader, especially those new to planning new care systems, to understand and appreciate the impacts of several forms of variation. In the following text, I will sketch out several of the forms and describe their impact on the planning and implementation of a PCCN.

As you read the following sections, keep in mind the goals and objectives of your specific PCCN, and how these forms of variation might impact your planning efforts. Regardless of the size, scope, and scale of your program, there will likely be some impact of some form of variation that may prevent the optimization of the care you wish to provide.

Also keep in mind that the analysis and study of variation is only applicable if you seek some level of optimization of your system, and/or your PCCN program is large enough to warrant it. You can, of course, plan and implement your PCCN without this analysis, but there are risks associated with doing so. Your resources may not be efficiently utilized, and you might find that there is less time to care for patients than you expected. You might also discover that you find yourself "throwing bodies" at the care strategies rather than effectively and efficiently assigning resources to tasks. As long as you fully understand the risks and challenges of both approaches, you can proceed as you see fit.

Process Variance

Process variation refers to differences in the way a process is performed or completed. This is of great concern, especially as it relates to important care and assessment steps. Process variance is impacted by many factors, from resource skill to the equipment used. Variance can lead to potential issues, some harmful and unnecessarily expensive, for instance, patient weight. If not measured correctly and precisely, variance can lead to incorrect clinical decisions.

Process variance is different than processing time variance, since the former refers to the variation in the actual *act of doing the process* rather than the time required to complete the process. (Obviously, process variance can lead to processing time variance if the variance in the way a process is completed also causes differences in processing time. However, these should not be confused or melded together, as both can be influenced through common improvement methodologies.)

It is therefore important to eliminate as much process variation as is possible. It not enough that resources *could* be trained to consistently perform the tasks, or work around variances as they erupt. Rather, it is critical that the tasks be set up such that as much process variance is eliminated as possible. This is especially true for nonclinical and relatively untrained communal resources. So, as a crude example, if patient weighing is conducted and read by six different resources on six different common bathroom scales, consistency and accuracy would likely diminish. The task itself might not be difficult, but its execution will be impacted by the process if the task and equipment are not set up and used correctly. Thus, proper instructions, equipment, and execution are important to ensuring quality information and correct clinical decision making, and thus the ongoing cooperation and trust of physicians and other clinicians. (We'll see how this can be achieved using trainers and the social–clinical network [SCN] in later chapters.)

Process variation can also depend on the patient's condition. Improving patient metrics may allow for a decreased utilization of clinical resources and an increased reliance on nonclinical resources. However, a deteriorating condition may have the opposite impact, increasing the need for purely clinical interventions rather than nonclinical resources. Similarly, an employed diabetic will require additional clinical and nonclinical support if alcohol or drug dependency is part of their overall health and wellness circumstance. Potential and acceptable process variation can be captured in the swimlane maps to a degree that allows for a complete understanding of the patient condition, the system's capabilities, and capacity requirements. Since this degree of process analysis is not common practice, advanced analytical tools such as swimlane mapping and simulation will be useful here. These can be aided by external expertise and/ or your industrial/management engineering staff.

Process Time Variance

Process time variance matters in our PCCN since multiple resources will interact in the care of our patients. If process times vary dramatically, resources will be less productive and the system may seem more chaotic. Fewer patients can be seen and fewer tasks achieved, in a given period of time. Therefore, the study of process time variance is important; especially if multiple resources and tasks are involved serially and/or if patient care or program effectiveness and capacity might be compromised by the reduced capabilities.

Process Time and the Impact of Variability

Process time is the time it takes to complete a given task. Process time variance leads to a direct impact on the system performance.[1] If significant enough, process time variance can lead to the quick and dramatic deterioration in resource productivity, effectiveness, efficiency, utilization, throughput, profitability, capacity, and ultimately system performance. Assuming a human is performing the task, there will inevitably be some degree of variance, since *all human process contains some degree of variability.*

Process Time Variance Example

Think of the simple process of going from your desk to get a fresh cup of coffee. If you do this process 100 times, you will not get your cup of coffee in precisely the same amount of time, each time, over the 100 replications. There will always be some degree of variance in the time it takes to complete the task. You might be stopped in the hall to chat, or stop at the restroom, or wash your dirty coffee mug, or have to wait for fresh coffee to brew. This is translated into variance in process time. If you perform this task many times during your day (as I do), or there is enough variance in the process time, coffee refills will have a significant impact on your total capacity to get work done. This might be reflected in missed phone calls, work being delayed, being late to appointments, and less total work done by the end of the day. Thus, variability in process time impacts the throughput, or capacity, of a process. If, on the other hand, your trip to get coffee took an exact and known amount of time, you could plan better for it, eliminate the hassles caused, and prevent it from impacting your work. But of course this rarely occurs in real life unless you are working with robots or very simple processes.

If we have several serial processes back to back, variance in each one yields reduced capacity of the entire system. Suppose that, as part of your coffee break process, you had to take the elevator from the top floor of your building and walk across the street to get coffee each time you wanted some (perhaps nothing but a Starbucks will do). Now, you have several processes that must mesh together in order to allow you to get back to your desk in the quickest time. The elevator must be there when you press the button, and the traffic lights must be in your favor so that you don't have to wait at the corner. The Starbucks must not be crowded causing you to stand in a long line. And the coffee has to be ready to pour and not require any brewing time (which can happen on occasion). Reverse the potential delays on the way back upstairs, and you have multiple opportunities for delay. A delay in any of the steps could yield delays in later processes and changes to the total process time. So, your simple task of getting a cup of Starbucks can now span anywhere from, say, 7 minutes to as much as 23 minutes!

Furthermore, this processing variance can, of course, be impacted by a number of external variables such as resource skill level and experience with the task, task complexity, number of processing steps in a task (e.g., filling out a short versus a long form), and so on. Without a thorough understanding of the variability in each task in your system, you risk the kind of unexpected delays that will frustrate both your resources and your patients. This is also why it is dangerous to use simple averages to quantify a system's performance.

Therefore, as part of the analysis of the tasks to be achieved, we need a thorough understanding of the tasks themselves, and how much time is required to perform each (including variances) since this will have a tremendous impact on the capacity of the care system we create.

Indeed, take a look at Table 5.1, which shows a comparison of the variability of three systems with a few processes in each. These sets of numbers all have the same average, but have vastly different highs and lows. This is a simplistic yet revealing example of the impact of variability on the decisions made with averages. If this were numbers of patients admitted to a unit on Tuesday afternoons, nurses would find the situation created by dataset 1 much less chaotic than that of dataset 3. Since the range of dataset 1 is very tight, between five and seven admissions, it will feel less chaotic than the range of dataset 3, which goes anywhere from 1 admission to 11. Think about trying to staff for the third dataset scenario versus the others.

Thus, what we see is that process time variation can make a tremendous difference in the way our systems operate, our ability to complete serial tasks within a given timeframe, and the capacity of our systems.

Table 5.1 Sample Datasets Depicting Degree of Variance around the Same Average Number

										AVG
Set 1	5	6	7	5	6	7	5	6	7	6
Set 2	3	6	9	3	6	9	3	6	9	6
Set 3	1	6	11	1	6	11	1	6	11	6

Interdependencies and Variability

If each of the processes in each of these small systems were independent of one another, and worked in complete isolation, the variance would not be as impactful. Think back to the coffee run analogy. The time it takes to get down to the lobby impacts what time you walk into Starbucks. If you leave at lunchtime, when everyone else is leaving, you might have to wait for the elevator. Likewise, an early morning run might yield a long wait time in line at the coffee shop, which would then delay your return to the building and cause you to just miss the next elevator up.

As an example of a PCCN application, imagine that a local synagogue took on the care of a few diabetes patients who were visited each Sabbath afternoon. Several members of that congregation agree to share in the responsibility, with each resource visiting a single patient to check in on specific care tasks, such as glucose levels, weight, general attitude, and so on. Since there may be only one visit per resource, the time required could be represented as a single number, most likely the average, since there was no previous or next task to influence.

However, if a single member of another congregation, perhaps the pastor or priest, were to take on the responsibility of visiting six diabetics each Sunday, the variance in the time of each visit would become much more important. This is because the variance in process times (inevitable in this case) can throw off the total processing time of the entire task series. Variability might therefore make the pastor late for the Sunday evening service, or force him to miss other important pastoral duties. Of course, a simulation can use both variability and averages to represent processes within a given system, so your choice is not one or the other. Indeed, if there is any significant variability in any of the important processing steps, resources, or other process attributes, a simulation model should be used, as described below.

Process Time and Patient Attributes

Process time can also vary by patient, due to patient attributes. This will be especially critical as we look to the care of patients whose care strategies might be more complex than others. Some patients will simply take longer and more effort to care for than others. These patients might be the morbidly obese or the very frail, or the mentally ill or impaired. These are *outliers within the outliers*, and are often the sickest of the sick. These are also the patients who need the PCCN the most and for whom the PCCN might be formed. Their more complex care needs are why we cannot use averages when calculating the resource requirements of our population. Similar to the above reasoning, using averages to surmise the resource demand would inevitably lead us to frustration and inadequacy if there are significant levels of variance in the population. In other words, if there is large variation in the patient attributes, which yield variation in the tasks and time required, the capacity of the system can and will likely be reduced, perhaps significantly.

Impact of Variance on Capacity

All this simply means that variability impacts many of the components of your program, including its capacity to care for patients. As process and process time variability enter your PCCN and the efforts of your resources, you will find that their work may be less productive and take longer, meaning fewer patients seen per resource or period of time. That is, reduced capacity.

As an old engineering colleague used to say, you can do two things to be more productive. One, do more work in less time. Or two, take less time to do more work. Of course, the third option is to properly account for the variances within the required tasks and properly align them with the resources available. Otherwise, your PCCN capacity may suffer.

Remember, of course, that the size, scope, and scale of your program will dictate the degree to which this analysis is necessary. For small PCCNs, you may need to recognize and be wary of this variability. For larger programs, thorough study may be required to prevent misallocation of resources and the hassles of constant realignment.

Tools for Analyzing Complex Systems

Swimlanes, while valuable for the analysis of process flows, resource allocations, task assignments, and interdependencies of workflow, are still *static* analytical tools. That is, because they do not change as a process might change over time or due to variances, they can only be quantitatively described by single numbers, usually averages. So, a process step in a swimlane map will ordinarily only be known by its numerical average attributes, such as average process time or average number of resources. The sum of these averages gives us an approximation of the total for a given attribute, such as total process time for a series of processes in the system. However, this is only as accurate as the accuracy of the degree of variance in each average in the total. The more variation there is, the less reliable the sum of the averages.

On the other hand, process simulation (aka *discrete event simulation* and other forms of process simulation) were developed specifically to account for the variability, interdependencies, and complexities of complex systems so as to be better able to analyze, test, and improve them. Simulation replicates complex systems in a computerized model so as to better study them. Simulations are normally built in order to run what-if scenarios to test alternatives and options in the computerized reality before implementing new ideas in real life. This prevents the hassles, frustrations, and unnecessary costs associated with real-life failures of new program implementations and improvement projects. Simulation can be quite useful if your PCCN has a lot of resources, patients, or interdependencies, especially if you want to truly optimize its functionality, resource utilization, capacity, and cost.

This, then, is the "engineered" approach to the PCCN we mentioned early on in this text, through which we can go to the next level of performance to attain insights into new program functionality and degrees of optimization heretofore impossible.

There are a number of texts available on the use of simulation in systems analysis. If this is of interest for your PCCN, consult with your hospital's industrial engineer (IE) or management engineer (ME) or seek out reference materials through vendors like Rockwell Automation or consultants like me.

Dynamic Standardization

Standardized work is jargon common to the Lean process improvement methodology. It refers to the preference for a single, standardized way to accomplish a given task, so as to eliminate internal process variability, which can lead to variance in outcomes, changes in quality, decreased throughput, and so on. However, as mentioned in the previous text,[2] external variation happens. That is, the circumstances in which our processes take place can change over time, making standardized work less effective and efficient.

Thus, too much rigidity in our structures and methodologies can yield their own inefficiencies, as variation butts up against our inflexibility. Furthermore, depending on the patient, resource, and circumstances, some degree of either process variation or process time variation, or both, may be expected or even required. This is because a process may perform well under some circumstances but not others, or may require a different resource mix under certain demand scenarios but not others.

Dynamic standardization is simply a methodological reaction to the need to account for variation. Using this methodology, processes can be performed differently, by different resources, or otherwise dynamically flex to meet variations in demand, capacity, or other inputs. These might have one or more standardized processes to achieve a single desired outcome. Dynamic standardization thus accepts that there will be variation in the inputs to the system, and accommodates them through different standardized responses.

For the PCCN, this may mean a different but still standardized care process flow for different seasons of year or patient loads. Or, different resource combinations might be used to accomplish the same clinical outcomes. Therefore, keep in mind that your PCCN may have multiple, yet still standardized, ways to achieve the same care strategies while remembering the need for proper standardization of work.

Data and Analysis of Current and Future States

In order to effectively analyze our current and future states, we'd prefer to have data. Rather than relying on anecdotes or "tribal knowledge" (information passed down through rumor, conjecture, and/or experience rather than objective analytics), data about the current care streams and demand patterns can teach us much about the changes we might want or need to make for the future state we want to construct. We would ideally like to have enough data to effectively analyze the patients we treat, the demand for care they generate, the processes and care streams via which they are treated, the resource utilization of caregivers, and the variation within all these elements. However, data for process analysis is often not easily obtained. More importantly, accurate and reliable data is often even more difficult to find. This of course brings us to the ubiquitous issue of obtaining useful data. Herein we'll focus on only two main types of data, which you can use at your discretion to evaluate your current system and plan for new ones. Of course, in addition to this and your analysis of your patient population, there is a wealth of additional potential analysis available for resource utilization and the other topics mentioned. You may or may not want to delve that deeply. But, remember, even a little data analysis can reveal tremendous improvement opportunities and benefits.

Process Data

Data on the actual number and flow of tasks required for the ideal future state should be readily available via the clinicians, chronicists and PCPs, and specialists involved. They can, with the aid of swimlanes and facilitators, envision a new world of patient care in a PCCN. This insight will aid in establishing how the PCCN should be structured in an ideal world of care provision. For the sake of the future PCCN organizational structure, this may be enough to create the future world via simulations and swimlane maps even if no other *actual* data is available.

Still, data for the tasks in the current state would be helpful in assessing the gaps between the current and BDP-based future-state systems, how much change is required, and what will be required to attain a new care system. However, data on the current tasks, process variance, and process time may only be available through complex and time-consuming patient record analysis, staff interviews, and work observations. These data-gathering steps would offer records of many if not most of the tasks performed, patterns of utilization of resources, timing of care provision, and so on. Of course, this might be too onerous a task, especially for a small PCCN. To avoid this data constraint, it may not be unreasonable to assume that either (a) tasks are being done as they should be, and thus only need realignment within the context of the PCCN resource pool, or (b) tasks are not being performed properly, and thus require both complete redesign and restructuring within the PCCN resource pool to ensure the anticipated and desired outcomes. Always remember, we are building a system to create new care capacity, so "blowing up" the current state and starting from scratch is acceptable if it is not performing as needed.

If you still want some actual process data, one compromise might be to examine the health records of only those patients known to be noncompliant or seriously ill. These are the outliers within the outliers. That is, they are the sickest of the sick, and may require additional resources over and above those of most of the PCCN patients. These patients may need to have their care patterns analyzed more thoroughly to gauge the degree to which care gaps exist and new resources are required, as well as determine what resources might be needed. This will lead us to a better understanding of the variation in the system and any resulting outcomes variation, at least as it relates to the most resource-intensive patients, which will likely teach us something about the other patients in the PCCN programs.

Remember, the PCCN structure is meant to provide a framework for care provision, not set in concrete the way it is implemented. Thus, you may find that your particular situation warrants these or other approaches to the data analytics and care provision issues. As long as the savings you generate can be shown to offset the cost of implementation and sustenance, you can select and analyze any population you choose.

Demand Data

By demand data, we mean the demand for care tasks by patients in the community. These might be the actual appointments, visits, and tasks currently being performed for patients, or the ideal demand for care tasks based on a perfect world of complete patient compliance, access, and care provision. The former would be used to gauge the current staffing requirements, while the latter is used for gap analysis and future state resource alignment.

If there is variability in the patterns of the current state demand data, especially at the aggregated level wherein all tasks for a particular resource are grouped, it should be reflected visually and graphically in some form of run or control chart (again, your IE/ME or consultant can assist here). This will allow for a visual representation and the understanding of variance over time. So, rather than reporting a single number for, say, the number of tasks for a visiting nurse during a given week, we would want to see the actual number of tasks over a period of several weeks. This would reflect the variance in activities performed from week to week, which might reflect a need for a change in the pool of available resources or a cleanup of tasks and wasteful practices. This will also aid you in understanding the totality of the demand and how it might be better managed via a more appropriate resource allocation (e.g., communal resources).

Importantly, and at the risk of beating dead horses, it is the degree of the variance that is the most critical issue here, since it is the degree of variance that will drive more of the performance level of the process and system. Small amounts of variance in demand patterns might result in only minor changes to the system's capacity requirements. Large variation is more indicative of broken processes and systems and would reflect a need for more dramatic interventions to control variation and better ensure care quality. And since variability will continue to happen, even in our most perfect world, we will need to account for at least some of the expected system variance in our future state planning. Even if you only have BDP swimlanes to help you assess the capacity, resource requirements, and so on, of your new PCCN, you will need to estimate the variation in key process steps, demand, task groupings, and other areas—wherever there is impactful variability.

Analyzing Community Demand

All the information gathered above and more could become analytical inputs for the development of the PCCN infrastructure. Though my preference is for discrete event simulation (DES) and other similarly advanced analytical tools, simple flow models can be constructed quickly to begin the process of resource, task, and system requirements analysis. These can be used as described in the following text.

Knowing the number of patients, the tasks required for the care of each patient, frequency and processing time of each task, and the resource(s) required to complete each task gives us many, if not most, of the inputs required for the *demand side* of a simulation model. Were we to use this information and simply total it statically, we would arrive at a glimpse into the average demand for resources over a given period of time. The equation would be as simple as the following:

Number of patients × number of tasks for each resources (based on frequency of each task during the time period in question) = total resource tasks

This would then be multiplied by the time required for each task. If we are going to use a simple static analysis and not a simulation model of some sort, an average processing time would offer the total task or processing time required of each resource. This would at least help us to get a glimpse of the resource utilization, though not the impact of outliers that will inevitably emerge from this (variable) system. For the purposes of our initial understanding of the community demand for which the PCCN is being created, we would typically use short time spans for portions of the analysis, such as days of the week or perhaps weeks of a month, so as to better understand the day-to-day operational and time requirements of the resources in the pool.

Of course, if you opt to use a more sophisticated analytical tool such as simulation, as described in this and other texts, the outputs of the analysis will be more accurate, specific, and informative. A simulation will allow you to more precisely understand the total processing time and total variance within a given series of tasks.

As you assess your community, its care needs, and requirements, and begin to map the care strategies for the population(s) you wish to serve, one factor worth considering is the patterns in the communal demand. In nearly every system imaginable, there are variances in demand. Demand for services varies by hour, day, and month, depending on a huge number of possible factors. Yet in nearly every system imaginable, whether emergency department arrivals, airport security queues, or the number of patrons in a store, there are patterns in demand variance. These patterns might reflect clinical needs (e.g., dialysis), or seasonal demand (e.g., flu vaccines). To the extent that we can discern any patterns in demand, we can begin to see how they impact our swimlane maps and resource requirements. And to the extent that data exists to depict these patterns, and the data is sufficient to describe these patterns mathematically, we can accurately depict the patterns as inputs into simulation models. This will help us to accurately portray our current system and give us confidence in the what-if scenarios we will build with models to analyze the impacts of change. Thus, where feasible, we need to look at our patterns of demand within the PCCN patient population to ensure that the assumptions built into our swimlane maps are validated and acceptable within the context of the real-life variance of the system. The patterns, and the possible outliers external to those patterns, tell us a great deal about how predictable the community demand is and may be over time. This will help you feel comfortable with any assumptions you might make or model outputs you obtain as to resource allocations, costs, and care strategies.

Finally, resource constraints (e.g., working volunteers who can best impact care after business hours and on weekends) will also need to be considered as you analyze your demand patterns and construct your swimlane maps. As you look to the resources you'll need, consider the realistic constraints that will impact volunteers and the currently employed so as to account for preferences in scheduling their assistance. These will be our *capacity patterns*, which will need to be matched with the realistic care requirements and BDPs of the PCCN patients.

Summary

As we produce an understanding of the demand side of the care continuum equation, we can begin to match the demand with our communal and clinical resources needed for the proper care of the patients in the PCCN. Remember, the size of your PCCN will be unique. Furthermore, there may be multiple PCCNs within a given geography, accountable care organization (ACO), physician group practice, independent practice association (IPA), or physician–hospital organization (PHO). This means that *each* PCCN will need its own demand calculations and, later, its own capacity matching.

Now that we have a solid understanding of the patients we need to care for and the totality of the tasks to be accomplished, we can begin the process of developing the communal resources required to meet their needs. This starts with an overall communal infrastructure assessment, followed by resource selection and assimilation, and then technology integration. Finally, we optimize the utilization of the resource pool as related to the patients we will be managing as we implement the PCCN.

Endnotes

1. For a thorough review of variability in systems, see P. Story, *Dynamic Capacity Management for Healthcare: Advanced Methods and Tools for Optimization* (Boca Raton, FL: CRC Press/Taylor & Francis, 2010), 7–36.
2. Story, *Dynamic Capacity*, 157–177.

Chapter 6

Building the Communal Resource Pool

Overview

As mentioned in Chapter 4, "Assessing the Community and the Patient Population," in order to build a pool of poly-chronic care network (PCCN) resources, you must first understand the community you wish to serve. This includes the disease state(s) you want to address, the population of patients to be managed, the assimilation propensity of the community and its poly-chronics, and the variation in the current demand and system operations.

To recap, without deciding which diseases and patients you want to treat (if not all of them), you will not be able to determine what each resource should do, when they should do it, and how many resources will be required to complete the necessary care tasks. You will not be able to effectively assess the needs of your PCCN, so you won't be able to accurately quantify the demand, either now or in the future. So, without understanding the total population to be served, you cannot properly identify and allocate resources and tasks from the pool. It is therefore important to assess the community as a first (or concurrent first) step. Once this is completed, you can move on to assessing and quantifying the possible available resources as a next step.

Commonly when we think of healthcare resources, we think in terms of clinical resources. But this may cause us to miss opportunities in community-based organizations and denizens we wouldn't normally consider. Indeed, other efforts in population health management have shown a lack of clarity and vision around the resources that are and could be available within any given community. The strategic framework for patients with multiple chronic conditions (what I herein call *poly-chronics*), published by the U.S. Department of Health and Human Services, spells out generalities but offers few details as to the resources required to change the current care systems.[1] Though these and other publications offer similar concepts, none that I have encountered have offered the specificity and detail that you see herein. Therefore, this chapter will assist you in broadening your horizons as to what could be considered a *healthcare resource*. See Figure 6.1 for a refresher sample of the PCCN resource pool.

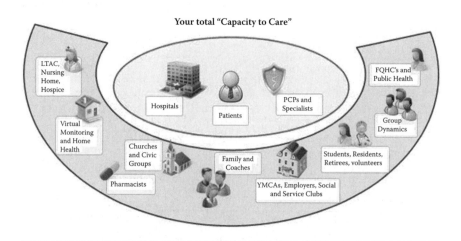

Figure 6.1 Sample PCCN resource pool.

A key strategy for the PCCN is to remember that not all resources will need to have letters after their names (e.g., MD or RN). So rather than asking, "Is this clinical resource capable of providing the necessary care?" we should be asking, "What can this potential resource contribute to the overall health and well-being of the community of patients we want to serve?" This requires us to become more creative in the use of available resources. So rather than asking, "Why would this person or group want to help?" or "Is this person qualified to help?" the better questions are "Why wouldn't they help?" and "How could they help?" and "What will cause them to be completely committed to helping?" This will help change your perspective on the types and numbers of resources available in your communities.

Indeed, there are likely a number of readily available communal resources in plain sight. For instance, many small communities have firefighters who aren't always heavily utilized. Ditto for ambulance and emergency medical services (EMS) and other similar resources with essential clinical knowledge. Have you considered retired healthcare workers, or local businesses with critical management and engineering talent? As you delve deeply into your communities, you may find there is a wealth of available resources awaiting an opportunity to make a significant difference in the lives and well-being of others, if only effectively directed, coordinated, and motivated. Indeed, volunteers may abound if properly motivated and incented to assist.

There may be existing, successful programs through local hospitals, Y's, and health agencies designed to engage the community in healthier eating, exercise, and other beneficial activities. In rural communities, you may not find organized efforts, yet there may be a general awareness of the need for healthier living that may in turn lead to opportunities to engage patients through a variety of local civic groups and religious affiliations. Such information will not only help guide you to existing infrastructure and volunteers who might assist your efforts, it will also assist you in understanding the degree of effort required to initiate and sustain a PCCN. A disjointed and lackluster community with little guidance or concern for population health will likely find greater difficulty implementing a PCCN (though such communities may be the most in need of its attributes and outcomes). In contrast, a community engaged and aware of population health issues may be quite willing to engage in low-cost, highly effective ways to care for patients.

Resource and Capacity Variance

Note: This section will probably seem like overkill for small PCCNs because those iterations will not need this degree of analytical power. Nonetheless, I encourage you to take the principles of the following sections and apply them to your efforts, however small.

Before we dive into resource availability, we need to keep in mind that capacity, just like demand, is variable in most cases. Furthermore, resource availability and capacity are influenced by the systems in which they work. The actual capacity of a resource to complete a given task or set of tasks is dependent on a number of factors, all of which can constrain or expand the resource's capacity for workload. These include the variance in the number of tasks required, as shown in Chapter 5, as well as the interdependencies among tasks.

There are other ways in which the capacity of resources might be altered. These include:

- Technologies that might increase or decrease a process takt time
- Travel distances between patient homes
- Number of resources deployed to a specific series of tasks (e.g., care teams)
- Education, familiarity, and experience with the task

- Resource-specific attributes, such as age, health and strength, mental capacity, and so on

All these factors mean that the average is once again a bad number to use when it comes to understanding resources and their capacity to care for patients. Failure to account for the cumulative impact of the variance in resource capacity will inevitably yield incorrect assumptions about the capacity of the entire system. Or, it will yield a recommended resource pool that is, at least to some degree, incapable of caring for the population in question.

All this is said to restate the obvious: as you begin to consider resource allocations, especially the number of resources and the task load they are to take on, understand that variability can and likely will have a tremendous impact on their productivity and workload. This should not only be accounted for in your resource estimates, but drilled into the brains of the resources used. Since it is such a critical concept for the capacity of the PCCN, all resources should have a thorough and complete understanding of the concept and its meaning.

Again, your local industrial engineer (IE) or management engineer (ME) can aid you with this and other similar analysis and planning.

Dynamic Demand–Capacity Matching

The concept of dynamic demand–capacity management harkens back to the previous text by the same name, and speaks to the need to effectively match the dynamic demand of the community (i.e., chronic disease patients) with dynamic capacity (i.e., the ability of the communal resources to provide the necessary care and task completion). Without an effective matching of the two, with consideration of the tasks to be achieved, the available resources, and variability in processes and takt time, there will be inevitable failures of care delivery and suboptimal outcomes.

Even if yours is a simple PCCN with only a few resources, it is nonetheless important to remember that both demand and capacity are *dynamic*—that is, they change constantly over time. Demand will increase and decrease with individual patient health, seasonal changes (e.g., flu season), and better/worse self-reliance and compliance. Capacity likewise increases and decreases as resources are added and dropped from the resource pool, space is constrained or expanded, technologies improve or constrain patient care, or takt times are reduced or increased such that the capacity of a given resource is expanded or constrained. Thus both demand and capacity are dynamic. The dynamism of the demand and capacity creates unique analytical needs for the effective allocation of resources. This is why simulation is so critical to this effort, as it is the only widely used tool that can effectively, accurately, and predictably match the two dynamic sides of the optimization equation.

As we start to match the variable capacity of the community with the variable demand, we will start to understand how, where, and why any excess variability and interdependencies impact the performance of the system and the possible breakdowns in patient care. In doing so, we can determine the optimal capacity of the system we create, its limitations, the circumstances in which system breakdowns occur, and under what conditions the system begins to deteriorate and patient care is imperiled. In order to build a robust and resilient system, we will need to be able to account for those circumstances in which excess demand meets unavailable capacity, and develop effective plans to preemptively mitigate those circumstances and any resulting consequences. This can be done quite effectively using simulation analysis and its what-if scenarios. Of course, small PCCNs will not use simulation as it would be analytical overkill. However, it might help to understand the concepts so you can more easily allocate your resources.

The Demand–Capacity Continuum and Simulation Capacity Analysis

If you'll recall, we've discussed ways to accurately determine the demand from the PCCN patients based on either the current or ideal state or both. This involved either simple calculations of average demand loads, or more complex but more accurate simulation modeling exercises. The result was the number of tasks to be achieved, the current or required timing/frequency of those tasks, the takt time status or requirements of each task/group, as well as some degree of understanding of the resource requirements of each task and task group. This is essentially the demand-side input to the model.

The other side of the equation, *capacity to care* can similarly be either assumed or derived. In your simulation model, your simulation programmer should allow for *direct* resource modeling or *resourceless* resource modeling. Let's understand the different uses, as your choice will have an impact on how you use this important technology.

In *direct resource modeling*, you enter a specific number of a given resource into the model. So, for instance, let's take a generic home visit task group. Assuming we have all the necessary information about the tasks involved, such as number of tasks per time period, takt time, and so on, we can place a specific number of resources to complete the tasks into the model. Whether or not this will be the right number is unknown until the model is run, and will be based on how effectively the specified number of resources can complete the tasks at hand. For instance, let's say we have 100 visits to complete in one week's time. And let's assume we enter five visiting LPNs into the model. The model will use the information about each visit and its variance, and each resource's capabilities. It will also use model inputs such as travel time or distance, task speed qualifiers, resource cost, and others, and depict how long it takes to complete all the tasks, the wait times for each task, and so on. From this information, you can gauge how well or how poorly that number of resources performed the tasks at hand. With this, you could rerun the model several times to determine the impact of using a different number or type of resource, different task allocations, reductions in takt time, and so on, to see if you can improve the performance in any way. These what-if scenarios are the reason that simulation is so widely used.

The outputs of the model will include the results of the many model replications. This will show the different outcomes based on the impact of the variability in the system. Thus, one iteration may show relatively effective resource use, while another might show long wait times due to the variance in resource performance, takt times, and other variables. The range of variability will depict how bad, and good, things can get with a given number of resources. This range is especially important as you test for clinically important tasks that cannot be avoided or delayed, because outliers should not be allowed to hamper activity in these cases.

A *resourceless resource model* performs differently. It takes the tasks at hand, and using some of the previous model inputs like takt time and travel time, counts the number of times a given resource is demanded during each modeled iteration. If one resource is busy with a task when another is required, a second resource appears and is counted (if only it were that easy in real life). As tasks are completed, the resource will then start the next task, or if there is none, will disappear and be subtracted from the model's working resource pool. The output of this model is a running tally of the number of resources required to complete the tasks throughout the time period in question, offering a glimpse into the highs and lows of resource consumption. Because the model automatically creates a resource anytime there is a need, there is no wait time. So, the system you create is the ultimate customer environment. As we all know, these systems are neither realistic nor cost effective, yet they tell us a great deal about how many resources will be required to create a customer-friendly environment.

Modeling of resource capacity offers us a more accurate and predictable way to staff the PCCN. Using simulation's what-if scenarios, we can determine a variety of potentially effective staffing models that will achieve the work required using different mixes of resources, task assignments, and costs. This gives us quantifiable differences that we can use for decision making, and thus offers realistic options from which to choose. This will be extremely helpful as you begin to select resources and staff and manage the PCCN over time.

Resources

Now that we have covered the basics of calculating the required resources, we need to evaluate and select the proper resource pools for our programs. We will first consider the care strategies that the resources will use, examine the various resource options we have, begin selecting and customizing resources for the program, and creating individualized care circles.

Using the Care Strategies

If you used a swimlane or similar mapping approach to your community's PCCN care requirements, you now have a detailed understanding of the *what, where, when, how*, and *how often* of chronic disease management. What you need now is the *who*. Since you will likely have options as to the resources you choose for each task (assuming both clinical and nonclinical task assignments), it is wise to begin the resource assessment process by looking broadly within your community for resources to complete the tasks laid out in your PCCN's care strategies.

For each task, you should have an understanding of some of the attributes of the resources to be used. These will include minimal clinical requirements (e.g., registered nurse [RN], licensed practical nurse [LPN], etc.), task groups into which the tasks will commonly be placed, time and travel requirements for each task and task grouping, number of tasks to be performed in a given period, and so on. Don't forget to include patient preferences. These qualifiers will help you gauge the requirements of each task and task grouping, into which you can plug the appropriate resource.

If necessary, there may be an additional step if you feel you have not adequately thought through the resource possibilities. Either now, or after you've assessed your communal resources for options, go back to the swimlane maps and brainstorm ideas for possible resource options. Start asking what-if questions about the tasks and resources in your swimlanes, such as the following:

- Could that particular home visit be handled via an interactive web platform and distance monitoring? Could a process be accomplished by a mobile LPN, or does it need to be performed in an office environment?
- Can a nurse pass off that task group to a nonclinical resource if follow-up was direct and specific enough?
- Might there be a technology solution for this task? If so, does it eliminate or assist in the task, or merely automate inefficiency? How much would the technology cost and is there a definitive benefit?
- Might this task group be better managed via group meetings?

Asking these questions will then drive you to the next questions, including which nonclinical or clinical resource would best handle those tasks or if a nurse is too expensive to use for that task, what other clinical resource has similar qualifications, enough to manage that specific task?

Or assuming physician interaction and sign-off of this step, does a nurse have to perform it or could a trained nonclinical resource manage it just as effectively and less expensively?

We'll delve into the customization and personalization of the resources for the patients in the PCCN later in this chapter. For now, we have the framework for a resource search, so let's look for options within our community.

Resource Options

Now you should be fully prepared to begin looking at resource options in your community. As you assess the available resources, consider at least the following:

- **Churches:** Already, congregations in the southeastern United States are banding together with local hospitals to help with patient care. Methodist Le Bonheur of Memphis, Tennessee has created a congregational health network to assist patients with transitions of care, disease management, and wellness. As another example, Inova Health of Virginia has created its own congregational health partnership with similar aims and ambitions. Churches are often ready-made for such assistance, since their members share a bond and are committed to one another through faith and friendship.
- **Pharmacies:** Hospital and local community pharmacies can lend a valuable hand in managing complex patient care through medication review and reconciliation. Even large retail chains such as CVS and Rite-Aid are committed to their communities and may be willing to commit resources. Pharmacists are a critical though constrained resource for the PCCN, as they will aid in ensuring medication compliance and duplication avoidance. Since they are constrained, like other clinical

resources, wise and effective use of their time and attention is required. Keep this in mind as you lay out your swimlanes and task assignments, to avoid overload. Also, try using pharmacy techs and other similarly educated resources where available.

- **Service and civic groups:** These might include Rotary, Kiwanis, Lions, Knights of Columbus, and others. As some of these organizations struggle for purpose in an age of electronic communication and the breakdown of social structures, you may find they are ready to serve their communities in new ways.
- **Meals on Wheels (MOW):** MOW often has very regular and friendly contact with patients. Why not have them check on a few specific clinical metrics as well, especially if the patient has some automated or easy-to-use virtual monitoring devices in their home?
- **Ys (aka YMCA):** Ys are already doing a great deal of work in helping communities get and stay healthy. This is particularly true of the elderly and youth populations. Ys are a good communal resource, already paid, and largely readily available in urban areas. Indeed, it is said that 80 percent of the U.S. population lives within three miles of a Y!
- **Hospital volunteers:** By tapping an existing group of committed volunteers, you may find additional resources come forth as the PCCN grows in popularity. Hospital volunteers are often recent and healthy retirees, sometimes retired healthcare workers themselves. With their commitment to the community and the local healthcare system, it would be reasonable to assume that they would be quick to participate.
- **Retired or semiretired healthcare workers:** In many communities, retired healthcare workers are available for local volunteer work, including blood drives and education fairs. Again, as knowledgeable and committed resources, these retirees could serve as

a tremendous addition to the existing, full-time clinical capacity.

- **Community colleges and other schools:** Often a ready source of ambitious passion, students may be looking for a way to make an impact on the community while they study for a career. This would be particularly true of students working toward health-related careers and degrees.
- **Residency programs:** These would include pharmacy, nursing, physician, and others. Often clinical resources in training seek out opportunities to get involved in patient care, and could be readily used to augment clinical and nonclinical task allocations.
- **Existing fire, rescue, and police:** As mentioned previously, many resources are relatively underutilized, though their presence is felt when needed. These resources are sometimes tapped to go to homes where elderly have minor issues, such as falls. These could turn into opportunities to help manage care and ensure safe home environments for home-bound patients.
- **Local businesses:** You will likely find that local businesses struggle in isolation with employee healthcare and the care of employees' extended families. Even a healthy, young group of workers has parents and relatives who require them to take hours and days off for healthcare-related reasons. Getting these issues under control is of great importance, particularly for small businesses with chronically ill employees and relatives. You may find willing assistance from small local businesses, even if it is only in the form of tech support!
- **Industrial (and management) engineers:** One of the key resources I've already mentioned is an industrial engineer who can aid in the analysis, modeling, and setup of the PCCN. Engineers of all stripes can be found in small and large companies and even state

and local government offices. Look for these as potential sources of assistance, especially for larger employers who might be willing to set up and support their own employees' PCCN.

■ **Clinics and Federally Qualified Health Centers (FQHCs):** These will be mentioned later as a space resource, but deserve mention here as a potential pool of clinical resources. If properly tied to the PCCN, clinic resources might aid in monitoring patients for medication compliance. Local doc-in-a-box employees may be willing to see PCCN patients to check key vital signs, such as weight, on a volunteer or low-cost basis. They will typically have an IT infrastructure that will support these efforts.

■ **Boys and Girls Clubs:** What better way to reach underprivileged kids than through the programs they rely upon. Special programs might be established to reach children here and elsewhere as their parents are reached through other communal resources.

■ **Other:** Of course, every community is different. Yours may have a nursing program at a nearby college, or a local Y, or a tightly bound ethnic population that can lend assistance. It will not be uncommon to see multiple PCCNs in a geographic zone, based on a subcommunity such as a large congregation or ethnic group, all tied to the same chronicist.

Since the scope, scale, and clinical challenge(s) of the PCCN have been decided and the potential resources mapped, you can move on to one of the two next steps: population analysis or resource allocation. We'll deal with the former topic in Chapter 9 ("PCCN Technologies"), as it is not always required and certainly is not required at this stage of PCCN development. If you want to use population modeling at this stage of the project, go to Chapter 9 for a review of its applications and come back after you've read it.

Resource Selection

This should be a natural progression from the previous tasks. Based on the work identified in the swimlane maps and/or simulation, you should have a solid understanding of the task requirements and the options for resources. Now, all that is required is selecting the resources from the potential pool that you have constructed. This may sound easy, yet there may still be several stumbling blocks in the way.

- Be sure to interview all the potential resources and ensure that they understand the distinct differences between simply being part of the PCCN and true assimilation. Ensure that they will have the same passion for the community's health as the PCCN leaders, and that they understand both the infrastructure and the learning requirements. You will likely find that there will be people within cooperative organizations who either cannot or will not make the necessary commitments to the program to make it successful. These people will obviously need to be culled from the ranks. Though they may be convinced later, be sure that negative attitudes are not allowed to infect the more willing members.
- Be sure to keep the individual patients' interests in mind, and not just that of the PCCN. Therefore, do not ignore potential resources that might only serve a very small number of patients, such as members of a small church congregation, or members of a single patient's family. These may be the best patient motivators, yet they may only be able to touch a few lives in their work.
- Don't lose your creativity as you discover gaps and new opportunities. As you seek out resources, you may become myopic in your resource selection. Don't. You'll need to constantly seek out new resources wherever they might present themselves.

■ Don't assume all resources are created equally. Constantly analyze each resource's potential variance, as it is easy to assume that all resources from a given group (e.g., Y, church, or community service organization) are equally committed to the cause. Thus, don't hesitate to cull resources, now and in the future, if their commitment, service quality, or capabilities fall short of expectations. I am not suggesting that there won't be issues with ongoing motivation, or that resources be "voted off the island" immediately upon any lapse. I am, however, suggesting that the importance of the goals and objectives of the PCCN demand a certain level of resource quality, and that this must be maintained at all times. Failure is not an option, regardless of the cause.

Selecting Physicians

Physicians are perhaps the most critical component of a PCCN, yet they are also the most constrained and the least likely to want to take on additional responsibilities, tasks, risk, and communications. Furthermore, there may be solid rationale behind the reluctance to use nonclinical and external communal resources in the management of patient care. Yet, the PCCN was developed to support physicians and their efforts to provide the best care and service possible. Physicians, once they hear of the advantages of the program and the benefits that will fall directly and quickly to them, are quite likely to sign up.

Importantly, the PCCN can be constructed in such a way as to support many physicians whose patients are primarily poly-chronics via a single communal resource pool. Thus, the issue of finding a single or a few physicians to act as chronicists is lessened or eliminated. Last, physicians at the helm of the PCCN needn't be masters of the entire domain; they only need to be cooperative members of the resource pool, which will be managed by the PCCN manager.

Therefore, in selecting the physicians for your program(s) there are several keys to consider:

- **Propensity to cooperate:** How willing are the physicians to allow a broader pool of care resources from the PCCN to assist in the care of their patients?
- **Propensity to support:** How willing are they to support the PCCN resources? This is a very important consideration, since using and/or controlling the PCCN's resource pool is not the same as supporting and enabling it. The latter requires an entirely different mentality, personality, and approach. The former is not desired, and should be avoided at all cost.
- **Current poly-chronic population:** Some primary care physicians (PCPs) already run chronic disease practices by virtue of their location, patient population, and/or preferences. These should be tapped, if possible, as they may benefit most from the PCCN's implementation.
- **Willingness to share, grow, and learn:** One of the key attributes of the PCCN, called for in the U.S. Department of Health and Human Services (HHS) document[2] on the strategic framework for poly-chronic management, is the enablement of a learning network to continue to expand the knowledge base of care providers. This will require a great deal of sharing, learning, and to a certain extent, humility. Some of this will come naturally to some, not at all to others. An aversion to the admission of failure has sadly been built into our healthcare system by malpractice litigation and a free-roaming and politically connected trial lawyers association. This makes finger pointing infinitely easier and much less risky, making for a difficult work environment that unfortunately lessens cooperation and trust. Nonetheless, physicians must be willing to share, grow, and learn from both successes and failures if the body of knowledge of poly-chronic care is to expand.

- **Passion for change and new ideas:** There are some, perhaps many, in your community of physicians who not only accept change but seek and embrace it. These are not typical, mind you, but they will be important for your implementation efforts. Finding those who challenge the status quo and make new ideas the hallmark of their practices is thankfully not difficult. They tend to stand out and make themselves known, and should be corralled into the network to the extent possible and necessary.
- **Propensity to accept new technology:** Some see technology as a savior, others as a detriment to their practices and a waste of resources. While the latter are not necessarily totally incorrect, the judicious use of technology in the PCCN is a requirement for its success. Thus, only physicians willing to take on and use the available technologies should apply.

Many PCPs will have incentives to participate in the PCCN, especially if they are willing to allow others to see their most difficult patients while they see others who might be more readily cared for. This would mean a more profitable practice while keeping the overall control of their patients.

PCPs within large group practices may have added motivation to release patients into the care of the group's own PCCN since the practice would not lose the patient revenue or long-term relationship. For this scenario, group practices may benefit from the concentration of patients into the care of a few, select chronicists while others in the practice are free to add less resource-intense patients to their rosters. Similarly, some specialty group practices may find that a limited number of physicians can cover the poly-chronics of the selected community without disrupting the flow and care of other patients, allowing colleagues to add new patients.

Last, the incentive programs put in place for both PCPs and specialists may entice some to participate who might have otherwise seen the PCCN as too difficult or cumbersome to deal with.

Selecting physicians will therefore depend on a number of factors, not the least of which are the propensities and attributes listed previously. Above all, remember to screen each one for passion and enthusiasm for the business models of the future, and select only those physicians who will fully support the goals and objectives of the network.

Creating a Care Circle Team

It is vital to the PCCN's functionality and long-term viability that a team environment be created. With this, there is risk that resources will drop or neglect their responsibilities, infighting and competition between resources will emerge, and a few resources will take over the entire system. To prevent this, it is imperative that the PCCN be set up and managed as a communal, team approach to care delivery. No one resource should have the power or the desire to take over the system, nor should resources feel they are being dictated to, used, or manipulated by the PCCN managers and physicians. All must attain and retain a sense of a communal "it's not about me" shared passion for the work being done. Neither physicians nor any other resource should assume their roles yield a fiefdom to be ruled.

However, neither should resources presume anything other than personal responsibility and accountability for their tasks. Since the level of trust given can be significant, the level of accountability should also be high. Governance structures are meant to ease the burden of the management of tasks, not hound resources into doing what they have volunteered to do. Resources should be self-motivated and supportive, while supporting others in the PCCN who are likewise motivated to help both the patients and other PCCN resources.

This team environment is one reason why the Core Action Values are so important. Joe Tye's approach promotes a true cooperative and passionate team work environment, and should be used to help develop the kind of camaraderie common mostly to military units and sports teams.[3]

The PCCN must therefore create a team environment of disparate resources while also creating a system of accountability, responsibility, and governance. Much like a team of remote programmers working on the same software from different areas of the world, the PCCN must utilize a wealth of resources while managing, motivating, and monitoring all simultaneously. This is even harder than it may sound, which is why the resource selection process is so critical to the long-term success of the program.

Personalizing the Resource Pool

As explained below, each patient may require (or sometimes demand) a slightly different mix of resources. Without knowing which resources can do which tasks, or the impact of adding personalization into the overall system, it will be difficult if not impossible to gauge the system's functionality within the personalized system. Furthermore, as you look to assign different resource mixes to individual patients, based on their preferences or other requirements, you will find that your system and individual resource capacity will quickly become an unknown. Furthermore, keeping up with task assignments, accountability, and other management duties will become very difficult and largely chaotic.

To avoid potential issues, you should analyze the personalization needed in the resource pool by completing the following steps:

1. Develop a *baseline* resource pool, based on the community analysis. This baseline pool is a standardized resource allocation, developed using either a simulation model or other simpler means and based on the community's available resources, which is sufficient to

care for the patients in the PCCN. Let's say, for the sake of the following example that it includes one nurse, two LPNs, three church members, and two ENT physicians.

Through discussions and interviews with the patients in the PCCN, you discover that one patient is particularly opposed to the use of church members in their care and refuses to allow the church volunteers into her home. You would then look to the other resources to see which might be able to effectively, and hopefully for the same cost, take on the volunteer's tasks *for only that patient.* Let's assume that the church volunteers would normally conduct one task group per week for this patient, which now must be done by another resource. Let's assume that the ENTs agree to split the task group between them, increasing their workloads by two task groups per month. The model will allow you to reallocate the specific tasks for a specific patient in the population, or simply increase the workload for the ENTs and decrease the workload for the volunteers by four task groups per month. The output of the model would depict the new time requirements for all resources in the resource pool, including the new demand for ENTs in the community. It would also depict the new additional capacity for the church volunteers, which might lead to another task allocation that would use the newly available time.

Similarly, let's assume that one patient has a recently discovered issue with depression. This might require the PCCN manager to seek out a new mental health resource to be part of the resource pool, even if for only this patient. Failure to account for this patient as an outlier within the outliers may lead to poor outcomes, additional strain on untrained resources, and potential capacity variance that might impact other patients in the PCCN.

As a final example, some patients will readily take to a group environment like a Y, while others will demand in-home care and more personalized attention. Thus, knowing the patients in the population is critical to both the successful use of community resources and the overall clinical outcomes of the PCCN.

2. Develop the variance from the baseline for each patient's requirements while pushing back as necessary on unreasonable or impossible requests. For instance, let's assume that a patient demands that only a physician see them for any medical intervention, and that no other resource type will do. This would, of course, not match the goals and objectives of the PCCN and thus would have to be addressed through patient education and assimilation rather than resource and task allocation.

Therefore, a manageable variation should be allowed, such that patients have legitimate choices without creating resource allocation issues. However, variance in the clinical roles should be avoided. For instance, physicians will necessarily be at the top of the care system to avoid confusion over care strategy development and implementation. However, nonclinical task allocation can be more loosely assigned.

Importantly, there is a difference between varying who performs the tasks and varying the tasks themselves. Tasks should not vary, no matter which resource is used. For instance, the primes might vary. One patient's prime might be a church member, another's, a social worker. In either case, the tasks of each resource classification (in this case the prime) should be identical. Too much variation in the tasks in the system will lead to a less predictable outcome. Thus the PCCN construct cannot and should not allow for customization to overtake the need for consistency in quality, outcomes, and reliability. Indeed, one can make one's system too customized, cause it to lose effectiveness and reliability, and lean more toward chaos than efficiency.

3. With the new, total task allocation, you can now test the resource pool's new capacity, looking for significant gaps or excess in resource capacity. What-if scenarios with the

model will then help you to match the capacity of the resources and care system with the personalized demand patterns of the patient population.

Fortunately, simulation and/or swimlanes are perfect for the kind of capacity optimization analysis needed to ensure that quality care is provided on a personalized basis to each patient, depending on their needs, desires, and requirements. Keep in mind that the baseline resource pool should be based on physician guidance, the patients in the population, and the resources available in the pool. Great degrees of variance should be avoided, as any degree of variance away from the standard inherently increases the complexity of the care system and the risk that tasks may fail to be completed.

Resource Assimilation

As we saw in Chapter 4, attitudes and motivation can have a tremendous impact on the expected outcomes of the PCCN. If patients refuse to comply with care strategies, you may find that no volume or intensity of services will assist in moving their metrics. In that chapter, I suggested several considerations for evaluating the community's assimilation propensity. As part of this analysis, you will want to consider the community's commitment to and attitude toward population health.

Resources, like patients, will need to be *assimilated*. We have already defined assimilation as a much stronger and far more intense commitment to the PCCN care processes and strategies, goals and outcomes, and population health of the patients served. Once selected, assimilating the resources of the PCCN will require education on the concepts, principles, goals, and objectives of the PCCN. Assimilation will require a new standard of commitment to quality, excellence, and service rarely attained heretofore in our society. These resources must be committed at a deep and intrinsic level, willing to do what is necessary to see the success of the PCCN and the betterment of their patients and their community. Not all resources will muster this level of commitment, of course.

Furthermore, do not be surprised if the initial excitement wanes over time, as frustrations, time commitments, personal interests and circumstances, and other life changes take precedence over the focus on patients. Therefore, do not be surprised by an ebb and flow of resources into and out of the service of the PCCN and the community. What might seem like a frustrating revolving door of short-term resources is actually a common and healthy occurrence in volunteer organizations. Resources, especially those who volunteer their time, are prone to moving in and out of interest and commitment over time. This, however, is not to imply that assimilation into the PCCN is not required. Even short-term resources who pledge their time during specific and limited periods of their lives must be assimilated into the culture of the PCCN and its principles and, should you use them, Core Action Values described in the following text. This constant change is one reason the management infrastructure suggested in Chapter 8 is so critical to the overall sustainability of the PCCN in your community. Without an infrastructure much like, if not precisely like, the one recommended herein, your PCCN risks becoming a flash in a disposable pan.

Resource assimilation is therefore based on a few key elements, all of which must be in place in order for the PCCN to be sustainable in the long term. These are detailed in the pages to follow.

Resources for the Resources

In addition to the bodies of knowledge already mentioned, there is a wealth of clinical information available to both the patients and the resources of the PCCN. This includes government-sponsored agencies and organizations that continuously crank out new research and perspectives, such as the Centers for Disease Control and the Department of Health and Human Services. There are myriad state and local government agencies involved in care enhancement, management, and research. University-based research programs study everything from behavioral sciences to new medications for stubborn chronic conditions. Volunteer organizations, such as the National Cancer Society or the Alzheimer's Institute, are excellent sources of information. All this could be valuable to your local PCCN resources and patients. Coordinating this information into a meaningful and helpful format for nonclinical resources will be, in part, the role of the PCCN management team, PCPs, specialists, and other clinicians. This information can be disseminated through the communication technologies discussed later in this text, or through initial and ongoing resource training.

There should be no limit to the learning opportunities available to PCCN resources, whether professional clinicians or community volunteers. The better educated the resources are about the diseases and patients they treat, the better and more effective the PCCN will be. It is therefore recommended that the PCCN management team develop a regular and accountable method for disseminating important care information to the PCCN resources, such that the knowledge base is fully utilized.

On the flip side, the PCCN can and should be the source of ongoing research into the care of poly-chronics. Much is still unknown about the care patterns and systems necessary to yield the best possible clinical and wellness outcomes for this population. It is not unreasonable to think, therefore, that your PCCN would collaborate with others around the country to develop new strategies and approaches based on the successes and advances you encounter. Because the technologies envisioned are powerful yet flexible, it should be possible to extend them well beyond your local communities to create broad *networks of networks*, through which PCCNs can collaborate, share, and exchange. And because of the social–clinical networking (SCN) platform that your patients and their families can tap into, patient-centered approaches to care delivery can be better attained.

To this end, as you will see in the technology section of this text, I recommend that your clinical resources in your PCCN connect with the best and brightest of clinicians across the country to aid them in advancing state-of-the-art in care delivery, medication management, and outcomes optimization. This is possible through either the health information exchange (HIE) platform or the SCN, or both. I also recommend that your patients and their families utilize at least the SCN to better disseminate ideas and strategies as well as to encourage mutual support and friendship among people with similar healthcare interests.

Resource Education

Resources in the community must be educated on the following topics:

- The PCCN concept and the reason for its existence
- Shared and personal responsibility on the part of both patients and resources
- "It's not about me" mentality as a requirement of service
- Their part in the system as an integral part of the greater whole

Additionally, they'll need to be trained in the following areas for their roles in the PCCN:

- Technology, such as the clinical networking, HIE, and any virtual monitoring equipment they will encounter
- Understanding the impact of variability and interdependencies with other resources in the care continuum
- Care strategies (conceptually)
- Organizational structure of the PCCN, and the chain of reporting and responsibility

- Any aspects of incentivization built into the PCCN
- Essential responsibilities, duties, and tasks required
- How to handle the patient population being served

And finally, they'll need to be supported with necessary clinical information and task education, as well as with constantly updated patient and disease management education. This would include the following:

- Individual care strategies (specific to their roles in the PCCNs)
- Changes in clinical protocols, instructions, or patient care guidelines
- Specific tasks relevant to their patients/populations

This shouldn't seem onerous or frightening to either resources or those who will conduct this training (see the PCCN trainer section in Chapter 8). Indeed, most if not all of this training is helpful if not essential to anyone who might want to simply better care for a loved one, friend, or family member. These topics are not difficult to teach, and should be seen as opportunities to advance population health within the communities via the resources in the pool.

Furthermore, resources should see this as an opportunity to learn how to better serve the community as well as their own families and friends. Since the education will be free for the taking (and indeed required as part of participation) it should be seen as a way to expand one's value in the community while learning something new about healthier living.

Setting up Educational Programs

Once the patient population and the resource pool are chosen, the heavy lifting of coordination and education begins in earnest. For this, there are a number of steps that each resource must go through, and in which the PCCN management team must be intimately involved. Under ideal circumstances, a PCCN trainer will be used to provide most if not all of the necessary training. This resource is one of only two recommended as full time for just about any size PCCN. However, note that each element listed here has an associated parenthetical training resource, which includes other members of the PCCN management team. These resources can be used as trainers if there is no full-time trainer, or if the trainer's role is limited by scope, task constraints, or knowledge. Also note that training resources are not set in stone, and can be flexible except where clinical resources are required. Therefore, as long as you provide at least the following elements in some way, the resources you use will be up to you.

These are the training elements important to a successful PCCN:

- **PCCN concepts and infrastructure (PCCN manager):** The PCCN will be explained, and its goals and objectives clearly defined and quantified for all participants. This is critical to the assimilation so necessary for the long-term success of the network.
- **Resource review and explanation (PCCN manager):** An overview of all the resources in the pool and the infrastructure that will support the care strategies the resources will implement.
- **Resource roles and responsibilities (PCCN manager):** Each resource must thoroughly understand his/her role in the care strategy, as it relates to the other resources, tasks, and outcomes. Thus, training on the various roles and responsibilities is critical to an understanding of the system.
- **Essentials of processes and systems (PCCN manager or IE):** This training, again for all resources in the PCCN, includes simple explanations of the working

of systems, the impacts of variability and interdependencies, and the roles of each resource within the broader care strategies of the PCCN. You will likely be able to find simple explanations of these concepts, some of which will be explained in a future publication by this same author.

■ **Technology (PCCN IT or technology resources such as vendor reps, etc.):** Obviously, to use the PCCN's technology, training must accompany any resource use. This training should include hands-on experience and real-life usage scenarios in order to prevent technology from becoming an inhibitor of the network's implementation.

■ **Risks and legalities (PCCN Manager or local volunteer legal counsel):** Clearly, there are some limited risks to the PCCN and its sponsors if sentinel events happen due specifically to the care provided by the PCCN resources. This is highly unlikely, even nearly impossible, given the infrastructure and the specificity of the task assignments. Nonetheless, each resource must thoroughly understand not only his/her role in the care processes but what not to do as well. Overstepping boundaries is a serious but altogether preventable error if proper training and certifications are provided.

■ **Clinically relevant information (PCP, chronicist, or clinical equivalent):** This information would likely be limited to those directly involved in the clinical care of poly-chronics, but might include the nonclinical but clinically curious. Indeed, it might include all the resources should the PCCN management team decide that clinical understanding by all is important to attaining the goals and objectives of the network. This training would include the specifics of the care strategies, the patient flow, clinical and nonclinical tasks, and goals of the patient's care. While this might be routinely revisited and personalized for a particular patient, an essential base

understanding by all is critical to the synergies of the
effort and the assimilation process.

■ **Core Action Values (Certified Values Coach):** Based
on the aforementioned Joe Tye's work, these Core Action
Values will help your resources in their roles in the PCCN
as well as in their day-to-day lives. These will easily and
readily match the values taught in most local Christian
churches.

Other training will be ongoing, and there may be elements
within your PCCN that require additional special consideration. These might include:

■ **Religious considerations:** This might include specific
requirements for working with poly-chronics of religions
different from those of the volunteers. Such training
would include how to speak with patients, what questions and issues are considered taboo, and restrictions on
male–female interactions.

■ **Dependencies and mental health:** Drug and alcohol
dependency, depression, and other mental health issues
are not uncommon among the poly-chronic population. Therefore, it will be common for resources to
encounter these conditions as they deal with and care
for their patients. Special considerations for language and
verbiage, signs and indicators of conditions, and so on,
will be important for resources to know well, as they may
develop relationships that will allow influence over behavior. Resources must be trained to take care not to overstep
their bounds and inadvertently cause harm while trying
to do good. This training should be taught by professionals knowledgeable in the science of substance abuse and
mental health treatments. Indeed, sub-PCCNs may need
to be created to deal with patients with these complicat-
ing conditions, as they might be outside the realm of
possibilities of general PCCNs and their resources.

- **Prison work:** Not all poly-chronics live in our local neighborhoods. Some live in prisons and mental health institutions, but nonetheless can benefit from the work of a PCCN. If your PCCN desires to take on the poly-chronics of a local prison, special training will no doubt be required from the institution's administrators. Training on personal safety, prison procedures and policies, and issue avoidance will be critical to the success of such programs.

- **Youth:** The youth of American face unique health and wellness issues. A frighteningly fast rise in obesity and associated chronic illness, coupled with a stubborn and steady percentage of smokers and illicit drug users bodes poorly for the next generation of Americans. Since chronic diseases often run in the family, obese and chronically ill parents may yield offspring with similar issues. Thus, it may behoove a community to set up a special PCCN through local schools and churches specifically for youth with and at risk of chronic diseases.

   Working with youth will likely require special training for the resources in the pool. Thus, trainers specializing in the management and improvement of youth health and wellness should be used for those resources that will interact with young patients and their families.

If there is no PCCN trainer involved, resource training will require organizational efforts on the part of the PCCN management team to ensure quality and positive outcomes, reduction of risk, and ongoing participation. Furthermore, it will behoove the PCCN to provide ongoing clinical and nonclinical training, refreshers, and opportunities to learn and grow for its resources. Doing so will require a vision of the needs of the PCCN patients as it relates to the requirements for resource knowledge.

Some of this training can be done online, some requires in-person interaction, and most if not all will require some degree of certification and documentation of capabilities and knowledge. This, too, must be considered as part of the management of the PCCN.

Leadership and Core Values

Assimilation can be driven by the motivation, passion, and commitment of the leadership to the goals and objectives of the PCCN. The PCCN management team will be responsible for the dissemination of the principles and values of the PCCN into the resources and community at large. This leadership must be more than direction and authority. It must engender a set of core values and principles that will not only ensure the successful direction of the PCCN, but will assist individual resources and patients in their own progress toward a better self and their own leadership qualities.

The leadership of the PCCN will also come, in part, from the clinicians, since they will be the inevitable go-to resources for important clinical decision making. They, too, will need to instill the values and principles of your PCCN. However, leadership principles should permeate the PCCN and all the resources, since they will have direct and influential contact with the patients. As leaders in their communities, the PCCN resources will have the best opportunity to instill the motivation, faith, and perseverance needed to help patients battle their diseases and come to a better state of physical, mental, spiritual, and emotional wellness.

Of course, many of the PCCN resources will be volunteers, unresponsive to the powers of authority common to the workplace. Volunteers commonly require a different set of motivators, benefits, and guidance mechanisms. Therefore, the PCCN leadership may need training on how to lead volunteers, since this can be much different than leading employees.

Your PCCN will therefore need a set of core, intrinsic values from which decisions are made and goals are set.

Without these, you may find that your PCCN is overtaken by the internal, often selfish agendas of key players and participants. This would at minimum inhibit the growth of your PCCN if not outright doom it to a troublesome and frustrating future.

I will therefore make a shameless plug for Joe Tye and his Twelve Core Action Values. These can be found on Joe's website, http://www.joetye.com. Joe is the author of several books, including *The Florence Prescription: From Accountability to Ownership*,[4] and *All Hands on Deck*.[5] Joe's philosophy, teaching, and approach could and should serve as an example if not a core component of leadership, service, and commitment principles for your PCCN.

On Joe's website, you will find, among other valuable resources, the aforementioned Twelve Core Action Values. They are as follows:

- Authenticity
- Integrity
- Awareness
- Courage
- Perseverance
- Faith
- Purpose
- Vision
- Focus
- Enthusiasm
- Service
- Leadership

These twelve are explained in great detail on his website, in his writings, and through his consulting and values coaching. I would highly recommend anyone interested in the PCCN and the use of community resources for the care of the indigent and poly-chronic populations use these values as the core foundation of your efforts.

Group Dynamics™ for Resources

Group Dynamics is a key supporting concept for the PCCN and its patients. Group interactions, support, and motivation are also critical for the resources in the pool.

I've worked from a home office for much of my career as a consultant, and only once worked in a busy office of cubicles and coworkers. While this has its advantages, there are a number of disadvantages as well. One is the lack of a feeling of connectedness with others in the office. Even though one might be connected electronically via email or, in the case of the PCCN, through social–clinical networking technologies, there may still be a disconnect among the resources.

To solve this, it is recommended that the resources in the PCCN gather periodically. These gatherings needn't necessarily include all PCCN resources, as this might prove difficult. However, there should be group meetings for a variety of resources on a variety of schedules. These meetings may be task focused, such as:

■ Meetings with clinicians to go over care strategies.
■ Group discussions regarding specific patients, whose metrics or attitudes or general health need additional focus. These patients may have become a frustration to the resources to whom they are assigned, and open face-to-face (FTF) meetings are the best way to work out solutions.
■ Generation of new ideas and strategies for the care of the PCCN's patients.

Meetings may also be more resource focused, such as the following:

■ **Motivational and personal growth:** Even the best of resources need to be reenergized periodically. This is difficult to achieve remotely or even via interactive technologies such as WebEx. This is best accomplished via FTF meetings.

Such meetings might include success stories, assistance with frustrations, promoting ideas for better patient engagement and care, and general sharing of patient improvements.

■ **Ongoing education:** It should not be unreasonable to expect that PCCN resources become "health evangelists" in the community, dispersing health-related information in their full-time jobs, with friends and neighbors, and the non-PCCN members of their communities. This, of course, requires ongoing education of these resources, which will allow them to help both their patients and their communities live better and healthier lives.

This education might include both clinical and non-clinical information such as how to help identify depression, how to manage a difficult patient, how to interpret particular clinical readings from virtual monitoring devices, or how to manage physician orders and recommendations.

■ **Resource expansion:** These group meetings might be used as a means to recruit new resources into the PCCN, when and where needed. Nothing is more motivating to an outsider than seeing the enthusiasm and passion of a group working on a project like this. Inviting outsiders to see what is happening and how the projects are impacting the lives of patients and the health of the community can drive new enthusiasm into the PCCN through new resource recruits. Success begets more success, which begets more resources for you to use.

By using the same group support methodologies and concepts common to group therapies throughout healthcare, it is expected that the resources can and will be aided, motivated, and lifted up as they care for the most complex patients in the population.

These meetings can happen in a variety of settings, depending on the community's physical space and the needs of the resources themselves. Whether in the local hospital or a resource's home, the resource Group Dynamics meetings should always be considered a unique and special opportunity to engage, encourage, and perfect the resource pool, providing a level of support heretofore unheard of in healthcare or community service.

Challenges and Obstacles

A number of challenges face the PCCN and its developers and managers. Here are the main ones worthy of consideration.

Legal Hurdles

If the government is serious about healthcare reform in the coming decades, legal air cover must be given to organizations that are willing to challenge the status quo. This includes the initial PCCNs that will rely on resources across a community to care for patients in a new way. Without legal protection, resources and the PCCN management may become skittish about the use of nonclinical resources, caring for patients using volunteers, and so on.

Legal protections can come in several forms in the existing environment. However, I would recommend that you consult with your organization's legal counsel to ensure that resources are adequately covered against liability for the care they provide. Regardless of your state's laws and legal precedence, it is likely that education, certification, governance and accountability, and strict adherence to resource roles will be important to ensuring a smooth and litigation-free existence. However, understand that there are lawyers who constantly seek enrichment from any source, however good and honorable its intentions. The trial lawyers may try to prey upon both the PCCN organization and its resources if they are not given the correct legal cover via documentation, written agreements with patients and families, and proper infrastructure.

Too Many Cooks?

The integration of many resources might dilute responsibility rather than promote it if the resources are not properly managed and led. Too many resources, tossed at a problem willy-nilly, will likely lead to a scenario in which chaos is overly prevalent, tasks are not completed, resources and patients are frustrated and unhappy, and quality and consistency suffer as care is placed at risk. Keeping this, as well as territoriality and infighting, out is like keeping black spot out of your rose garden. It requires constant vigilance, preventative measures, and the assumption that bad events and circumstances lie unseen and waiting for an opportunity to disrupt the beauty you've worked so hard to create.

Thus, again, the need for team accountability, Group Dynamics meetings, knowledge of and respect for the infrastructure, core values training, and a distinct "it's not about me" mentality. All this must be ingrained in each and every resource in the pool in order to avoid the potential chaos of many resources being thrown at a very big problem haphazardly. Even the best of fire departments would fail to effectively douse a fire if they just showed up and started squirting water. Organization, regimen, and accountability are all vital to the PCCN's success.

Summary

Resources in the PCCN, whether clinical or volunteers, are the life's blood of the system. Without enough of the right resources, the provision of care still suffers and your PCCN will fail from lack of support. Understanding what and how many you need, where, and when, is critical to success. The engineered approach to the PCCN's resource and task allocations help to ensure the right resource mix for your patient population. By using the above guidelines to develop your own resource pool, and training it well in the art and science of PCCN care management, your network will be assured of the best chances for success.

Now that you understand the necessary resources mix, it is time to delve more deeply into the governance structures that will form the foundation of the accountability, communication, and team dynamics of your PCCN.

Endnotes

1. "Multiple Chronic Conditions: A Strategic Framework: Optimum Health and Quality of Life for Individuals with Multiple Chronic Conditions," U.S. Department of Health and Human Services, December 2010.
2. Ibid.
3. www.joetye.com
4. J. Tye, *The Florence Prescription: From Accountability to Ownership* (New York: John Wiley and Sons, 2010).
5. J. Tye, *All Hands on Deck* (New York: John Wiley and Sons, 2010).

Chapter 7

Build It and They May Not Come

Am I suggesting the construction of a new and unique business model with no payment model to go with it? Yes, I am. But that's OK, for a lot of reasons. Importantly, it is quite possible to start this new concept based on the old payment models. Let's walk through this notion.

Think about who is paid in the current fee-for-service (FFS) system. The primary care physicians (PCPs), specialists, hospitals, nursing homes, and other ancillary services are the primary recipients of the current funding. In the initial stages of the poly-chronic care network (PCCN), however, who would receive the funds? Well, until new payment models are developed, the recipients would largely be the same. Here's why this is both important and yet not a "show-stopper."

Since the PCCN is based on a broader network of resources, it is capable of achieving the Five Pillars through the expansion of clinical capacity and the effective allocation of clinical and nonclinical resources to care for an ever-growing population of patients. Yet, many of these newly utilized resources are either (a) already paid through some other entity, such as the YMCA or social workers, or (b) volunteers who do not demand compensation for their efforts (e.g., church congregations, civic groups, etc.). Thus, the expansion of nonclinical capacity can come with a surprisingly low budget.

Furthermore, because of the engineering approach to the issue, the PCCN allows for the optimal use of the available (paid) clinical resources, such that their capacity is optimized and maximized without undue stress or additional work-load. As workload and workflow are dispersed throughout the resource pool, both can be better managed through the PCCN's technologies such as the social–clinical network. And by engineering a supportive team of resources to aid these clinical resources in the management of care, the PCCN ensures that the available capacity of currently paid resources is used at the lowest possible cost.

Protecting the Herd

In the short-term, fewer oxen are gored than one might imagine. Rightfully, providers are concerned that innovative delivery models will result in a reduction in their income. For example, short-sighted detractors say the risk of bundled payment arrangements with payors is a "race to the bottom," in which hospitals and physicians begin to compete to be the lowest-cost provider in exchange for preferential referrals from large employers and payors. This, they say, yields an inevitable deterioration of pay rates, even for those not participating in the bundled payment competitions, as payors reduce their payouts as a result of ongoing competition. However, there will inevitably come a day when the diagnosis-related group (DRG) will be expanded to include bundled and capitated payments for diseases and entire populations as healthcare is transformed from the old *volume* incentive systems to a new *value-based* approach. Thus, whether we like it or not, the inability of the current system to sustain the current payment model begs for innovation, yielding a pressing necessity to use similar business models to approach cost, quality, and system capacity.

Until then, and as the PCCN is tried, tested, and altered, the FFS model will be protected in the PCCN implementation. This is particularly true of the specialists, upon whose expertise the system greatly depends. While bundled payments and capitated payment models will ultimately arise for the poly-chronic population, specialists will likely continue to be paid on some sort of service-based model, in part because the specialist is only involved in the patient's care on an intermittent basis, during which services are provided and paid. Coordination of care delivery and the proper task allocations will aid in the "downstream" care management of the population, which ultimately aids the specialist as well as the others in the network. And while a capitated and population health model (aka accountable care organizations [ACOs] and health maintenance organizations [HMOs]) must allow for some use of specialists, utilization will be increasingly but carefully managed to prevent (a) cost overruns that have been indicative of the current broken system, and (b) disenfranchising the much-needed specialist community.

The hospital is the entity perhaps at most financial risk, though there is less downside than one might expect. Several issues emerge as hospitals consider this business and care model. First, hospitals may find themselves unable to control decreased volumes. Since physicians direct patient care, and can help steer patients either to or away from the hospital doors, the hospital is somewhat at the mercy of its physician referral base. If the PCCN works as it should, the PCCN will preemptively manage the care of the poly-chronic populations and patients will see their physicians before their condition unnecessarily warrants hospitalization or an emergency department (ED) visit.

Secondly, a fully functioning PCCN will result in reductions in ED volume, unnecessary readmissions, and length of stay (LOS) for inpatient and intensive care unit (ICU) stays, and other related ancillary impacts (e.g., reduced testing, radiology, and preventative services). While this is good for the patients and the community, it is not necessarily good for the hospital. Hospitals that desire a reduction in, say, unnecessary readmissions may find that other admissions are also reduced, thus offsetting what might be a negative financial impact with undesirable volume outcomes.

Therefore, these desired impacts can be viewed as positive or negative, depending on one's perspective. Hospitals will need to make up for the potentially lost volume by accounting for the offsetting capacity and potential improvement in margins. We'll discuss the financials of the PCCN in greater detail in Chapter 10. For now, take a look at some examples of financial impacts.

■ Reduced ED visits (and perhaps thereby increased physician office visits) will certainly reduce revenues, but will also free ED capacity for better community service, and result in reductions in staffing and workload, streamlining of care provision, overall ED LOS reductions, and reduced (unnecessary) admissions.

■ While no one denies the trend toward reduced reimbursement for unnecessary readmissions, identifying at-risk patients is perhaps easier than preventing their return. Now that the Centers for Medicare and Medicaid Services (CMS) is providing increased motivation, the financial incentives now exist for using communal resources in the battle against readmissions, even those that CMS does not yet classify as unwarranted. Hospitals can assist by targeting patients at risk for unnecessary readmissions by working with the PCCN community resources upon patient discharge, ensuring a smoother transition to the home or care site and helping prevent the readmissions, which will do it the most financial harm.

■ Proper and community-wide use of end-of-life (EOL) planning and education has been shown to greatly increase patient and family gratification, and can also impact ICU and inpatient margins. As an example, Gunderson Lutheran Health System, through their Respecting Choices program, signed up 90 percent of eligible patients for EOL planning and advanced directives, simplifying and smoothing the care process for both patients and practitioners. While direct cost reduction associated with EOL planning is a touchy issue and often not well tracked, there is clear anecdotal evidence that EOL planning does impact total cost of care, especially for chronic disease patients, through minimizing the improper use of ICU resources. Analysis of the cost of care delivery for the chronically ill during EOL stages of treatment may reveal opportunities for the hospital to both trim unreimbursed DRG costs while improving care and community gratification.

This all means that the cost savings associated with the PCCN should not be alarming to hospital and physician practice administrators who plan effectively for the changes in volumes and patient care requirements. Transitioning to the new models will require strategic planning, some financial activity–based cost accounting, and management vision (again, see Chapter 10 for more detail).

Physician Participation

In order to make the PCCN work, there must be physician participation at some significant level. The incentives for participation can be high, depending on how the PCCN is structured and viewed.

Of course, physicians may want to participate simply to help their poly-chronics deal with their diseases more effectively, easily, and at a lower cost. Participating patients should be much more satisfied with the coordinated care they receive, and thus may be more willing to self-manage. If so, physicians can have a greater impact on their patients and their communities.

Physicians can also directly benefit from the ongoing communication with communal resources. This ongoing dialogue should assist them in disease management and patient contact, and offer greater *care efficiency* by helping them see patients who need it most while expanding the number of patients they manage. By passing certain care tasks to community resources who can more readily and easily manage them, physicians can increase their own capacity without giving up clinical control and guidance. Physicians may also see an increase in their number of appointments as patients are preemptively managed and see their physician rather than going to the ED or hospital.

Additional revenue offsets, such that they are required, may be available through *shared savings programs* similar to that offered through other CMS demonstration projects (e.g., medical homes, wherein physicians receive a per-beneficiary, per-month stipend).

Risk, Payors, and the Government

One of the largest issues facing healthcare costs today is risk. Payors and government both wrestle with risk as it impacts cost, premiums, and capacity. However, we have typically dealt with risk of the outliers in the population by surrounding them with a larger, lower-risk population to offset their cost. The more low-risk patients we have contributing to the system, the lower the risk that a single patient in the population might outspend available monies. The low-risk patients thus pay for the high-risk patients. And since legislation prevents the kind of risk-based premiums so common among other types of insurance, the risk is spread as higher costs to everyone. Assuming there are enough of them, the low-risk patients dilute the risk such that the overall, total cost of the system (and its risk) per patient goes down. However, this model needs serious reconsideration in light of the current healthcare systems.

Given a poly-chronic patient population, and its relatively higher cost and care requirements, segmenting it from other patients will actually serve to remove risk for everyone. Since our poly-chronic patients are *all* likely to require extensive medical treatment, their costs are both known, transparent, and expected to be high. This can be anticipated if we utilize our population modeling technologies so as to predict disease prevalence and types amongst our populations. The future (long- and short-term) trends in population health can then be studied for impact on risk as well as resources. This will allow for the risk of the PCCN population to be managed more effectively.

In a typical fully capitated business environment, one would want the low-risk population to cover the costs and risks for the high-risk population. This is why, for instance, it is recommended that the ACO model encompass no fewer than 50,000 covered lives. This high number means that medical risk is spread more evenly, allowing the necessary insurance cushion against catastrophic illness or chronic disease.

However, if poly-chronics are fully segmented out, and their current and future healthcare needs known, we could create a new risk pool for which the actuarial risk would become less murky. By more accurately predicting total cost, and understanding future disease prevalence in the community, we would allow for better management of those costs both in the short and long term. By removing the poly-chronics from the general population's risk pool, both groups become more predictable. This lessens the risk to the general populace, thus removing premium costs, while concentrating cost control measures on the populations that need it most. Additionally, efforts to control costs within this population would more readily be seen in the results generated, without the statistical interference of the other 80 percent of the general population.

This means that the poly-chronics could and should make up their own healthcare subsystem and risk subsegmentation. By grouping them together, rather than trying to mix them into the general population (and hoping the 80 percent's premiums can cover the 20 percent's high costs), the risk and cost of the poly-chronics are separated out. This makes the risk more visible and manageable, and would allow for its own capitated business model, complete with its own risk pool and management structures.

Importantly, this would allow for a better use of government funds (assuming the government wants a continued role in care design, delivery, and payment). If government entities were to focus on the high risk and high cost in the capitated yet "encapsulated" environment of the PCCN, costs to taxpayers could be more predictable and transparent. Meanwhile, the 80 percent of the population could go to the private market for their insurance based on a variety of currently proposed reforms (e.g., purchasing insurance within small groups, across state lines, or not at all). Gone would be the risk factors that require individual mandates for insurance (à la Massachusetts and the Patient Protection and Affordable Care Act [PPACA]) since the risk for the general population would have gone down dramatically. And by focusing efforts on the Five Pillars, the care of poly-chronics would be enhanced yet less expensive, leaving taxpayers with a better overall package.

Future PCCN Model Alternatives

Thus, even government could accept this PCCN subsystem as a viable policy alternative. If this were carried to the next step of evolution, I could envision that the PCCN might become privatized, with professionally managed PCCNs offering the best of management expertise in exchange for accepting the risk of care delivery. Large national employers, such as IBM or Deere, in cooperation with hospitals and physician groups, might roll their local PCCN communities into larger structured organizations that allow for economies of scale in technology and organization, thus further reducing the cost while impacting important worker and population health within communities across the country. Indeed, perhaps there is no better place to start the PCCN than within large employers struggling to make both their workers and their communities healthier.

Other PCCN models might link multiple PCCNs together through large, multistate and/or for-profit health systems such as HCA or Catholic Healthcare West. These entities could tap the power of the PCCN concepts while sharing best demonstrated practices (BDPs) and expertise throughout their provider networks. The economies of scale in technology and the learning networks that might be enabled make this a viable and promising road for the PCCN.

Summary

Hospitals and physicians are critical participants in the PCCN infrastructure. Without their buy-in, the PCCN is sure to die, assuming it ever starts. Consideration of the financial risk and political implications of the various models is critical to the long-term viability of the PCCN model. Therefore, it is incumbent upon the PCCN management team to ensure that all players' issues, reservations, and constraints are fully accounted for and thoroughly vetted. Let's take a look at some of the issues of governance and technologies that will assist the PCCN implementation, and then we'll go into how to pay for it all.

Chapter 8

PCCN Resources and Governance Structures

In the previous chapters, much mention was made about the various roles and responsibilities of the resources in the poly-chronic care network (PCCN). These include references to the PCCN managers and trainers, PCCN management team, primary care physicians (PCPs) or chronicists, and industrial engineers (IEs) or management engineers (MEs) and engineering staff. These general roles play a critical part in the formation, resource training, and ongoing management of the PCCN.

However, there are quite possibly an infinite number of actual structures one could use to implement a PCCN. Indeed, as long as the core philosophy, values, and technologies are the same, the PCCN concept supports a variety of infrastructure and governance designs. This is by design, of course, since all communities are slightly different, and will not have identical resource pools or circumstances. Key to all these models are several core attributes that the PCCN and its resources should exhibit, without which it may falter:

- Accountability
- Personal responsibility (for both resources and patients)

■ Ownership mentality with respect to the patient and the PCCN

■ Strict adherence to clinical instructions, protocols, guidelines, and communications

■ Maintenance of the limitations of one's scope of duty, work, and role

■ Respect for others, especially clinicians, patients, and the governance structure

■ Outcomes-focused approach (which is defined as both patient- and resource-centered)

In this chapter, I'll outline a few possible governance structures, from which you can select or derive your own. Keep in mind that these structures are flexible, and meant to provide guidance as to the level of accountability and management that will be required for an effective organization.

Also remember the issues of size as you think about your PCCN. Depending on the scale and breadth of services, you may need all or just one of the following resources and duties. In a small PCCN, such as one servicing a single, small ethnic group, a single PCP and staff can effectively run the network. If the PCCN is based in a large physician practice with hundreds of patients, all of the roles and multiple resources of each might be required.

Let's run through a few of the key roles and their responsibilities.

Poly-Chronic Care Network Roles

PCCN Management Team

The PCCN management team would likely be made up of some or all of the following:

1. Key clinical decision makers (including representatives from independent specialty practices)
2. Chronicists (if any, see later)

3. PCP and specialist representatives
4. Manager (see later)
5. Trainer (see later)
6. Community representatives from key volunteer organizations (e.g., Lions, Rotary, churches)
7. Patient representatives
8. Employer representatives (in an employer-based PCCN)
9. IT representatives
10. Hospital representatives (especially if the PCCN is hospital based)
11. PCCN legal counsel
12. PCCN finance liaison

The role of the PCCN management team (MT) is to direct and guide the overall delivery system; assist with issues that arise from training, logistics, internal disagreements, IT infrastructure, costs, patients served, and so on; and generally offer both vision and direction to the PCCN resources. In other words, the MT is to be the governing body for the PCCN. The makeup of the MT should be made flexible, to account for a variety of circumstances, patient populations, resource pools, and other parameters.

For instance, a population of poly-chronics with a large mentally ill and substance abuse population might include more social workers and psychologists. A rural MT might include more individual volunteers and churches rather than representatives of community service organizations. An ethnic- or religion-based MT might have special members including clergy or experts in the group's culture and social norms.

Regardless of its members, the MT is envisioned to be less a *dictatorial council of elders* than an *advisory body* that helps the PCCN continue its ongoing function and attain its goals. Thus, it should avoid elected officials or their representatives, as they may create more issues than they solve. Union representation, too, should be avoided, as their interests are too heavily focused on supporting the interests of their membership and not enough on the bigger picture of changing the delivery system.

Additionally, employer representatives should be kept to those whose vested interest is in the employees' health and wellness and not in the employer's income or costs, since the latter might intimidate the other members of the MT in an employer-sponsored program. Therefore, care should be taken to avoid an employer-led oligarchy in which the interests of the employer are the only ones that truly matter. Lastly, representatives of hospitals and large physician practices should be limited to those who are focused on the patient outcomes rather than their constituents; else there will be too much *politicking* and not enough vision and guidance. This means that representatives of these organizations should represent the larger aims of communal health and wellness rather than solely the interests of their entities or their financial well-being.

Overall, the MT should consist of those who can objectively and wisely coach and guide the PCCN resources through difficulties and set and maintain the PCCN's vision and mission, while serving as the ultimate authority in dispute resolution and challenges to the PCCN's work from the community. A few of the key players on the MT are discussed in detail next.

Chronicists

A *chronicist* has been defined herein as a physician specializing in the care of poly-chronics. Chronicists may or may not show up in your PCCN, depending on the organizational structure you select or devise, the willingness of local physicians to realign their patients' care within the PCCN, and the reimbursement systems in place.

Note: This role is expected to exist if and only if some or all of the PCPs attached to the PCCN and community are willing to "give up" their poly-chronic patients to another physician, at least in part. This might be the case in countries where the fee-for-service business model is not as predominant as it is in the United States, where there is tight integration among employed physicians, or where there is a bundled or capitated model. If this is not the case in your community, you can easily read this and other sections of this text and substitute PCPs for the more specialized chronicist role. Wherever you see *chronicist*, simply substitute *dedicated and knowledgeable PCP* in its place.

There are a number of potential backgrounds for a chronicist. Of course, the chronicist must be a physician. Backgrounds might include a PCP who has worked with poly-chronics in his/her own practice; or gerontologists, internal medicine, or other similar specialties who routinely deal with this patient population. The background is not set in stone, and in fact is meant to allow for flexibility within the many community types this business model will encounter. Regardless of the background, there must be sufficient respect for the skills, knowledge, and capabilities of the chronicist within the local physician, patient, and provider community, such that they can lead care strategy management and promote change as required.

The chronicist is meant to be at the top of the pyramid. The role focuses on what physicians do best—direct and manage care strategies—for this specific patient population. The chronicist, as a *resident expert* in the care of poly-chronics, will collaborate closely with specialists, experts from across the country and around the globe, and poly-chronic patients, community resources, and families to ensure the best care and care strategies possible for each patient in the population. The chronicist, therefore, is the locus of clinical decisions, care strategy development and implementation, relevant information dissemination, and clinical collaboration. Whether they see a few or a lot of patients as physicians, their role is to focus on the health, well-being, and clinical optimization of the poly-chronics under their care.

Governance Structures and the Chronicist

There are a number of ways the chronicist might be used in your PCCN. These will largely guide the governance structure you select, since the chronicist, in whatever role you select, will be the central clinical figure for the PCCN system. Thus, the role you select for the chronicist will dictate the type of governance structure your PCCN will have.

For example:

A. The chronicist may act as an integrator, collaborating heavily with other PCPs and specialists, taking instructions and disseminating them to the broader resource pool.

   In this sense, the chronicist does not take over the care of the poly-chronics, but rather collaborates with others to iteratively develop care strategies and then implement them as a clinical leader (see Figure 8.1). In this scenario, the chronicist will manage the care strategies but develop them collaboratively. Ultimate responsibility for the care strategy's success or failure lies with the chronicist, as does all clinical guidance and instructions. Other physicians can and should offer input. However, once the care strategy is developed, other physicians should respect the role and step out

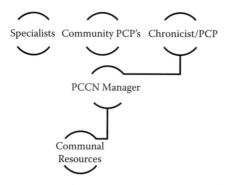

Figure 8.1   Chronicist as integrator of physician resources in care strategy development.

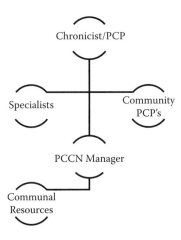

Figure 8.2   Chronicist as leader of care strategy development and implementation.

of the patient's management and allow the PCCN to do what it is designed to do. Otherwise, the chronicist role becomes that of a meaningless and powerless bureaucrat.

B. The chronicist acts as the leader and sole authority for the care strategies of the poly-chronics under the PCCN's care.

This version of the role (see Figure 8.2) is more of a benevolent dictator than the aforementioned open collaborator. This role would be used in circumstances where patients are placed in the direct care of the PCCN, with few "strings" back to their PCPs, as might be the case with a population of urban poor or uninsured who have no PCP, or patients whose PCP prefers the PCCN as the source of care management. Of course, the chronicist would collaborate with specialists and other chronicists, and base clinical decision making and instructions on their input. But those decisions and guidance would emanate from this chronicist rather than from a broader group of clinical leaders.

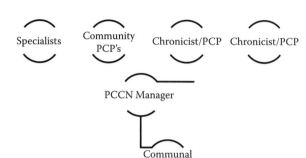

Figure 8.3   Groups of chronicists and PCPs using a single group of communal resources and a PCCN manager.

Again, this scenario is highly unlikely in the current fee-for-service world here in the United States, given the strains already on our PCPs. However, this may work in other, non-FFS systems where task and patient allocation is more easily managed among local physicians.

C. Chronicist groups/multiple PCPs: In certain situations, a number of chronicists may manage smaller groups of poly-chronics within a broader community of disease prevalence (see Figure 8.3).

This might occur in small group practices wherein physicians opt to continue to see their own poly-chronics and perhaps a few additional poly-chronics from the other physicians, while maintaining services for their entire patient panel. These chronicists would align with chronicists in the community to utilize the same communal resource pool and a single manager. Thus, several chronicists with relatively small poly-chronic populations would tap into the same communal resource pool, MT, and manager to assist in the management of their poly-chronics. This might also be the case with a relatively small population of patients from a church congregation, neighborhood or geography, individual nursing home or retirement community, and so on, who tap into a larger organizational structure for assistance. This allows for a sort of micro-PCCN to emerge, specific to a small population or subset of a larger community.

Naturally, such a scenario requires additional resource management, since resources might get pulled in too many directions if there are conflicting needs amongst the various chronicists. This is why a strong manager, MT, and strongly aligned resources are important to the continuity of care provision and prevention of misaligned interests. Thus while feasible and reasonable, you should be careful to ensure that services can be readily provided to all chronicists tapping into your community of care. This is where some of the swimlane mapping and simulation technology will come into play, as it will help guide your resource and task assignments to optimize utilization despite the more complex operating environment.

D. You may find that your PCCN "clinical authority pyramid" is more Mayan than Egyptian in shape, with a flat top upon which rest several (physician) clinical resources.

In this scenario (see Figure 8.4), your chronicists share responsibility for a large population of patients, acting as more of an executive council than individual decision

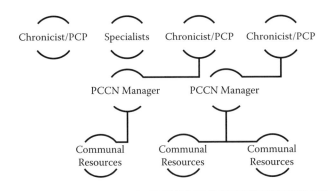

Figure 8.4   Multiple chronicists and PCPs with multiple resource pools and PCCN managers.

makers. This would be more commonplace in scenarios in which large group practices with specialists and PCPs develop teams of chronicists to serve entire communities. Imagine the largest of physician practices aligned with the local major hospital(s), a major payor, and employers to provide capitated/bundled payments. The chronicists in this case may tap into multiple resource pools with multiple infrastructure designs, since the population's poly-chronics may be served by many resource pools. In this scenario, collaboration and communication becomes much more complex and multiple managers collaborate to manage demands for cross-PCCN collaboration. While not impossible, this clearly begs for the use of the most sophisticated resource and task allocation tools and methodologies. Otherwise, you may find the coordination of the resource pools to be difficult if not impossible. Such a scenario might also entail the use of full-time management engineers and other performance improvement specialists to ensure the ongoing and optimal functionality of the system created.

As mentioned above, the chronicist might see a few or a lot of patients. In some scenarios, the chronicist might merely direct the care of many patients, only some of whom are seen on a regular basis. Of course, since the community resources and PCCN technologies are meant to greatly increase the capacity of the system, it is likely that many chronicists will increase the number of patients on their panels while providing them all with better and more holistic care. This is achieved through the use of additional care resources that will deflect some of the demand from the chronicist onto other care resources, allowing the chronicist to see only those they need to see for important clinical reasons. (This, by the way, is one of the obvious reasons that a new payment model is required, since much of the work of the chronicist is currently unpaid under the traditional FFS and even new quality-based payment models.)

Since chronicists are, in some of these scenarios, likely to pull patients from other practices, it will be critical to ensure that relationships are built and maintained, and that the PCCN does not become a pariah in the community. Indeed, it is likely that, if successfully implemented, the PCCN will pull patients from other PCPs and practices in the community as word spreads about the unique results attained and methodologies used. Therefore it is critical that there is a collaborative and communal spirit within all the work of the PCCN, such that issues of competition and patient theft are mitigated.

Thus, chronicists will do more than sit atop a throne and bark out orders for all to follow. Rather, they will be a resource, guide, mentor, and inspiration for the community and its many resources.

Specialists

Of course, without physician specialties, the PCCN would not be able to function effectively. From gerontologists to podiatrists to hematologists, specialists direct and manage a great deal of care of the poly-chronic population. Yet even though they already see the poly-chronics, their care may not necessarily be coordinated well with others, such as PCPs, hospitals, social workers, and others in the community of care. Thus, if nothing else, the PCCN will bring structure and coordination to their work.

More importantly, the PCCN and the chronicists will bring new resources to aid the specialists in patient management; technologies to make their monitoring more efficient, cost effective, and quicker; and systems to increase their already strained capacities, allowing them to maximize their productivity and practice revenues while simultaneously holding down costs.

To achieve these ends, specialists should be involved, to the degree appropriate, in the PCCN. More specifically, they should be involved in the MT's decisions on goals and approaches, and the development of care strategies. In return, specialists must be willing to accept some degree of coordination of care delivery, and input into the patient's treatment from the chronicists and other specialists. Care strategies will involve, but not revolve around, the specialists as they are brought into the patient's care. And while this might seem like loss of autonomy and a potential loss of income, neither should occur.

The role of the specialist within the governance structure may depend more upon their employment and practice affiliation status than their importance to patient care. While it is recommended that some representatives of the specialist community be part of the MT, independent specialists may find themselves outside the MT core group if a hospital-based PCCN prefers its own, employed specialists to be involved. Likewise, multispecialty practice-based PCCNs will likely keep the MT representation limited to its own physicians, rather than using external resources. To avoid conflicts in the community and keep the community's poly-chronics at the center of attention, the manager and others invested in this care model should strive to keep all possible doors open, even if the initial efforts are limited in scope and scale. Prevention of exclusionary policies in the early stages will allow the future expansion of the PCCN throughout the community as its impact is seen and felt.

PCCN Manager

The PCCN manager's (hereinafter manager) role is to take on the organizational, logistical, and flow maintenance and monitoring tasks of the chronicist, other physicians, and PCCN leaders. Indeed, it is the manager's role to take the direction of the MT and turn it into action. This includes but is not limited to the following duties:

- Recruitment and coordination of resources
- Task, compliance, and alert monitoring
- Accountability audits and follow-up
- On-boarding, training, and dismissal of resources
- Communication to and with resources
- General financial oversight and management (though the role is not expected to serve as an accountant or other financial officer)

Small wonder that this is envisioned to be a full-time position within the network. These responsibilities might normally be expected to fall upon a physician leader or his/her office staff and management. However, remember that it is our goal to ensure task dispersion and the focus of clinical resources on clinical tasks. Therefore, few if any of the actual managerial tasks of the PCCN should fall on any of its clinical resources, especially the physicians or their practices, unless specifically and intentionally structured as such. Rather, the manager should be focused on the holistic vision of the PCCN's objectives and the attainment of a new level of community and patient wellness.

The manager plays a critical role in the maintenance of the PCCN, its ongoing functionality, and goal attainment. Without this, a large PCCN would likely flounder as its resources struggle for assistance, communication, and direction. While the manager is not meant to be the sole resource for questions and management within the PCCN, he or she is expected to serve as a central management hub. Note, too, that the manager may or may not have a clinical background, since the clinical direction is to come from the physicians and other clinical resources. Rather, the role calls for operational management of disparate resources and the enablement of clinical direction, and thus is more similar to a manager for a large physician group practice than a hospital nurse manager.

It will be common for the manager to come from and be paid for by a local hospital, large physician group practice, physician–hospital organization (PHO), or other organization able to fund the FTE. These larger organizations will likely have a strong vested and financial interest in the success of the PCCN, and therefore should be willing to invest in the talent to ensure the endeavor's success.

The manager will be in constant contact with all facets of the PCCN's resources, from its volunteers to its physicians and specialists. Using the PCCN communication and social–clinical networking (SCN) technologies, the manager will push new information to the resource pool, facilitate discussions, maintain accountability, and generally encourage and enforce compliance. In order to maintain order and consistency, the manager will be a key part of the management team, taking direction from both it and the physician leaders. As a liaison between clinical and nonclinical resources, the manager must maintain relationships with all parties, intervene where necessary, and inspire all participants to achieve the goals in the face of both troubles and successes.

PCCN Trainer

This is perhaps the most critical role of all. Even if a small PCCN sprouts from a church congregation or ethnic neighborhood, there will be need for a trainer resource to ensure smooth implementation. Depending on the complexity, scope, scale, and breadth of coverage of your PCCN, your trainer may be full time, part time, merged with another role, or handled through volunteer resources.

Regardless of how you set up your training resources, you will need to have them achieve the following:

- Train new communal resources on the following:
    - Software to be used (e.g., SCN)
    - Virtual Monitoring (VM) systems to be used (if necessary)

- Troubleshooting process steps and solutions
- Roles and responsibilities of resources
  - Do's and don'ts of care
  - Appropriate use of the SCN and other software (if any)
- Clinical basics of patients in the PCCN
- Operational structure, reporting, and communications
- Hierarchies, escalation processes, etc.
- Tasks, requirements, and impacts of failure
- Legalities (to the extent necessary)

■ Train physician office staff on the following:
- Software to be used (e.g., SCN)
- Interactions with communal resources
- Operational structure, reporting, and communications
- Hierarchies, escalation processes, etc.
- Tasks, requirements, and impacts of failure
- Legalities (to the extent necessary)

■ Train patients and primes (likely in group settings) on the following:
- Software to be used (e.g., SCN)
- Communal resources and their roles
- VM systems to be used (if necessary)
- Troubleshooting process steps and solutions
- Personal responsibility requirements
- Operational structure, reporting, and communications
- Hierarchies, escalation processes, etc.

Patient's Primary Communal Resource

Every patient will need a single, go-to individual who will ultimately be responsible for watching over the patient's care. This isn't meant to be a clinical role, nor take the place of any clinical decision making and management (though clinical expertise is certainly not excluded from the job description). Rather, this would be a patient's close friend, relative, or committed and motivated health partner who will oversee the care delivery, ask questions, get answers, and generally make sure that everything goes smoothly toward outcomes optimization. Since the patient's communal resource (hereinafter prime) will serve as a sort of *patient advocate*, there would ideally be some familial or emotional tie between the patient and the prime, so that concern is high and care strategy scrutiny remains intense.

Roles and responsibilities will vary, depending on the patient and their need for such advocacy, support, and oversight. For instance, if the patient's needs are not being met by a given communal resource, the prime makes sure that the PCCN manager is aware and that action is taken. In another example, a physician office care manager requiring information about the patient's current condition would turn to the prime as the source of new information. In another, the prime ensures that the various communal resources are effectively communicating with the physicians and executing instructions properly. In many ways, then, the prime acts as a *communal care director* for a specific patient. While not personally giving clinical care, they will ensure that proper care is indeed administered.

The prime might also serve other needs, such as assisting the manager in securing new and additional resources, helping manage patient and resource expectations, and generally aid in the management of the patient's care. The prime might communicate with the pharmacist on medication reconciliation, attend physician appointments with the patient, interact with the patient's care circle resources about the care strategies, and so on. Again, while not a clinical role, the prime will act preemptively to help optimize patient outcomes.

Since this might be a family member or close friend, advocacy should come easily. However, it is important that the resource be local to the patient. While a distant relative, such as a son or daughter living in another city, might make for a good advocate, the lack of immediate physical contact would make their role as prime difficult. The prime will need to have quick access to the patient and the resources serving him/her.

In cases of the lonely elderly who have no available or capable resource to be a prime, the prime may be an unrelated volunteer from the community. This should be noted with the manager, such that these primes are monitored more closely to ensure that their roles are effectively administered; otherwise the manager risks becoming a prime for some of the PCCN patients.

Education of the Community

Tantamount to the success of the PCCN and assimilation of patients into its concepts, methodologies, technologies, and approaches is proper patient and community education. Patients in the PCCN are special, and require special care. They are not *special* in any other sense of the word than their struggles with health and wellness. Their illnesses may have been brought about through genetic ties, aberrant behavior, bad living, poverty, or mental health disorders. Regardless of how they came to be in the condition they are now in, they now require unique amounts and types of resources, and will need a special care system to adequately provide those resources. For many, it is too late to change their fate, as their diseases have set the course for the rest of their lives. However, even they can have their circumstances mitigated through a more effective care system. For those able to turn the corner and change the course of their disease, the PCCN offers a unique opportunity to seek greater and more focused assistance, localized and familiar care partners, and compassion that may not exist within their current treatment options.

The PCCN is not merely a cost-cutting or utilization-reduction tool. Indeed, it is meant to offer patients more and better care rather than lesser or worse care. Education of the community to be engaged on these critical points is vital as we try to engage and assimilate community members and patients who might suspect ulterior motives. Some might believe it is merely a plot by insurers to reduce the cost of care, or reduce their access to PCPs. Others might think that the system is designed to get them out of the traditional care system and into one that offers lower-quality or reduced access. Some may even insist these are "death camps" into which the chronically ill are placed. These myths must immediately be busted, or else the PCCN is doomed to struggle with its communal reputation, if not fail entirely.

PCCN patients must be convinced that the system is being customized for their needs, rather than the needs of everyone else, particularly the insurers and local hospitals whose costs they drive up. Because they are sicker than most, they require special care that simply cannot be effectively provided by the traditional care triangle, physicians, hospitals, and to a certain and limited extent, patients.

Furthermore, the systems being put in place will help local friends, community members, and congregations assist in their care, increasing their access to assistance and meaningful, educated care delivery while involving physicians and other providers all along the way. Thus, patients are given increased attention, where, when, and how they want it most. This is the kind of messaging that must come across to patients to prevent suspicion and distrust.

As patients become assimilated into the PCCN, their education should be ongoing, consistent, and positive. Of course, we will need to educate the resource pool as well, as discussed in Chapter 6 and elsewhere.

Governance as a Practical Matter

The control and direction of multiple resources within the community will require substantial "moral authority" and the willing release of control from some of the normally controlling entities, such as hospitals and individual physicians. The PCCN and its governing body(s) therefore must have the backing of all the large players in the organization in order to be recognized as legitimate and worthy of respect. This will help engender the respect and ongoing cooperation of the volunteers and other communal resources. Thus, the major players, from hospitals to key physicians, must buy into the approaches, methodologies, goals and objectives, tools and technologies, and infrastructure design of the PCCN. It goes without saying that without this level of support from key players, the PCCN risks loss of effectiveness via a loss of participation.

Governing authority will therefore likely be based on the respect for the individuals and groups represented in the MT, the "purity" of their motivations to participate, and the openness of the governing bodies to new ideas to advance the cause. Respect is earned, not demanded or assumed. With the respect for the players represented on the MT, and the ongoing repetition of the outcomes-focused nature of the PCCN, even the most skeptical can be turned.

More on Governance Structures

If you have the proper components of the PCCN structure, the way your PCCN is governed can vary somewhat. As mentioned above, the governance structure will likely follow the role you give to the chronicist. For instance, if the chronicist takes on complete responsibility for the care of the patients in your system, the governing systems will be a traditional pyramid shape with a chronicist on top.

Regardless of the role the chronicist plays, the PCCN leadership will ultimately guide the communal resources, ensure quality care, eliminate gaps and lapses in care provision, and encourage patient self-management when appropriate. There are several key elements to this role that will need to be part of the role of the governing body.

1. **Resource management:** By this, I mean the education, oversight, encouragement, and correction of PCCN resources. These should encompass *all PCCN resources, including chronicists and physician leaders.* The resources are, to borrow a phrase, the life's blood of the PCCN, without which it would be a meaningless exercise. However, because their responsibilities deal directly with the health and well-being of their fellow citizens, it is important that they (1) are properly trained and educated on an ongoing basis, (2) certified for their role, (3) "own" their patients and their responsibilities, and (4) are dealt with properly in the instance of failure.

   Training is critical, of course. Indeed, there should never be an instance in which a resource is placed into the care and management of any patient, even a family member or close friend, without proper training on the technologies, procedures, diseases, and so on, that will impact their roles and patients.

   Encouragement is a must, since many of these resources, especially volunteers, will want to help but may have some reluctance to do so. It will be important to promote the mission, objectives, and successes of the PCCN through social–clinical networking and resource group interactions, so as to constantly encourage and motivate them. Having dealt with volunteers for many years as part of the management engineering and quality communities, I can profess that the ongoing motivation of volunteers is difficult particularly when their work is frustrating, tiring, and troublesome. It is easier to motivate volunteers when their own lives are going well than when there is trouble in their families, jobs, or health. Yet, these volunteers are critical to the mission at hand, so theirs is a role that cannot be diluted or left to chance. Encouragement, promotion, and recognition are all tantamount to success.

Of course the latter, dealing with failings, is the most difficult for *any* manager, especially for volunteer managers. Because they have little or no financial or other vested interest in their roles, volunteers can (and sadly do) quit, often abruptly. Worse, they often just fade away without warning. This often yields a gentler management of volunteers, since their free will and mobility makes it more difficult to be harsh and stern with them. Yet there are ways to deal with failing that do not include harsh reactions. This is why the Joe Tye Twelve Core Action Values training is so critical to the success of the PCCN. Joe's work (found at http://www.joetye.com/twelve-core-action-values.html) is the basis of a better and more engaging leadership method that is sure to work better for the PCCN than anything I have encountered. Managers and others in the PCCN should be trained in the Twelve Core Action Values, and train others in the organization as well.

2. **Guidance and mission setting:** Just because your PCCN cares for some of the sickest in the community doesn't mean you have finished your business. If yours starts with, say, diabetes management of a select community, the next part of your mission may be chronic obstructive pulmonary disease (COPD) in another subset of the population. Furthermore, remember, the ultimate goal of the PCCN is education of the healthy and reduction and mitigation of the impact of disease prevalence, so caring for the ill is but part of the goal of the organization.

   Thus it is the role of the PCCN leadership to guide the mission and purpose of the PCCN toward goals that will most impact the health and well-being of the community, as well as its costs of the provision of care. Your PCCN, as part of a larger PCCN *community of communities*, is trying to remake the entire healthcare system and its many traditions and habits. It will be important to remember the breadth of this ultimate mission as you seek to determine the goals and aspirations of your providers and their communities.

3. **Community engagement and communication:** Just because you construct and staff your PCCN, it may still be rejected by the community if its purpose, goals, and mission are not communicated effectively. Worse, it may be seen as a means to ration care in local media. Thus the PCCN could quickly gather mistrust rather than support from the community, quickly leading to its demise.

   Thus, early on in your efforts, you should bring in key members of the local media, community leaders and influencers, and even politicians to garner support and enthusiasm for the project. This may sound easy to do, but I've seen excellent ideas die on the hill of bad public relations before. For instance, your PCCN may start in a given community or geography, but its expansion could lead to issues if there is underlying resentment or mistrust between communities or key players. As another example, just because one group of physicians works well together doesn't mean that others will cooperate to the same extent, creating barriers to expansion and implementation across community boundaries.

   It is therefore imperative that your PCCN leadership conduct ongoing media and public relations campaigns in order to prevent and stop bad press; update the community on successes and progress through the media and other marketing venues; prevent misunderstandings and misinformation among the communities and patients; praise volunteers, clinical leaders, and patients as even minor successes are seen (especially early on); promote volunteerism and patient participation; and encourage better health and wellness.

This campaign should be ongoing and never ceasing. It might even be wise to consider adding a member of the press or a public relations (PR) expert to the leadership group, or at least creating a channel to constantly update local press members and community leaders on activities within the network.

4. **Disburser of funds:** Of course, if there are funds to be disbursed as part of the PCCN implementation, such as shared savings or capitation payments, the PCCN leadership and its governing structures will be responsible. Such disbursements will no doubt require some degree of legal agreement and contractual obligation, especially for physicians, but may not be as complex as one might imagine. Since many of the players in the PCCN are already involved in the care of the poly-chronics, the additional payment mechanisms are mostly incentives and rewards for new milestones, objectives, and clinical outcomes. These will most often be based on group results, and are much easier to administer than more complex individual performance contracts. Furthermore, since many are volunteers who may not wish to be paid for achieving the group's milestones and outcomes targets, there may be less to do than one might first imagine.

Nonetheless, assuming a reimbursement model follows the PCCN business and care model, there will necessarily be a means by which to disperse shared savings and capitation payments. This may require the leadership group to form special legal and tax organizations and structures, hire external legal and accounting advice, and otherwise set up the means by which to administer the funding without running afoul of government entities and external lawyers. These decisions will need to be made, and perhaps changed, over the course of the implementation of the concept, as services and populations are expanded beyond initial trial efforts.

These tasks may seem like a lot for a single, small group of leaders and this isn't even the full extent of their roles. They will also have to act as a legal barrier or resource to the communal resources, and a grant and endowment administrator, among other possible roles. But given the potential and importance of the program, the leadership should willingly devote time, energy, resources, and passion to its implementation.

A Word on Group Dynamics™

The concept of Group Dynamics can be traced specifically to the work of Professor Muhammad Yunus and the infamous Grameen Bank. I credit him and a few others who use group interactions to better manage the care of chronic disease patients with the ideas expressed herein. In case you don't know the history of Grameen, it goes back to 1976 when Professor Muhammad Yunus, head of the Rural Economics Program at the University of Chittagong in Bangladesh, launched a research project to examine the possibility of designing a credit delivery system to provide banking services targeted at the rural poor. The Grameen Bank Project (Grameen means *rural* or *village* in the Bangla language) came into operation with the following objectives:

- Extend banking facilities to poor men and women.
- Eliminate the exploitation of the poor by money lenders.
- Create opportunities for self-employment for the vast multitude of unemployed people in rural Bangladesh.
- Bring the disadvantaged, mostly the women from the poorest households, within the fold of an organizational format that they can understand and manage by themselves.
- Reverse the age-old vicious circle of low income, low saving, and low investment, into the virtuous circle of *low income, injection of credit, investment, more income, more savings, more investment, more income.*

Thus was born the concept of the *microloan*. A smashing success (and since copied by many of the world's largest banking institutions), Grameen grew in size and notoriety over the years. In 1983, the Grameen Bank was formed from the research project through a government decree. And in 2006, Professor Yunus and Grameen Bank were jointly awarded a Nobel Peace Prize for their efforts to create economic and social development from below. And though the bank has recently come under attack, their mission and values stand as a reminder of the power of independence and freedom to impact the lives of even the poorest of people.

One of the keys to the success of the Grameen Bank program is its use of group accountability. In the Grameen methodology, which has been honed, changed, and improved over the years, groups of approximately ten loanees are brought together weekly for meetings and loan payments. Representatives of the bank come to the group meetings to collect loan payments, but the group is really there to offer accountability, support, peer pressure, and coaching to all the individuals. Those refusing to participate in the group interactions are not given loans, as it has proven such a powerful means by which to maintain loan repayment, and more importantly, encourage successes.

So successful has this model been that Grameen has developed an entire methodology around it, and offers it widely to the world through a division called Grameen Research.[1] This methodology and structure, combined with the existing innovations in healthcare group interactions and therapies, is the basis for Group Dynamics.

As a conceptual structure, Group Dynamics brings groups of similar patients together, face to face and via the SCN, to interact, support, cajole, pressure, and encourage one another. Similar interactions have proven highly successful in the management of diabetics, and should be an integral part of any PCCN implementation. Furthermore, Group Dynamics could and should be used with communal resources to provide a way to offer ongoing support, task and role accountability, and learning opportunities to otherwise disparate resources.

You will need to structure your Group Dynamics meetings based on the patients and resources in your population, their willingness and ability to travel, location of communal meeting space, distance and time requirements, and so on. In rural areas, you will need to be very creative to accommodate distance, time, and cost. In populations with frail elderly, you will need to think about special transportation issues and the realities of the patients' conditions. However, whenever and wherever possible, you should try to add Group Dynamics to your PCCN methodology and tools, just as you would software and resources.

Making Room for Skeptics

I have always found it helpful to listen to the most vociferous of critics, since it is they who will speak the harshest of the path taken. In this case, skeptics and naysayers will likely abound initially, and may become frustrating by their negativity. Nonetheless, within nearly every negative statement there lies a potentially positive action—a way to analyze and further optimize your performance. In this case, then, we should constantly look to detractors for new ideas for improvements, further optimization of care delivery, and if nothing else, a pulse of part of the community at large. Just as we readily make room for those who spur us on, we should make equal room for those who would pull back on the reins.

Governance as a Legally Binding Concept

I'm not attorney and wouldn't want to be. Most lawyers are, to me, an occasionally useful but otherwise troublesome lot. In this case, your attorney can give you good guidance on the legal structures required to develop, maintain, and run a sound governing body as described here. The governance of the PCCN may take on its own liabilities, and thus this will need to be considered as the MT is established. Legal protections are commonly similar to those provided to other group practice settings in which medical decisions are shared and joint accountability is the norm.

Summary

The governing body of the PCCN will simultaneously serve as its guide, mentor, vision, and control. To achieve the level of trust and confidence required for this group, the management team should be pulled from across the community of care, encompassing as diverse a group as necessary to obtain sufficient insights and perspectives on the optimal means for caring for the population. The MT should therefore pull from clinical and nonclinical staff, volunteers and paid employees, and physicians and health service workers. The only groups to be intentionally excluded are those who might taint the goals and objectives, shift the focus away from outcomes, or have the wrong motivations for their input and assistance. Within each community, you will likely find all of the above. It will be up to the key sponsors to decide how to deal with each, such that the result is a functional, widely respected, and selfless body of passionate contributors.

Endnotes

1. See the Gameen Research website: http://www.grameenresearch.org.

Chapter 9

PCCN Technologies

Introduction

Since the poly-chronic care network (PCCN) relies heavily on certain enabling technologies, these systems deserve their own special section in this text. In this chapter, you will become familiar with several key technologies that are suggested or required in the infrastructure of the PCCN. These technologies, pulled from whatever vendor you might select, are tantamount to the successful implementation and long-term success of the PCCN. Without at least a basic infrastructure, you'll find it more difficult to support a PCCN on a large scale.

There are, of course, a number of ways in which the technologies can be layered in. Some PCCNs, with many clinicians and large populations, will use all these technologies and more. Some small, low-budget systems will be successful with only the bare necessities. The technology strategy and infrastructure of a given PCCN will depend upon the volume of patients, the number of resources, the existing technology infrastructure and future plans, and the financial capabilities of the support players. You will need to find the appropriate mix of technologies and supporting infrastructure components to best serve your patients and community.

Infrastructure Options: Overview

The following are several key ingredients in the PCCN technology infrastructure that, with the exception of the SCN, can be used as needed. Each will be expounded upon later in the chapter.

1. **Social–clinical network (SCN):** Think of this as a private Facebook for poly-chronics. The SCN provides patients, caregivers, and their specific communal resources with a means by which to communicate, share, exchange, and learn. The SCN envisioned herein is a web-based networking tool that allows for ongoing communication among the members of patient care circles while ensuring patient privacy, personalization, and connection preferences. The SCN can be used as follows:

   a. As a communication platform for interactions among physicians, patients, and clinical and communal resources. Aided by private messaging, web-based social networking, and interactivity, the SCN will allow for quick and efficient communications on the ongoing care and well-being of patients via their resources and clinicians.

   b. As a private social network for patients with similar disease states and clinical conditions, both locally and eventually across the country wherever PCCNs exist.

   c. As an extension of Group Dynamics™ through which patients and resources can communicate with and support each other.

   d. As an information dispersion system through which patients and resources can be kept informed on PCCN news, relevant clinical research, policy issues, and other communal information.

   e. As a general PCCN information source wherein PCCNs from across the country can collect and disseminate information relevant to patients and providers.

The SCN is the only required technology for the PCCN (and in the smallest of configurations, even this might be optional). Since it can serve multiple functions and purposes, the SCN can be either the main central information and communication hub or a piece of a larger technology implementation in which it plays a specific and limited role.

2. **Simulation software:** As mentioned several times in this text, simulation is the means by which we can examine the implications of the variability in component and system performance; conduct realistic and informative what-if scenarios to test alternatives to the current and future systems; and determine the best possible combination of parameters to yield the results we seek. Simulation also lets us determine how and when outliers might impact us, how we might react to these situations to best mitigate negative impacts, and current and future resource requirements.

    Simulation is therefore handy in the construction phase of the project. It then comes in handy again as the system morphs and changes over time and we need to examine new options for better solutions for the new realities.

3. **Health information exchange (HIE):** The HIE is an optional but potentially important add-on to the necessary base SCN technology, and serves as a broader information source. While the SCN is only meant for communication and doesn't actually store patient or clinical information, the HIE is a true clinical information exchange platform. An HIE serves as the plumbing that links all the resources, space, and software together across disparate systems and locations, and can serve the PCCN well.

4. **Chronic disease management system (CDMS):** The CDMS is a very different and much more complex system that often includes clinical decision-making

applications, workflow automation, clinical alerting, and other capabilities. This will enhance the PCCN's ability to care for its most complex patients by assisting physicians with development and ongoing maintenance of care strategies, providing consistency in treatment regimens, preempting clinical deteriorations with optimal interventions, and tracking outcome metrics over time.

5. **Virtual monitoring:** These technologies are rapidly becoming standard in the marketplace as their popularity continues to rise. These include everything from home glucose monitoring to education and interactivity, to active patient tracking that monitors where a patient is within their home at all times. These will aid in the communication with patients and the monitoring of their day-to-day activities, so as to ward off potential clinical deteriorations and issues, and aid in reducing the resource costs associated with in-home care.

There are, of course, other technologies that might aid the effort, such as mobile apps. However, with just a few of the above, you can make your PCCN function. Let's look more deeply into the various available technologies to explain how they integrate with the operations.

Using the SCN

In the lowest-cost environment, the SCN will serve as the base communications platform. Here, the SCN can act as a central hub for non-patient-specific clinical information, patient-specific clinical communications and instructions, and a means by which patients with similar life experiences can engage one another from the comfort of their homes or institutions.

Patient Connectivity

Much like Facebook and LinkedIn, the SCN of the PCCN will be a connective bond that ties many patients together with those who will best understand their issues through the sharing and exchange of personal information. Patients who are able (mentally and physically) to communicate via a social networking platform can link with other patients with similar diseases and conditions, exchange stories, offer support, and generally bond with those in similar circumstances. This will augment group interactions, which are widely known to have substantive impacts on care provision. Commonly, a patient's selected communal resources will be included such that they can join in the support and communication, offer input and ongoing advice, and monitor the patient's activities, moods, and well-being on a very regular basis. Clinicians might also be included, depending on how the patient wants his/her contacts structured.

As is common in these platforms, patients will determine who will join their care circle, much like selecting friends on Facebook. These care circles can be made up of whomever the patient chooses, and can be expanded and contracted as necessary. Patients can also have multiple care circles, for example, one that might only include fellow patients and one that might only include their caregivers and communal resources. This allows the patient to have total control over their interactions and with whom any personal information is shared.

Disease-specific *care communities* can be formed that will allow willing patients to be grouped for easier connections with one another. So, if Ms. Jones, a chronic obstructive pulmonary disease (COPD) patient, agrees to be part of the SCN and the PCCN, she would set up her profile to reflect her availability for connection to the COPD care community. This will allow other COPD patients to quickly and easily find her and connect with her. It is important to remember that patients will only be offering as much information as they want, and will not be subjected to the behind-the-scenes mysterious data accumulations suspected of other social networking systems. Indeed, it is recommended that security and data integrity be among the highest priorities of your SCN. Therefore, these communities will likely be "walled off" to prevent the broad dissemination of patient-specific information.

Patients within disease-specific care communities can also expect ongoing information feeds, including everything from research on new remedies to coupons from local medical suppliers to announcements of gatherings and significant community care events.

If working with a known set of patients from a given hospital or population, these care communities can quickly be populated from patient records (as permitted by the patients). A single data dump can provide the core information on all of the patients in the population, which is only made accessible when and to the extent that a patient agrees to be part of the PCCN and SCN communities.

Patient–Resource Connectivity

As one might expect, resources will be using the SCN for a variety of functions. The SCN can serve as a means for resources to keep in touch with their patients, their disease-state care communities, and other communal resources.

Here, the patients and their respective resources, particularly their prime, can communicate on an ongoing basis to further expand the connections. Resources might only visit a patient once per week, but might interact via the SCN daily or as needed. While this, of course, is not meant to take the place of the direct, face-to-face interactions, it can allow for another means by which patients can connect with their resources. Importantly, patients can connect with a larger group of resources simultaneously, via the previously mentioned care communities and care circles. So, if Ms. Jones wakes up with a strong headache or a cold, she can relay this information to more than one of her communal resources at a time, allowing for quick and coordinated responses. Under the current state of affairs, at best Ms. Jones might phone the doctor's office or perhaps a friend, but would not be able to easily reach out to a broader group of resources for assistance and advice. This will streamline care while encouraging the ongoing dialogue between patients and their various care providers.

Additionally, resources can more quickly follow up on patient expectations, such as medications. While, again, a phone call might serve a similar purpose, the SCM allows more than one person to see that Ms. Jones is being reminded of her medications. This in turn increases awareness of her issues with medication compliance and also increases the compliance accountability on both Ms. Jones and the community.

Lastly, this allows the physicians (and office staff) in the care circle to see how and when patients are engaged in their care, interacting with resources, and being cared for in their communities. They can see that Ms. Jones didn't go to the Y this week for her diabetes group meeting, but can also see that she was visited twice by a local emergency medical technician (EMT) and her prime, a church member, and is doing fine.

Resource–Resource Connectivity

Resources will be able to form their own circles in which they can exchange information, ideas, stories (good and bad), tips for dealing with noncompliant patients, and generally discuss issues that do not involve a specific patient. Of course, resources will be well trained on the proper and legal use of the SCN in discussing patient-specific information, and will be required to follow very specific guidelines. This will aid resources in bettering their care provision, encouraging one another, promoting accountability for care, and generally supporting the goals and mission of the PCCN.

The SCN can also serve as a place for educational materials for resources on disease regimens, the concepts and specifics of care strategies, disease information, and guidance on care provision. It is hoped that the PCCN managers, physicians, trainers, and other resources will constantly update the SCN with relevant information from which both resources and patients can benefit.

PCCN Management: Resource–Patient Connectivity

One of the important goals of the PCCN management team is to constantly educate their communities about the diseases they treat. To achieve this, the SCN can serve as an information hub into which reference and educational materials and links can be placed. This might include everything from the basics of the diseases treated to current articles on treatment regimens to efforts to control quality, access, and cost for the underserved from around the country. In this way, physicians, care managers, and office staff can keep the community abreast of the latest in disease management, helping both the patients served and the general knowledge of the community on the diseases they will battle.

This is perhaps one of the best long-term benefits of the program, in that the education of the community writ large will hopefully aid in the early self-management of the conditions, habits, and personal activities that lead to chronic diseases. With this, it is hoped that education will bring self-awareness and self-motivated change before diseases have a chance to set in.

Resource–Clinician Connectivity

Perhaps the most important function of the SCN is the connectivity between resources and clinicians. Here, the SCN will serve as the means by which communal resources communicate with clinicians about specific patient issues, and receive instructions and guidance in reply. As resources see patients in their homes or other settings, they can send private messages directly to clinicians about the patient's condition and current clinical status, and ask questions about specific issues being seen. Such interactions should aid in promoting speedy interventions, thus reducing the need for more drastic actions such as emergency department (ED) visits and hospital admissions. Responses can come in the form of additional tasks to be completed, phone calls to the patient and/or resource, instructions for other communal resources (e.g., visiting nurse), or a request for a physician office visit. Resources can then ensure that proper action is taken, such that the patient's issue doesn't go untreated, appointments are scheduled, and follow-up is ensured.

Since these communications are private and secure (as designed in the current system), specific information about the patient is kept guarded and away from the rest of the community or care circle until permitted and/or necessary. Again, education on the proper use of private messaging and the importance of the privacy of patient information will be instrumental to the patient's comfort with the program.

Since in a large-scale PCCN there may be literally hundreds of resources and thousands of patient interactions every week and month, some means of standardized communications will be required. Thus, in larger-scale implementations, specific instructions will need to be provided to resources on how, when, and under what circumstances communications should be escalated. This will help clinicians avoid messaging overload while ensuring that pertinent patient information is transmitted on a timely basis. This is yet another reason for the need for full-time trainer and PCCN manager roles.

Of course, clinicians have the responsibility to follow up with communal resources. This might seem a simple, no-brainer task, yet it is quite possible that communication breakdowns occur on the physician end. Busy offices can let communications lapse if they are not seen as an integral part of the overall patient care system. Resources need to know that clinicians are on their side and support their ongoing efforts; thus, each and every transmission of information should be met with an appropriate response, even if it's only a "thank you for working hard to support Ms. Jones' health!" As part of the broader care team, resources deserve respect from physicians, who should view them as partners in the patients' well-being and ongoing disease management efforts. Thus, messaging should be two-way and constant.

Example of a SCN Use Case

Ms. Jones is an 82-year-old widow who lives alone. She is an arthritic, asthmatic diabetic who has battled depression since her husband passed away four years ago. She attends the New Hope Evangelical Church when she can, but is mostly homebound. She sees her doctor intermittently, but misses more appointments than she keeps due to transportation and other issues. Her physician has assigned her a care manager who does her best to manage Ms. Jones via telephone. Previous attempts to have Ms. Jones use home monitoring systems have failed due to her inability to use the devices. Her doctor asked her to sign up for a new pilot PCCN being run in conjunction with the local hospital and several church congregations around town, and she agreed. Though she cannot use a computer, she is willing to participate and let the community resources schedule visits with her in her home to lessen her need to see the doctor.

The new PCCN management team, through their own contacts and relationships, has already tapped into several local civic organizations, a local community college medical training program (pre-nursing), several local churches, and a Federally Qualified Health Center (FQHC). The local hospital is very supportive of the concept, and has purchased a one-year license of the SCN software to see if the PCCN could become self-sustaining within that period.

Ms. Jones' name and clinical information is forwarded to the PCCN manager. The manager analyzes the care strategy put together by her physician, and looks for variances from the standard care plans of similar patients. She also reviews the physician's goals and objectives for Ms. Jones' health and well-being, and quantifies the outcomes the physician hopes to see. She reviews with the physician's case manager the social, personal, familial, and other issues and challenges Ms. Jones faces in the management of her conditions, as well as Ms. Jones' preference for a prime, her son-in-law. From this, the manager then knows what will be required of the resource pool, and what qualifications are required for each resource.

Upon attaining agreement from available resources on her list, the manager reviews the new care strategy and task assignments with the physician and care manager, and patient. Upon agreement, the care manager reviews the information with Ms. Jones' son-in-law, and obtains agreement on his role as a prime. She then reviews the care strategies, goals, and objectives with the new prime, as well as her choices for communal resources.

With Ms. Jones' permission, the manager sets up a care circle in the SCN for Ms. Jones, and includes her in the existing SCN communities for diabetics and asthmatics. Ms. Jones is very sensitive to her battles with depression, and thus wants that kept secret. The care circle includes the prime, the physician office care manager, one pre-nursing student from the community college, an EMT (a member of a civic club), and a close friend and member of New Hope. The pre-nursing student, approved and recommended by the head of the pre-nursing program, has not been through training and will thus require certification via the trainer before providing any assistance to Ms. Jones.

Each member of the care circle is given tasks to accomplish for and with Ms. Jones, from visitation to medication review to appointment maintenance to outcomes monitoring to food intake review. Schedules are set, and reporting expectations and accountability are put in place. This care circle will then communicate on their interactions with Ms. Jones, relay any changes in her condition to the physician (and the others in the care circle, as appropriate), encourage physical activity and getting out more, and generally be the eyes and ears of the clinicians within the patient's home. The prime, who actually lives about two hours away, will monitor the activities of the other members, ensure compliance via the SCN, and communicate with the care circle team about Ms. Jones' ongoing condition. Since he has a personal and vested interest in Ms. Jones's health, the prime will make sure that tasks are completed and reporting is timely and informative. Additionally, a local dietician has agreed to provide training and coaching to care circle members on Ms. Jones' dietary requirements, and will update them monthly on changes she recommends based any changes in Ms. Jones' condition. Lastly, the physician has agreed to make weekly diabetes updates available to the care circles, which are posted on the SCN each Monday morning. These help educate the care circle members and aid them in understanding their own task requirements. Lastly, Ms. Jones' goals are monitored monthly by the care manager (and physician, as needed) and compared to a baseline.

Upon checking in on Ms. Jones, as he does every Tuesday and Thursday, the EMT notices that Ms. Jones has missed a couple of regular meals, and has not been regularly checking her blood sugar. He inquires about her testing and diet regimen and she explains that she hasn't felt like eating but has snacked a bit. Furthermore, she explains that the cold winter air has prevented her from her usual walks up and down the driveway of her home, making her largely sedentary. Unsure of her current status, he logs into the SCN from his smart phone and sends Ms. Jones' physician's care manager a private message. The care manager then instructs the EMT via phone on next steps, which he completes. He updates the care manager, who then follows up with an SCN message to the group about the need for heightened awareness of Ms. Jones' diet and testing regimen. Her New Hope friend lets the group know that she'll be able to go by to visit Ms. Jones every day in the coming week, beginning tomorrow, and will be sure to go through the medication and dietary instructions with her again. The pre-nursing student promises to drop by over the weekend, and will give an update if anything changes. The prime chimes in, and lets the student know that he and his wife will be dropping by and spending the weekend, hoping to add some cheer to Ms. Jones' winter, so he'll take care of the weekend duties. All agree to be vigilant in the coming weeks, and monitor her mood more carefully. If her mood slips, the care manager suggests a visit from a local volunteer psychologist.

Thus Ms. Jones might be saved from clinical deterioration at a very low cost.

Another SCN Use Case: Discharge and Care Transitions

Mr. Adams is admitted to the local hospital for treatment for COPD. At 66 years old, Mr. Adams is a lifelong smoker. He lives with his wife in the retirement community home they purchased several years ago. He hasn't been to the doctor in years because there is not a local primary care physician (PCP) that is taking new Medicare patients. His condition deteriorated due to lack of proper treatment.

Upon report of the admission, the hospital case manager contacts the PCCN manager and alerts her of a possible significant gap in postdischarge coverage. Because there are so few PCPs who will take new Medicare patients in the community, and knowing he lives with an older wife, she fears that Mr. Adams will not get the care he needs quickly enough. Though his MMRC scale is 1 and he has a borderline BMI (21), he could quickly return to the hospital if his medication regimen isn't followed. Mr. Adams is approached with the PCCN concept on his second inpatient day, and he agrees to participate in the program.

Using some retired nurses, volunteer EMTs, and volunteers from the local Knights of Columbus (KoC, in which Mr. Adams was once an active member), the PCCN manager constructs a care circle within the SCN to help Mr. Adams with his postdischarge lifestyle changes. Since Mr. Adams is familiar with the group, he agrees that the KoC member will be his prime. She works with the case manager, a care manager from one of the local PCP offices (willing to see at least some new Medicare patients), the hospitalist seeing Mr. Adams in the hospital, and the pulmonologist to develop a reasonable care strategy for the communal resources. This will include visitation, weight and medication monitoring, and education on diet and exercise. A local PCP is contacted and agrees to work with the rest of the care circle to expand his capacity in order to care for and properly manage Mr. Adams' condition. Since the care circle includes a retired nurse and an EMT, there is much that can be done for Mr. Adams' without excessive, expensive, and time-consuming office visits and excessive work for the PCP and his staff.

Simple yet important goals and metrics are set forth for the care circle to achieve. The group uses the SCN to collaborate on visit schedules, proper tasks for each member (based on qualifications and training), metrics management, and the possible use of home monitoring. Visits are scheduled periodically throughout each week, with each member of the care circle agreeing to monitor specific elements of the care strategy. Updates on visits and metrics are regularly sent to the care circle, which includes the case manager, the pulmonologist's nurse assistant, and the PCP's care manager. The pulmonologist works with the PCP via the hospital's electronic medical record (EMR), and both transmit instructions to the entire care circle, the prime, and/or individuals within the group.

Mr. Adams also uses the SCN to reach out to fellow COPD patients with whom he now has much in common. Using this small community of new friends, Mr. Adams finds comfort and support that he might not otherwise have had, given his short tenure in the community.

It is hoped that Mr. Adams's disease progression can be slowed, his life made more comfortable, and expensive ED visits and admissions minimized.

Using Simulation

Simulation may be a requirement for large-scale PCCNs, whereas in a smaller iteration it may be unnecessary. Resource allocations in a large PCCN will require greater coordination and synergies across a larger patient population, which could lead to confusion, inefficiency and misallocation of resources, and frustration if not well planned and executed. This is where simulation will shine as a planning and strategy execution tool.

Since these simulations can be quite complex, their development should not be taken lightly. Though Rockwell Automation's Arena Simulation software is relatively easy to use (and the one I always recommend), it will require the expertise of an industrial or management engineer (IE/ME) in order to ensure a proper model build. However, by the time you read this text, much work will have already been done to develop the simulation models with which PCCNs can be created and optimized. I would therefore suggest you consider looking to existing models before venturing out and creating your own from scratch. Indeed, Arena allows for models to be moved back and forth between disparate locations, so as to help with the dispersion of models and the easing of the model coding burden.

Simulation is to be used primarily when the number of resources, tasks, and/or patients is such that optimization of care and efficiency is hampered in some way. If you want your many disparate resources working like a well-oiled machine, each performing tasks when, how, and where they should, you will likely want simulation to help develop your care strategies implementation. In urban areas where the numbers of patients can quickly get into the hundreds or even thousands, organizing resources to optimize the care streams can be impossible without the kind of thorough analysis of resource and task allocations that simulation provides.

While there is no cutoff size or scale beyond which you need simulation, you will know when you need it by the degree of complexity of your PCCN infrastructure. If yours is or is becoming difficult to manage, or if your resources are complaining of redundancies, errors, and misallocation of tasks, you know simulation is in your future. If you don't have one, or cannot "borrow" one from a local employer, hire an industrial or management engineer for the task, either full time or part time. They will assist with building and properly using a model for analytics and planning. (I highly recommend IEs for any hospital and health system interested in optimum efficiency throughout operations. Therefore, you might consider hiring one for multiple purposes if you haven't already.)

Using the HIE

With its universal "pipes," the health information exchange (HIE) can gather, store, and transmit many different kinds of data from many different systems, including images, documents, and text. Indeed, if used correctly, it could provide for both patients' clinical data from disparate sources (the original intent of the HIE concept) and a private communication path between physicians and communal resources. Much like the SCN, the HIE could provide the necessary exchange of instructions and guidance from clinicians as well as ongoing patient information updates from communal resources. The benefit would be having this all in a single system, rather than relying on both an SCN and an HIE. Since the SCN is not meant to gather and house clinical information, the HIE would be the system of choice if it could be configured correctly.

An HIE platform, properly configured, would integrate data from virtual monitoring systems and communal resource communications into a larger and more holistic patient dataset. Proper management of resource messages and communications would permit a more continuous stream of patient information, creating a more complete picture of the patient's care, lifestyle, and individual circumstances. This more complete picture might help physicians to hone their care strategies and develop specialized interventions.

The downside is that few if any of the current HIEs on the market are being configured for nonclinical interactions. Indeed, the previously discussed holistic patient management system doesn't exist today. Certainly, the SCN concept does not exist within current HIE systems. While some HIEs have their own "patient portals," these are not meant for wider, external use like the SCN. Permissions, accessibility, and privacy are all concerns that make current HIEs potentially difficult to use in their current formats. This is no small feat to correct.

A simple solution might be the integration of the SCN into the HIE in much the same way that an HIE is integrated with an EMR. Since, for the immediate future, the SCN will be used no matter what, given its usefulness in patient–resource connectivity, it may make sense to allow for integration of SCN communications and data streams into the HIE rather than configuring the HIE to do what the SCN already does.

This, of course, adds cost and will need to be analyzed within the context of the overall potential savings of the program and available resources.

If you or your state already have an HIE, investigate its functionality before investing heavily in new platforms or technologies. It is likely that you will need the SCN as an adjunct. If yours is a small PCCN, it is unlikely that the clinical information access is worth the investment in an HIE unless it is for other reasons.

Using the Chronic Disease Management System (CDMS)

The optimization of care strategies can be achieved through the wisdom and experience of good physicians. However, the goal of the CDMS is broader than simple clinical instructions. Its benefits are in the increased efficiencies in care strategy development, faster interpretation of clinical data, ongoing monitoring of patient trends and medical conditions, and the general management of patient alerts, interactions, and medications.

In the PCCN, this might be considered a "nice to have." However, given the complexity of the patients in the PCCN, physicians may learn to appreciate the ongoing assistance of CDMSs in care strategy implementation and maintenance. Assuming that the CDMS has the capabilities to help manage the complexities of the PCCN population and not just a single disease state such as diabetes, then it may be a tremendous help.

There are a few systems, particularly some from Europe, which have already integrated CDMSs into HIEs. This integration is likely a trend in the industry, as HIEs blend with EMRs and add in the intelligence of the CDMS. This will bode well for the PCCN, but will add to its long-term cost. If the HIE, the EMR, and the CDMS can come together for *all* patients in a given population and region, the need for customized solutions for the PCCN decreases dramatically, and thus can be managed as part of the overall cost of care delivery for the entire community. As long as the PCCN can be *sectioned out* from the rest of the population's systems, I would welcome the combination of technologies to lower the overall cost of their use. However, if the complexity of the patients in the PCCN population cannot be assisted by the use of a CDMS due to the complexity of their care requirements, its overall advantages are greatly diminished.

Using Virtual Monitoring

Virtual monitoring (VM, aka home monitoring) has the potential to greatly increase the flow of information from patients to their care providers without increasing the demand on clinical resources. Virtual monitoring allows clinicians to check weight, blood pressure, and other important vital signs and metrics without actually visiting the patient in their care location. Some systems even allow physicians to chat with the patient via webcams, and educate patients via streaming videos. Integrated with home computers and even smart phones, these systems are revolutionizing the efficiency of home care delivery while managing the resource cost and capacity constraints. VM systems are commonly linked to the web, whereby they are linked to EMRs and can transmit clinical information instantly to physicians. This permits more timely interventions when needed.

The PCCN is, in many ways, perfectly suited to a synergistic use of these devices. Communal resources are greatly aided by the availability of the technologies that allow them to more precisely monitor their patients' important metrics. These systems also permit resources an easy way to transmit important clinical information via the web-enabled, linked technologies.

Importantly, the use of VM systems is also aided by the communal resources. Many patients may find these technologies intimidating or confusing, or may not be able to effectively use them due to physical or mental disabilities. Resources, trained in the technologies, can therefore help patients use VM and thereby ensure monitoring compliance, accuracy in measurements, and assistance with follow-up instructions. Without this assistance, physician offices and hospitals may find themselves paying for unnecessary home nursing and office visits. Furthermore, inaccuracies and the resulting increased risk caused by poor data collection and/or the misuse of equipment can be reduced or eliminated as communal resources better monitor patient usage, ensure precise measurements, and retrain when errors arise.

Also, as communal resources see patients in their care locations (whether home or elsewhere), they can add a more holistic perspective to data and even add webcam interactions. By scheduling patient interactions via webcams to coincide with resource schedules, physicians can better use distant interventions with a knowledgeable resource in the room to assist with examinations, questions and answers, and ensuring complete patient understanding. Thus, the resources act as a communication aid to the physician, allowing instant perspectives and a hands-on knowledge of the patient's current condition.

Finally, PCCN resources could expand the use of the monitoring equipment while controlling cost by sharing equipment among their patients. This would also aid in ensuring that the equipment is functioning properly and is well maintained. Indeed, it is not out of the question that a group of communal resources, such as a church, might share a pool of devices that are used for their specific PCCN populations.

Thus, the use of VM systems may be greatly improved via the PCCN infrastructure as the synergies of the goals of efficiency, optimal quality, and reduced cost come together at the patient bedside.

Who Pays for It?

While this question will remain to be answered by each individual PCCN management team, it begs for some brief discussion here. The technology infrastructure can run into the millions of dollars in setup costs, and upward of $500,000 per year in maintenance. And that's just for the software. Those numbers don't include ongoing PCCN staff costs (at minimum, a manager and trainer to the tune of about $250,000 per year, fully loaded), additional IT resources that might be required, or extensive VM installations. (Take a look at Chapter 10, "Financial Considerations of a PCCN Implementation," and the website link therein for more info on the cost of a given project.) Even a minimalist implementation consisting of nothing more than the SCN can cost over $100,000 per year plus the aforementioned PCCN resources. Thus the cost of the IT portion looms large. While there may be scenarios in which the various systems, such as the HIE, are purchased through state or federal grants so that at least some of the cost is covered, rarely is there a free pass to the infrastructure.

Even if there is a willing buyer, the critical catch-22 is that the "savings" generated can be seen in both lost revenues and some margin improvements to the hospital, as well as varying financial impacts on physician practice revenues. Depending on the focus and resulting impacts of the PCCN, both can either make or lose money. So, remember:

> *If your ox is being gored, you're unlikely to want to pay for the knife!*

One of the larger issues is the cost of the implementation. Depending on the software and technologies you choose to add, implementation costs can run near $1 million. It quickly becomes difficult to gain that back unless you have either (1) a benevolent benefactor such as the government to fund your implementation, or (2) a very large population from which to pull savings.

Even if the PCCN were as financially desirable as it might be for physicians, it is unlikely that even the largest physician practices can afford to pay for the very large costs of a full PCCN IT implementation. Thus the brunt of the cost will likely fall on the hospital (and the government, if they are willing), and to a lesser extent the physicians, to the degree they are willing. Therefore, the PCCN's focus needs to be structured to create a healthy balance between the financial needs of the hospital and the communal needs for better care at a lower cost per patient year. This can and should be done through a holistic approach that includes attention to the current critical financial metrics that a PCCN can impact (e.g., unnecessary readmissions, excessive intensive care unit [ICU] and ED length of stay [LOS]) along with the needs of the patients in the community (e.g., better care delivery in local, less expensive settings) and the financial needs of "the system" writ large (e.g., dramatically reduced cost of care delivery). This balancing act is difficult but achievable if the right focus is attained, and all parties can agree on mutually beneficial goals and approaches.

Of course, as the financial models change over time (and they will have to), movement toward capitation and reduced reimbursements will change the revenue streams. Yet, of course, the cost of IT and PCCN staff will remain, and will therefore need to be evaluated within the context of the new models. If reimbursement goes the way it is expected, I anticipate that the PCCN will become an even more valuable part of the care system as its ability to control costs in a capitated environment becomes increasingly critical.

How to Save on Implementation Costs

Technology advances at an incredible rate, bringing costs down as functionality goes up. It should therefore not be surprising that bright and clever entrepreneurs would develop inexpensive, integrated systems that can do what the SCN and other technologies can do for far less. Whether web- or cloud-based, created via open-source or proprietary software, if the market demands it, someone will build it. If this concept catches on and achieves what I believe it is capable of doing, it is my fervent hope that software innovation will bring down the cost of the PCCN implementation and make it more palatable for even the smallest communities. If you are of the mindset that this idea has merit, and have the wherewithal to produce such innovations, consider this book a "higher calling" to move forward and develop something new. When you do, be sure to let us all know via my website, http://www.capacitystrategies.com.

PCCN Resources and the Technology Infrastructure

This text is meant to be a blueprint for the development and management of a PCCN in your community. Since IT is such an integral part of the PCCN, it will need to be an important part of the initial and ongoing focus. The IT implementation will require the assistance of several parties in the community, from hospital and office IT staff to vendors and PCCN staff. Thus the management of the IT implementation will very likely come from the PCCN management team, which of course includes hospital and physician representation. If necessary, special consulting or IT resources can be deployed to assist.

Regardless of how your IT planning is structured, make sure you plan early for the implementation; else you risk significant delays and frustrations in the PCCN initiation. Delays can come from disparate efforts to implement state-required HIEs that conflict with local efforts to install large-scale EMRs. Add to this the SCN, and you have a recipe for a revolt in your IT department. Asking for another IT implementation therefore might sound the death knell of your PCCN venture if it plans for a high degree of IT utilization. IT departments are often understaffed and overworked, and with too many project requests to manage another. Whether true or not for your specific facility, hospital IT departments are in high demand and usually inundated. This is commonly also the case with physician group practice IT staff, if they even exist. If your IT plans include the need for integration with EMRs and other IT systems, keep the inevitable delays in mind as you plan the implementation timeframes. IT may also need to be involved on an ongoing basis for maintenance and upgrades to your various systems. While vendors are commonly responsible for these efforts, IT will commonly need to be engaged. Be sure to work with your IT staff early on as you make plans for your PCCN implementation, engaging them heavily in the initial "visioning" discussions. Above all, if you are considering this idea for your population, start immediately on an IT strategy to ensure timely deployment of the necessary tools.

Of course, the IT implementation goes far beyond the wiring of systems. Various PCCN resources will be in charge of training communal resources on the ongoing use of the systems they touch. This should not involve IT staff unless upgrades significantly change the functionality of the systems. However, training the trainers will need to be part of the plans for rollout of the PCCN infrastructure. This will include training on software and VM systems, as well as ongoing updates. Depending on the complexity of the systems you choose, you may need to deploy vendors, consultants, PCCN trainers, or even specialized IT resources to ensure proper ongoing use.

Furthermore, troubleshooting plans will need to be laid out so that IT and the communal resources have a way to solve issues in the field. Depending on your IT system selections, this might be done via vendors and customer service, or IT, or both. Make sure that your troubleshooting processes do not inhibit the communal resources, since many of the volunteers will have neither the time nor the desire to become IT experts and solutions providers. If the systems you have do not function as promised, or create more hassles than benefits for patients and resources, you can be assured that your PCCN will be hampered at best, or fail at worst. This of course means that direct and ongoing contact between the IT team(s), PCCN management team, and trainers will be required, especially in the early stages of visioning, development, and deployment.

Summary

Your IT systems are important to the ongoing functionality of the PCCN. Without them, you will have difficulty achieving any large degree of scalability and improvements toward the Five Pillars. Managing the cost and financial responsibility for IT will be critical to the long-term success of your efforts. This may mean effectively aligning the goals and improvement strategies of the PCCN with at least some of the financial interests of the key players, such as hospitals and physician offices. Metrics impacting current and future hospital revenues, such as unnecessary readmissions, unnecessary and extended ED visits, and excessive ICU LOS will need to be considered as part of the implementation strategies in order to attain support from hospitals (whether financial, resource, etc.).

Thus planning the use of and payment for the IT systems is a critical step in the strategic planning process, and should be initiated very early in the PCCN planning process.

Chapter 10

Financial Considerations of a PCCN Implementation

It goes without saying that the poly-chronic care network (PCCN) must be financially sound and self-sustaining. Its infrastructure, technologies, and resources must somehow be paid for via offsetting savings or additional revenues if it is to warrant serious consideration. If not, it will be far too easy to postpone implementation or cut off funding during tough economic times.

In this chapter, I hope to offer insights into the financial implications of a PCCN implementation. Since each scenario will be very different, and each community will have very different needs, financial conditions, and financial require-ments, you will need to study your community and the impacts a PCCN could have on its poly-chronics. From there, you may want to structure your disease and patient selection and care strategy objectives to align community health impacts with current and future improvement efforts of the key players (e.g., hospitals), such that the outcomes of the PCCN positively influence their financial objectives to the extent possible.

This will help you more readily sell the concept to those who have the most to lose and gain from an implementation. It is important to cross this hurdle early to avoid making the PCCN about money rather than outcomes and population health.

To see an example of the costs associated with a single PCCN implementation, go to my website, http://www.capacitystrategies.com, and seek out the PCCN section. Therein you will find a link to the PCCN Sample Financials spreadsheet, which you can download and review. Upon examination, you will quickly see that there are a variety of costs that need to be covered each year, including technology and staff. In this very brief chapter, let's examine these costs, and then discuss how they might be justified and offset by the outcomes of a PCCN implementation.

Cost Analysis Assumptions

There are several sheets in the Sample Financials workbook. The first several sheets refer to the start-up costs of the PCCN implementation. These numbers make several assumptions, which are as follows:

■ Consulting services are required but flexible. If you read this text and follow its guidelines, you may find that you don't need these services at all. Excellent. Your small investment in this book has already paid off in spades. However, if you are not comfortable with the implementation of this very new system in your community, or if you don't have the resources and time to deploy, you may want to invest in implementation and even management expertise. This would include expertise in volunteer management, deployment of resources and technologies, and the requirements for the infrastructure. The need for assistance should be taken seriously if your PCCN is to get off on the right foot and avoid early damaging missteps and failures.

Conversely, you may find that your PCCN requires more extensive consulting, to include physician office efficiency and staff utilization, process and systems optimization, culture change, and leadership and strategy execution. Firms like PRISM (a nonprofit consulting firm) focus specifically on physician relationships, change management, and office productivity optimization. PRISM would be critical if you think your physician office productivity needs improvement to be able to handle the new PCCN patients; or if simply implementing the PCCN will result in too much change for the physician offices to handle, or will require significant alterations in flow, processing, staffing, and so on. Likewise, you may see the need to instill a new culture in your community, hospital, and physician offices, such as one that supports "ownership" of patients. This can be done very effectively through training programs offered by Joe Tye (also mentioned elsewhere in this text). You might also need general simulation services for your hospital's flow and efficiency, such as that offered by ArchiSim, or basic process improvement assistance offered by myriad firms.

Consultants are listed among the line items in the workbook to show a fuller implementation cost should they be required. Use them as you see fit for your particular situation.

■ There are no immediate reductions in a new PCCN patient's base cost. The financials assume that the base cost of care of new patients entering the PCCN remains relatively steady over the three- to four-year period, and that the PCCN's existence does not reduce the cost of care delivery for *all* patients in the community. This means that a patient entering the PCCN during the first year will have a given average base cost of care, which is to be reduced as they participate. Of course, this reduction in cost of care delivery is what we seek.

Subsequently, however, new patients entering the PCCN will have the same, original base cost, as it is assumed that nothing has happened to change the cost of their care delivery. This is only for simplicity, since we actually hope that there will be ancillary impacts of care delivery costs that go beyond those patients enrolled in the PCCN. As time goes on, and more and more patients are brought in and costs are further reduced, the total average cost of care delivery should drop as the PCCN begins to impact the total cost of care delivery for the entire community.

◾ There will be one PCCN manager and one trainer position, both of which are permanent. In the smallest of PCCNs, these roles may be taken on by a physician office care manager/patient navigator, hospital case manager, or even a single volunteer in the PCCN. Unless your PCCN is very small, however, you will likely find that these are full-time roles, even if unified into a single resource. In larger iterations, you may find that one of each is not enough, and that several trainers and/or managers are required. Thus, again, the scale and breadth of your PCCN will drive your total permanent resource cost.

◾ Travel cost assumes some degree of external consulting, and an ongoing expense of the trainer. The spreadsheet can account for external consultants that might be required to assist with your implementation. (Per the above, if these are not necessary, you can save quite a bit by eliminating this travel cost. Conversely, if you need additional consulting resources or more trainers, travel costs will increase.) It also accounts for the need for the PCCN trainer to be out in the field working to train new resources and office staff.

◾ Training and marketing materials will be required. Eventually, you will be able to download these from the PCCN section of the http://www.capacitystrategies.com

website and print them yourself. However, herein it is assumed that these materials will be created specifically for your PCCN and printed locally. While minimal, these expenses are ongoing.

■ The contractual spreadsheet assumes that you will have a relatively extensive technology infrastructure. This includes the social–clinical networking (SCN) platform (a near must-have for any PCCN) and simulation (also a near must-have for any large PCCN). In the spreadsheet you'll find that there is no assumption of the use of a health information exchange (HIE) or chronic disease management system (CDMS), but of course these can be added.

■ The spreadsheet assumes a cost for a per beneficiary per year (PBPY) benefit to the physicians. This is especially volatile, since there may be no need for such compensation. As we have discussed, it is likely that physicians might see their capacity and patient volumes increase or at least remain stable rather than decrease. It is therefore unlikely that the PCCN implementation will result in a significant loss in revenues to the physicians. This remains to be seen, and will depend on the community, the patients, the patient mix, and the physician practice patterns. So, unless the Centers for Medicare and Medicaid Services (CMS) funds it, it is unlikely that the PCCN management team (MT) will immediately agree to the outlay. However, for the sake of this analysis, we will assume some degree of payout to the physicians to better gauge the potential total cost of implementation.

It is worth noting that a relatively simple implementation that includes only the basic consulting services and a full SCN will still result in roughly $1.5 million in start-up costs (over three years) and roughly $120,000 to $450,000 per year in subsequent years. The only way to significantly reduce these numbers is to obtain a free or very low-cost SCN, or reduce or eliminate full-time PCCN staff. In the end, you will have to spend money to create and maintain a PCCN. The question becomes how much you need to now justify, and how to justify the expense.

Creating Your Own Cost Analysis

Early on, you will need to create your own financial analysis. Start with the potential populations, their total cost of care delivery, operations and care stream processes, volumes, and growth potential. Begin to analyze how the key players interact with these patients, and the financial implications of the current care model. If, for instance, your local hospital derives significant inpatient revenues from "frequent flyers" in the poly-chronic populations, look at how costs of care delivery might be reduced such that both payors and the hospital win in a new care paradigm.

You will also need to seriously consider the scale and scope of your PCCN, since this will impact both the cost of PCCN operations and any potential benefits derived. A single, small church congregation focused on diabetes using two single primary care physician (PCP) practices will have little impact on a large tertiary health system. Thus, there may be little stomach for high cost and financial risk.

Additionally, you will want to consider the long-term implications of PCCN deployment. Though difficult to quantify, there are significant impacts from community awareness and education, promotion of personal responsibility for disease management, and an awareness and appreciation for palliative care and end-of-life planning. These will be important to both your community and the overall cost of healthcare system management in the future.

Lastly, no matter how you construct your analysis, be sure to include at least the elements shown therein, including technology, marketing, resources (both permanent and tempo- rary), and even PBPY if you think you can get it from a payor.

Impact of the PCCN on Hospital Financials

Changes in both costs and revenues should be expected in a PCCN project, with much of the revenue impact hitting the hospital's bottom line. Your hospital may have very different financial needs and situations than others. Yet all hospitals deploying this program are likely to see similar "tacks" if deployment is successful. That is, the direction of change in costs and revenues in each affected area should be similar between facilities and implementations. Let's look at some of the potential revenue impacts from a successful implementation first.

■ **Reduced emergency department (ED) visits for poly-chronic patients:** Whether it is good or bad from a revenue viewpoint, the reductions of ED visits is a key indicator of a successful PCCN implementation. Patients who might otherwise have gone to the ED for care are now either receiving care in a less expensive location (e.g., a physician office or outpatient clinic), or have had preemptive interventions that eliminated the need for care altogether. Since the ED is the "front door" to the hospital, this also impacts inpatient visits.

■ **Inpatient visits:** Again, preemptive interventions, proper and timely follow-up on clinical instructions, and better disease management should all lead to a reduction in the need for inpatient stays (often associated with ED visits in the poly-chronic population). If the outlier visits can be eliminated, the total cost of care delivery for the entire system should be reduced. However, this could mean reduced revenues to the hospital.

■ **Reduced intensive care unit (ICU) stays:** As you now know, part of the PCCN approach is an emphasis on end-of-life (EOL) planning and palliative care. This, along with the preemptive care strategies, should mean reduction in some ICU stays, particularly those outlier lengths of stay that can run up such tremendous costs. If palliative care is approached correctly within a community and its PCCN(s), there should be some perhaps significant reductions in unnecessary ICU admissions and length of stay (LOS) and greater cost control for patients with increasing morbidity.

■ **(Unnecessary) readmissions:** I say *unnecessary* parenthetically since not all readmissions are created equal. Anecdotally, I've chatted with a number of chief financial officers (CFOs) who quietly profess a strong reliance on some readmissions to drive revenues. Without these, they say, many hospitals would struggle to survive. That said, the CMS will drive much of what is considered necessary and unnecessary in the future as they strive to drive down taxpayer costs for wasteful and unnecessary spending. Thus, hospitals that want to thrive will need to focus on preventing the readmissions classified as unnecessary to avoid financial penalties as well as nonreimbursable expenses. The PCCN will drive down some admissions, some of which might be classified as unnecessary. This could benefit the hospital's efforts to comply with new CMS regulations and reimbursement strategies. Indeed, proper alignment of focus and disease management should help to address those readmissions considered unnecessary among the poly-chronics.

■ **Improved discharge processing and care transitions:** PCCNs can assist in the placement of discharged patients and the transition from hospital to home or other care facility by offering additional care resources, transportation, and contact points for patients newly discharged. If planning occurs early in the inpatient stay, as it always should, discharges can become smoother, more predictable, and readily scheduled throughout the day. This of course has upstream impacts, as better discharge planning has been shown to yield additional capacity throughout a facility, reduced ED LOS, and reduced post-op wait times.

This can even impact surgical throughput, as beds are freed up in a way that allows for freer flow from surgery to the inpatient units, which in turn prevents surgical delays due to bottlenecks in post-op. (This is the concept described in detail in my previous book, *Dynamic Capacity Management for Healthcare: Advanced Methods and Tools for Optimization*).[1]

■ **Case Mix Index (CMI):** If your PCCN is large enough, and its impact on the community significant enough, it might actually alter the CMI. This, of course, could result in ancillary short- and long-term impacts to your hospital's financial health. Your CFO should evaluate this closely to determine any potentially negative impacts.

In addition to potential revenue impacts, there are also direct (especially variable) cost impacts. For instance, with fewer admissions and ED visits, staffing might be adjusted to reflect the new volumes and case/patient mix. Long-term fixed cost might be altered if the impacts to the poly-chronic population yield a future reduced need for certain types of inpatient capacity. Again, as with revenues, the scale of the PCCN will determine the total cost impacts.

The downstream results are potentially significant impacts on the hospital's bottom line. In order to get buy-in and the necessary financial and logistical support from your hospital, these costs and expenses must be reconciled against the current realities of fee-for-service (FFS) and diagnosis-related group (DRG) reimbursements, and aligned with the hospital management's strategic plans and objectives.

Impacts on Physician Office Costs and Revenues

Office costs will vary depending on the amount spent on infrastructure (e.g., technologies for the PCCN implementation, staffing for care managers, etc.). Many offices have already committed fully to the concept of a care manager to assist with chronic disease management and patient navigation. Some have fully integrated electronic medical records (EMRs) in place that could be augmented by the technologies of the PCCN. Thus, there may be little additional infrastructure expense, assuming the PCCN managers and trainers can work effectively together.

Some might argue that a PCCN will yield additional practice responsibilities and activity-based costs since time and effort are required to monitor resource communications and remotely manage the poly-chronics in the community. Indeed, these activities will increase if the practice expands its care capacity or patient panel. For instance, physicians will likely find that they spend time developing the new holistic care strategies that include the communal resources, some of which will take place outside their offices and thus will not be reimbursed. Similarly, physicians and their care managers (if any exist) will need to spend time reviewing correspondence from resources, communicating instructions, and working closely with the PCCN managers to direct care. None of this will be reimbursed in the current FFS models.

However, PCCNs should be viewed less as an activity-based cost and more as a reduction in long-term healthcare costs, greater efficiency, future patient revenue through expanded capacity, and most importantly, better care for the patient. As the PCCN expands physician office capacity, physicians will have a larger number of patients under their care, which would logically mean greater potential revenue (assuming there is any capacity and willingness at all to see these patients). The key is to redesign the practice to allow for the new processes and business models while paying attention to the tasks for which the practice is directly compensated.

Furthermore, in the PCCN model, poly-chronic patients will have additional care resources in the community to aid in disease management, and thus will see their physicians only as directed and necessary. This should reduce unnecessary visits, leaving capacity for patients in greater need of direct interventions. In theory, then, physicians remotely would manage a larger panel of patients while directly intervening with only those patients who need to physically visit them. Management of the cost for the physician practice will therefore lie in how physicians use their time and internal and external practice resources to balance the new interventions available to them.

This brings us to the revenue side and the potential for PBPY (per beneficiary per year) and other compensation systems. If you implement your PCCN today, physicians will be paid on a FFS basis, since there is no PBPY compensation method. Thus, physicians and their offices will have to work to alter their current practice patterns, task allocations, and work breakdown structures to best manage the various new and necessary communications media and PCCN workload. As per the above discussion, some of this work will technically go uncompensated, even though there are long-term benefits in better use of the physician's time and energy. Therefore, it is imperative that office efficiency be optimized to reduce process waste, redundancy, and so on, to allow for changes to patient interactions and to manage resource time to optimize both compensation and patient care. This can be achieved internally, or through management engineering methodologies, or through external experts and consultants.

This office cost-revenue-utilization optimization is important not only for the PCCN but for all future models of care delivery. Whether through business models such as accountable care organizations (ACOs), and/or payment models such as Premium Support, offices will begin to see compensation based on something other than volume. Quality, outcomes, and PBPY compensation systems are already in the works, and are here to stay. Thus, it behooves physicians to adopt process and systems improvement methodologies immediately to be as efficient as possible as these changes take place. Otherwise, they may struggle to keep their doors open as high overhead cost and inefficient resource utilization take their toll on practice margins.

Offices should also recognize the importance of the trends toward remote care and management, and build these efficiently into the office work streams. In the PCCN, remote care processes would include the review, screening, and prioritization of communal resource communications to allow the physician to properly select the information that corresponds to the need for their time and attention. If woven correctly into the workflow, this can become an important and cost-effective part of the physician's management of their now-larger patient panel.

Of course, in an ideal world, CMS and other payors would compensate the physician for their time and attention to these distant patients. Indeed, PBPY compensation systems beg for the use of such care management programs, as they allow the physician to increase the number of patients managed while reducing the total per-patient cost of care delivery. As has been shown in previous demonstration projects, CMS is quite willing to experiment with PBPY plans and will likely continue to expand their use as efficacy is shown. If this trend continues, the PCCN will mesh nicely with new compensation models, and allow physicians to profit from the dispersion of workload to a broader and properly directed resource pool.

This, of course, is one of the many, many benefits of the PCCN concept.

PCCN Cost Justifications

Even if your PCCN can or will do great things for the poly-chronics in your community, it means little if the cost of operations cannot be justified or the program cannot be made economically sustainable. While the community service of a PCCN would be a worthwhile justification of any expenditure, I prefer a sustainable model that does not rely on external funding, special grants, or government benevolence to ensure ongoing operations.

If you hearken back to our earlier discussion of ox gor-
ing, you'll recall that I stated, "If your ox is being gored,
you're unlikely to be willing to pay for the knife!" Thus, in
order to examine the cost justification issues, we determined
who might win and lose under a PCCN model. This will now
help us create financial strategies that can be aligned with
the community care strategies we want to promote, thereby
eliciting support from the key supporting players, such as
hospitals.

It will help to recall some of the goals of the PCCN, including preemptive care management to prevent unnecessary and
wasteful care provision, more extensive use of less-expensive
venues and resources to manage quality care delivery at a
lower cost, involvement of families and patients earlier in the
poly-chronic disease state to ensure opportunities for appropriate clinical and spiritual late-life decisions, and ongoing
patient engagement to help with the optimization of disease
management. All these plus other aspects of the program
should result in and be driven by dramatic changes in the
care processes and thus the cost of care delivery. But until
a new compensation/reimbursement system is developed, we
will have to make the PCCN work within the confines of the
current, flawed system. And as we all know, one entity's cost
is another entity's revenue. Therefore, the key is to turn these
opportunities toward those areas that will have the largest
financial impact for the key players.

Let's explore some of the many ways in which the PCCN
can be cost-justified for the key players in the community.

■ **Total cost of care optimization:** A holistic approach
   to care delivery, which includes the use of communal
   resources, palliative care and end-of-life planning, physician office capacity optimization, patient engagement,
   and personal responsibility, will result in the reduction
   in the total cost of care delivery for a given poly-chronic
   population. With this, the total cost of care delivery can

be optimally reduced, regardless of the larger business and reimbursements models used.

■ **Bettering physician relationships:** One advantage to hospitals is the building and strengthening of relationships with physicians, both PCPs and specialists. By contributing to the PCCN, which ultimately assists the physicians, their patients, and their communities, hospitals can demonstrate an understanding of and contribution to a truly community-wide approach to population health improvement efforts. By collaborating closely with physicians on palliative care programs, hospitals can strengthen ties and create mutually beneficial synergies among independent and employed physicians. These will be important as the relationships evolve over time as new healthcare business models take shape.

■ **Ancillary impacts:** If your PCCN performs as it should and could, you will clearly impact the care requirements of the participating poly-chronics. However, many ancillary impacts are felt upstream and downstream from the actual day-to-day management of chronic disease. Changes to the way poly-chronics are cared for also alters the care of all other patients in the system, at least to a limited degree. So, for instance, if you are able to reduce the need for certain surgical interventions among your diabetics, surgical capacity will be freed for other procedures. For example, podiatrists might take on other surgical procedures and appointments from private payers to replace the "lost" business from fewer diabetic patients.

To effectively plan for these complex interdependencies, you will need to do the following:

■ Precisely map the care processes (as you would have in your care strategies planning sessions).
■ Examine your maps and look for changes in the care brought on by better health and wellness of the poly-chronics in your population.

- Quantify (to the extent possible) the expected *degree of change* in the processes, operations, costs and revenues, and resource utilization of patient care (e.g., how many fewer appointments will we need if this patient is better cared for in their home?).
- Quantify the net new and additional capacity, financial gains and losses, resource utilization reduction, and so on, made available, remembering that the new may not be the same as the old (for instance, two fewer diabetic appointments with a PCP might yield fewer or more appointments with other patient types). Remember, too, the interdependencies of your care strategy maps. For instance, reductions in ED visits might increase the number (and thus the cost) of physician office or urgent care visits. So, one cost reduction can be offset by an increase elsewhere, and thus should be calculated as a net improvement/loss.
- Calculate the actual total expected impact of the changes, such as impacts to episode or total cost; resource time; physician, specialist, and hospital gain or loss, etc.

With this information, you can then begin to quantify the justifications of the PCCN based on expected ancillary impacts in a more holistic way. Go through the following list of possible ancillary impacts, looking for the interdependencies with each and quantify the outcomes of change brought about by the PCCN implementation. When finished, you can total the results and see how you might add to the justification of implementation.

- Increasing capacity for surgery and other profitable lines
- Reducing total ICU LOS, thereby reducing ED LOS for patients awaiting an ICU bed
  - Calculated in part by examining the relationship between ED LOS and wait times for ICU beds by ED poly-chronic patients

- Reduced total ED LOS by reducing LOS outliers (which impacts all patients in the ED)
- Reducing ED visits, especially those visits considered excessive, overly expensive, or uncompensated
- Reducing per-patient expenses, especially for the ICU
- Hospital LOS cost reduction (though this might be less than you expect; hospital LOS may be of little consequence due to the way it is often calculated, which places very little cost on the final day of stay)
- Earlier discharges from inpatient visits
- Better coordination of care transitions to new locations of care delivery
- Better planning for ED visits and admissions (rather than admitting through the ED)
- Reduced use of ambulance services to get nonurgent patients to the hospital for admission
- Optimized use of medications and treatments (presumably means *reduction*)
- Optimized use of clinical resources, inclusive of all hospital and physician resources (presumably means *reduction*)
- Optimizing the physicians' patient panel size, thus optimizing the overall total system capacity

With this information in hand, you will be able to begin a serious discussion of the cost and benefits of the PCCN implementation and determine how much, if any, it would make sense to spend on the program.

Outcomes and Incentives

As is obvious by the current FFS reimbursement system of U.S. healthcare, financial incentives can drive behavior, sometimes even self-destructive and counterproductive behavior. For example, while PCPs and experienced nurses often try to do a good job of seeing *the whole patient*, the rest of the medical community is less holistic in its approach to care delivery. This is largely due to the government-imposed and industry-supported FFS payment structure that has so blinded providers to both the actual cost of care delivery as well as long-term outcomes of care delivery. Clearly, for this or any other business model innovation to become reality, there needs to be wholesale removal of the old habits, thinking, and payment systems. The PCCN, as at least one of the ways in which the healthcare system might be salvaged, has a vested interest in the successful improvement of population health. Saving the few will aid the many. But this becomes difficult if not impossible in the long term without changing the incentives of care provision.

Thus in order for the PCCN to work effectively and obtain its expected results, the entire resource pool will have to change their focus away from financially focused FFS mentalities and a myopic, task-oriented approach to care provision. Doing so will require an entirely different approach to care delivery and resource support, one which supports the PCCN, is enabled and supported by the PCCN technologies and infrastructure, and is paid for with a new payment and incentive model.

For a number of reasons, this means a gradual shift toward the idea of *capitation* and *bundled payments* and away from FFS. First and foremost, the patients in this population are, for the most part, unlikely to be cured of their ailments. Their care strategies involve mitigation of future deterioration, improvement in existing conditions, maximizing the potential to lead meaningful and pleasant lives, and reduction in the overall cost of care delivery without compromising quality, access, or gratification. Yet, this does not necessarily equal *cured*. Indeed, many will eventually die of the diseases they have contracted. It is how this inevitable decline takes place that makes up the driving objectives for the PCCN. Thus a holistic and long-term approach that includes everything from disease management to end-of-life planning is required if the needs of these patients are to be addressed. Because of this longer-term approach, and the holistic nature of its care and service delivery, the goals of the PCCN and its care strategies simply do not blend well with a FFS payment model in which volume drives the motivation for patient care delivery.

For instance, the improvement of patient weight or hemo-globin levels must be measured and gradually improved over the course of months and years. Therefore, the PCCN payment system should reflect this longer-term focus, with the goals and any related shared savings programs and incentives of the PCCN aligned with long-term, outcomes-focused care strategies rather than a number of visits or tests in a given cycle.

Secondly, the new care systems currently being considered must approach these patients holistically, as poly-chronics, rather than as isolated users of individual services. Indeed, for these complex patients, there is no other reasonable and effective way to approach their care and develop the plans by which they will be treated. Physicians and every other caregiver in the community must therefore lower their territorial walls and focus on the patient rather than their individual financial and related self-interests. This will require the "It's not about me!" mentality mentioned earlier in this text, as well as a payment system that rewards long-term efforts and the holistic while creating disincentives for the isolated treatments of the past.

Given the dollars to be saved, there should be ready access to incentivization monies. These payouts should be carefully crafted to enable a system that is more about rewarding quality than throughput; outstanding service rather than the volume served; and extraordinary care rather than filling out forms and checking the correct boxes. While volume is a factor and should remain as a metric in our systems, it should never be the only factor determining relative success or failure. However, quality and financial returns to the payors (particularly CMS) should not be the sole focus either. *Quality* for this patient population is a relative measure, and might prove difficult to quantify. Quality metrics should therefore be included, but again, carefully constructed to match the long-term nature of the diseases being treated.

And certainly all savings to the payors (and taxpayers) is not derived equally. Simply reducing the amount of care provided is not the goal of the PCCN. Rather, cost reduction could be thought of as a by-product of the efficiency rather than an explicit goal of the system. Thus, shared savings from the optimization of care provision should be rewarded based on attainment of a number of key milestones for most if not all patients in the PCCN population. Those milestones should include everything from health improvement or maintenance, to cost reduction for each patient, to new patient enrollment, and overall community engagement in health promotion and PCCN participation.

Of course, as mentioned earlier in this text, we are creating a business model for which there is no payment model. However, since this and other business model concepts are already catching on, it won't be long until there are new ideas in payment and incentive models to help save the system. I predict that we are on the verge of a great degree of energy and motivation for new care and business models both here and abroad.

Who Pays for What?

Fortunately for this model, not all resources in the PCCN will have their proverbial oxen gored by the capitated or bundled payment systems made possible through an implementation. Because many of the resources in the PCCN are already employed in jobs that involve caring for PCCN patients (e.g., social workers, YMCA staff), additional pay may not be necessary. Their role is to focus at least some of their current time on the PCCN population, which may not require any change in their efforts. (Indeed, the technologies and communication systems put in place may actually aid their efforts and make them more productive.) There may even be situations in which these resources can dedicate all of their time to the PCCN for only a small amount of incentive or additional pay.

Other potential resources, such as church members, may be voluntarily doing some of the work of the PCCN, but in a disjointed and uncoordinated fashion. Many, in fact, try to help care for the PCCN's patient population, either as friends, relatives, congregation members, or a service organization, but have no direct tie to the work of others. Thus, their efforts, while laudable, are not as effective as they could be. They would likely demand little remuneration, again finding the PCCN's collaborative environment and technologies as a benefit to their efforts. However, organizations such as church congregations who dedicate time, resources, and even money to the task at hand should be compensated fairly for the results they help achieve. This can be optional and will no doubt be customized, depending on the resources in a given community and the infrastructure constructed.

Some resources will be short- and long-term volunteers, tied to no specific organization or group, and may only require minimal, if any, incentivization. Certainly, we do not want volunteers signing up just to get paid, as this is absolutely the mentality we want to steer the PCCN away from. Other resources, however, will definitely need to be compensated for revenue losses. These might be PCPs, who may need to change a great deal about their practice patterns in order to head up the PCCN. The necessary changes to move a PCP's practice from one focused on volume and throughput to one focused on outcomes and efficiency for a small population will often be enormous. This would normally mean serious decline in income to the practice, coupled with a large IT and training investment, making the PCCN concept unacceptable to most if not all. Therefore, PCPs will need to be "made whole" from the savings generated via the PCCN's cost savings.

The specialists, on the other hand, might be incentivized in a number of ways. For some, and in certain communities, the patients of the PCCN are already their "bread and butter." Many see primarily Medicare/Medicaid patients, and thus are paid at the reduced rates common to these programs. To avoid further reductions in their compensation, and given their limited role in the management and operations of the PCCN, their compensation should be aligned with the time they spend, the services they provide, and the outcomes they produce. While this will require a realignment of incentives, accountability, and measurement, we anticipate that at least some of the specialists will remain more or less tied to a sort of FFS payment model. There are options for this, however.

Depending on the percentage of PCCN patients as part of a specialist's practice, physicians may opt for a partial or full salaried arrangement. Some are already employed and paid by local hospitals, and their compensation might therefore be more directly tied to the more typical quality, throughput, and outcomes measures of the PCCN and current management systems. Others, who might be part of multispecialty practices that include PCPs who are involved in the PCCNs, might arrange for payments as part of a PCCN capitation payment model.

Furthermore, hospitals stand to lose significant and important revenue if they fail to effectively manage the impact of the PCCN. As we've seen, hospitals can target interventions to simultaneously help the community's poly-chronics while helping their bottom line through utilization control. While it is doubtful that payors will agree to directly compensate hospitals for their "losses," it would not be out of the ordinary to see incentives created for the management of chronic disease at the hospital level.

Of course, these payment arrangements will likely need to be customized for each iteration of the PCCN and each physician community. To try to prescribe a single, fixed solution for each and every PCCN across the United States and the world would be preposterous and preclude the innovation I hope this concept will drive. Thus, the payment methods, and who gets paid for what and when, will be developed as part of the overall infrastructure as the PCCN itself is built. Payors will therefore need to be an integral part of the conversation.

Summary

This chapter is meant to get you thinking about the inevitable "What's in it for me?" questions you will face as you try to implement a PCCN in your community. Without solid answers to the financial questions of cost, who pays, and compensation for services rendered, your PCCN will likely never make it off the ground.

Each scenario will be very different, and each community will have very different needs, financial conditions, and financial requirements. Study your PCCN, the impacts it could have on your community and its poly-chronics, then structure your efforts to align the community health impacts with current and future improvement efforts of the key players, such that the outcomes of the PCCN positively influence their financial objectives to the extent possible.

Endnotes

1. P. Story, *Dynamic Capacity Management: Advanced Methods and Tools for Optimization* (Boca Raton, FL: CRC Press/Taylor & Francis, 2010).

Chapter 11

PCCNs, Palliative Care, and End-of-Life Planning

If a truly holistic approach to care provision for chronic disease patients is to solve for quality, cost, and patient gratification, we must necessarily address some of the most costly and difficult periods of a patient's life as well as the entire disease progression process. This includes the end of life (EOL) and the pain and suffering that occurs throughout the disease episode. Often confused for one another, palliative care and EOL care are two concepts born of the same general principle: caring for patients as they wish in a dignifying and personalized way, while providing relief from pain and the distress of symptoms. If we are to address the Five Pillars, Triple Aim, three-part aim, and so on, within the context of the poly-chronic care network (PCCN), we must necessarily integrate EOL and palliative care into our program strategy.

Palliative care and EOL planning and care are important for a number of very different reasons. EOL is most commonly noted due to the costs and inpatient capacity associated with the dying process, particularly for Medicaid and Medicare patients, and specifically poly-chronics. As we'll see in this chapter, EOL care can unnecessarily use tremendous resources while often offering little in the way of substantive outcomes or patient and family relief. Furthermore, EOL care is often associated with difficult familial decisions for patients who have left few, if any, legally and morally binding instructions for their care. Alternatively, proper EOL planning and care implementation have been shown to greatly improve gratification and even quality outcomes. Similarly, palliative care has grown in popularity due to its profound impact on patients, which is the result of its holistic focus on the patient's condition as advanced diseases progress. Both are important to the overall health and well-being of the poly-chronic patient population. And fortunately, both can be readily integrated into the PCCN care model.

In this chapter, we'll address the need for these concepts in the overall schema of healthcare delivery for poly-chronics, and describe the process by which integration into your PCCN could take place. Keep in mind, of course, that the PCCN model remains flexible and can accommodate a number of different configurations, and can therefore be structured to handle a variety of EOL and palliative models and resource allocations.

Palliative Care: Definition and History

For those who are not familiar with palliative care, it is one of the fastest growing components of healthcare systems across the globe. Since it was adopted from the United Kingdom in the 1980s, millions of U.S. patients have used palliative care as part of their disease management regimen and/or EOL treatment. The word *palliative* is taken from the Latin word *palliare*, which means "to cloak." Palliative care focuses generally on relieving and preventing the suffering of patients, whether physical, emotional, or even spiritual. Medications and treatments are said to have a palliative effect if they relieve symptoms without having a curative effect on the underlying disease or cause, and thus can be a vital part of the palliative program. This can include treating nausea related to chemotherapy or using morphine to treat a broken leg or ibuprofen to treat aching related to a flu infection. Unlike hospice care, which focuses specifically on care of the terminally ill, palliative medicine is appropriate for patients in all disease stages, including those undergoing treatment for curable illnesses and those living with chronic diseases, as well as patients who are nearing the end of life. Though commonly associated with patients having acute or chronic diseases, any patient with significant pain and suffering, mental anguish, and other symptoms would be a candidate for its use. Palliative care is also a broader care process than hospice or EOL care that can begin with the knowledge of a disease and extend throughout the curative process all the way to death and bereavement. Still, as you'll see in the generally accepted definitions and models in this chapter, it remains commonly associated with EOL care and the very sick.

Since its roots are in the United Kingdom, let's look at the UK definition of palliative care, taken from the UK's National Institute for Clinical Excellence (NICE), and the World Health Organization (WHO).[1]

> Palliative care is the active holistic care of patients with advanced progressive illness. Management of pain and other symptoms and provision of psychological, social, and spiritual support is paramount. The goal of palliative care is achievement of the best quality of life for patients and their families. Many aspects of palliative care are also applicable earlier in the course of the illness in conjunction with other treatments.
>
> Palliative care aims to:
>
> - Affirm life and regard dying as a normal process
> - Provide relief from pain and other distressing symptoms

- Integrate the psychological and spiritual aspects of patient care
- Offer a support system to help patients live as actively as possible until death
- Offer a support system to help the family cope during the patient's illness and in their own bereavement.

By way of contrast, a World Health Organization (WHO) statement describes palliative care as:

> An approach that improves the quality of life of patients and their families facing the problems associated with life-threatening illness, through the prevention and relief of suffering by means of early identification and impeccable assessment and treatment of pain and other problems, physical, psychosocial and spiritual.[2]

Most palliative care occurs in the acute hospital setting due in part to the equipment, medication, and monitoring requirements. The prevalence of palliative care teams in U.S. hospitals shows steady growth and indicates a rapidly rising trend. According to the most recent data analysis, 1,568, or 63 percent, of U.S. hospitals with more than 50 beds have a palliative care team—an increase of 138.3 percent since 2000. Eighty percent of hospitals with more than 300 beds have palliative teams.[3]

Palliative medicine typically utilizes a multidisciplinary approach to patient care, relying on input from physicians, pharmacists, nurses, chaplains, social workers, psychologists, and other allied health professionals in formulating a plan of care to relieve suffering in all areas of a patient's life. This multidisciplinary approach allows the palliative care team to address physical, emotional, spiritual, and social concerns that arise with advanced illness.

The Origins of Palliative Care

The concepts of palliative and hospice care originated in the United Kingdom in the 1960s, with slow adoption in other parts of the industrialized world. Led by Dame Cicely Saunders, it began with research at St. Joseph's Hospice, where Dame Cicely was allowed to experiment by giving regular dosages of drugs to four patients. This apparently simple practice was a novel approach at the time, and was even observed with some skepticism. However, skepticism soon turned to interest as the results showed a marked improvement in the quality of these patients' lives. By the time Dame Cicely left St. Joseph's, she had observed and documented over 1,000 cases of patients dying of cancer. Her scrupulous records provide the basis of this fundamental area of research.[4]

Dame Cicely's pioneering work was soon followed by others. In 1963, Professor John Hinton recognized the physical and mental distress of dying in the ward of a London teaching hospital.[5] He later authored groundbreaking work on the progression of the awareness and acceptance of dying over time—one of the few longitudinal studies conducted with terminally ill patients and their families.[6] His research revealed different patterns of progression, influential factors such as depression and anxiety, and the relationship between patients and their relatives' awareness and acceptance.

In the early 1970s, palliative care in the United Kingdom saw its first large-scale epidemiological survey, led by Professor Ann Cartwright and her team. Drawing from a random sample of deaths in 1969, she reported the experiences of 785 patients and their families in the last year of life, which would later be compared with those of 639 patients in 1987.[7] In this comparative study, several changes were recognized: "increasingly people were dying alone, older and with prolonged and unpleasant symptoms, in institutional and hospital settings, with improved home help though with fewer home visits, and with a greater awareness of the disease and dying."[8]

Palliative, hospice, and EOL care utilization is growing rapidly across the globe, as caregivers and patients realize the benefits and health systems see the results on key metrics, including cost and quality. In the United States, groundbreaking work was being done in the latter 1980s and early 1990s, and is moving rapidly forward.

Resources for Palliative Care

In any business model, including the PCCN, palliative care will require additional, trained, and specialized resources. However, these resources should meld well into the overall PCCN infrastructure such that the communal resources are included and used as needed, and the entire resource pool is supportive and engaged in the palliative care model of delivery. The number and type of resources depends on the goals of the program, the locations of palliative care delivery (hospital or elsewhere), and the availability and use of any available communal resources. Since palliative care is such a unique service, its complexity should not be taken lightly. Thus, any communal resources added to your palliative program should be specially trained, even if only used in a volunteer or temporary capacity.

From the information above, we can see that a number of potential palliative resources might be required. Fortunately, these include many resources already expected to be part of the PCCN, which is testament to the ease of integration of various models. Pharmacists, nurses, chaplains/clergy, social workers, and psychologists, some specializing in palliative care, are added to the list of PCCN clinical and nonclinical resources. Since these resources might operate within the hospital rather than the community, proper integration into the PCCN will require additional effort and collaboration. In this case, PCCN managers and trainers will need to create an atmosphere and camaraderie with hospital staff that is conducive to external participation by PCCN communal and clinical resources. If, however, palliative care programs extend beyond the walls of the hospital, PCCN resources might be substituted and used as part of an integrated palliative–PCCN approach.

End-of-Life Planning and Care

What if you were asked, "How would you prefer to pass on—hooked to a machine in an intensive care unit (ICU), or at home surrounded by family and friends?" Few, I'd guess, would take the first option. Yet, one of every three people who died in 2007 in the United States was in the hospital for treatment at the time of death. The cost of their hospital stays was about $20 billion, which was significantly more than that of discharged patients.[9] According to the same Agency for Healthcare Research and Quality (AHRQ) research, the following statistics represent the patients who die while hospitalized.

- 32 percent of all deaths in the United States in 2007 were inpatient hospital deaths.
- The inpatient death rate in 2007 was 1.9 percent. However, these hospital stays ending in death were responsible for 5.1 percent ($17.6 billion) of all hospital inpatient costs.
- Average hospital costs for a stay ending in death were $23,000, about 2.7 times higher than for a patient discharged alive.
- Medicaid had the highest costs for a hospital stay ending in death, $35,000, nearly 5.5 times higher than for a Medicaid patient discharged alive. However, Medicaid had the lowest death rate among payers, 0.8 percent.
- Medicare had 67 percent of all inpatient deaths, with a total cost of over $10 billion, which accounted for 6.9 percent of all Medicare inpatient costs.

- Approximately 12 percent of all inpatient deaths were for elective admissions, with a death rate of 0.9 percent.
- The leading principal diagnosis for inpatient death cases was septicemia, which was the principal diagnosis for 15 percent of all deaths; 17 percent of patients with septicemia died in the hospital. Other leading causes of inpatient death included stroke, pneumonia, myocardial infarction, congestive heart failure, and malignancies.[10]

Some patients die in hospitals simply because their medical conditions leave them with nowhere else to safely go. Others die there because they have given no other explicit instructions about end-of-life preferences, or because familial wishes cause extended stays and extensive treatments. Some even pass on there because there is no coordinated way to move them to a different care setting for a more peaceful departure. Regardless of the reasons, it is clear that the full one third of Americans who die in hospitals do not need to or would not want to die there. If given a choice well in advance, and if properly consulted about their conditions and the options for passing on, patients routinely opt for a much different fate.

Yet, EOL care is a highly sensitive subject. Discussions are not easily or lightly had, especially with the poly-chronics whose mortality daily stares them in the face. Physicians, who one might think of as a good source of feedback and advice, often prefer to be at arm's length from these discussions. Theirs is to heal, not to discuss the failure to heal. Patients are thus often left without an effective means by which to plan for their own desires to be carried out in the event of their demise. This can lead to someone else making what are sometimes emotionally charged decisions.

There are a number of potential ways that patients can communicate their wishes to care givers, ranging from do-not-resuscitate agreements dealing with specific and singular points of care, to legal advance directives and more broad and sweeping advance care planning (ACP). In some states, such as

Oregon and West Virginia, physician orders for life-sustaining treatment (POLST) are used.[11] All have their uses and nuances. For instance, an advance directive is often a long legal document, full of typical legalese, and may only partially cover the specificity of a patient's long-term care goals and wishes. By contrast, advance care planning is more comprehensive, and may deal with many aspects of care as a patient lives through many stages of disease progression. And POLST documents accompany the patient's medical record and augment the ACPs.

In order to effectively establish attention to EOL care, you should first consult with your attorney on the specific state laws and regulations that govern your patients and the expression of their wishes, since state laws can differ significantly. Once you have done this and understand fully what can and cannot be achieved in the advanced planning of patient care, you should strive to use both palliative and EOL planning as part of the PCCN program. This planning should be as comprehensive as possible, using trained facilitators to lead both patients and caregivers through the EOL planning process.

Example: Gunderson Health System

Perhaps the best example of a long-term and successful program in the United States is in Wisconsin at Gunderson Lutheran Medical Center in La Crosse.[12] Gunderson has two related programs, one of which is known as Respecting Choices, which began in 1993 as a community-engaging effort to reduce the frustration, angst, and fear of planning for one's own death. Programs copied from Gunderson's model have shown up in other states like Minnesota and countries like Singapore.

Gunderson's goals for its ACP programs are as follows:

■ To provide qualified assistance to individuals in making informed healthcare choices appropriate to their stage of illness and their goals, values, and beliefs;

- To create plans that will be effective in providing personalized care—plans that ensure that individuals receive *all* the treatment and *only* the treatment they desire; and
- To develop strategies to communicate these choices to those who need to know (e.g., healthcare agent, family, physician, other healthcare providers).[13]

Gunderson learned all along the journey to its currently successful and ongoing program. As Gunderson's community worked through the education processes, they discovered many of the issues related to the implementation process. This includes educating both physicians and patients in the development of realistic and doable ACPs in order for patients and families to be happy and clinicians comfortable in the ACP execution. For example, a patient's home or living situation may not allow for the kind of EOL scenario a patient might prefer. He/she may have unrealistic expectations of caregivers or resources, desire outcomes that are unattainable, or even request services that are considered immoral or illegal (e.g., euthanasia or physician-assisted suicide). Or, facilities and resources may simply not exist to execute the patient's wishes exactly as they would like. For instance, the patient may want to receive all his/her EOL care in their home, yet their disease state may require hospitalization as their disease progresses but before they are ready to pass peacefully on. Thus a sort of ACP coordination and regimen is required to ensure that the processes that a patient desires can be implemented effectively and according to their wishes. And lastly, whenever possible, families should be intimately involved in the ACP planning process.

Importantly, patients must have records that can follow them throughout their care interventions. At Gunderson, this meant modifying the electronic medical record (EMR) to allow for the ACPs to be included (Gunderson also adopted the aforementioned POLST paradigm, which records the legal preferences of the patient). This allowed patient wishes to be followed anywhere in the Gunderson Catchment area.

To compensate for a need for resources to work with patients (and relieve physicians of the responsibility), Gunderson created advance care planning facilitators. Their responsibility is to engage patients, families, physicians, and other community resources in the necessities of proper planning, and ensure that realistic and reasonable advance care plans are developed such that physicians and families can comply. These are part of both their palliative care model and an EOL care model. Other resources in the patient's care continuum are part of the ACP discussion, such that a communal knowledge and appreciation for the importance of patient wishes is obtained and sustained.

Data on the ACP and POLST programs shows great success. Per a study of 2007–2008 patient deaths, 90 percent of adults who passed on in local Gunderson County facilities had an ACP in place; 99 percent have a care plan in an accessible medical record; and those care plans were followed as prescribed 99 percent of the time.[14] While not the specific goal of the program, the ancillary benefits of reduced cost (via reductions in unnecessary or unwanted treatments) and improved patient experience are beginning to show up in the analysis.

Integrating EOL and Palliative Care in the PCCN Model

In order to integrate EOL and palliative care into the PCCN framework, there will need to be a commitment on the part of physicians and other clinicians, hospital management, and the affected patients and families. While the communal resources may be of lesser value to patients in the hospital (where they are already receiving ongoing care and constant supervision), the PCCN care circles can still support and encourage their patients. The PCCN care circle can also become immediately engaged as patients leave the hospital and move to other care settings, such as home, hospice, or nursing facilities. Furthermore, the PCCN communal resources can remain as the patient's advocates and ensure that the goals of the care strategies align with and are promoted by the EOL and palliative care process. Indeed, the EOL and palliative care processes should be part of a patient's care strategy once the need for those services is recognized (more on this later). Lastly and importantly, the PCCN can offer a smooth transition to alternate care settings, expanding the reach of these services beyond the traditional hospital and hospice settings. Thus, the PCCN should serve as an extension of palliative services, offering greater resource support, care, spiritual, and monitoring assistance, and flexibility in care settings.

The Gunderson example demonstrates several key points relevant to the PCCN integration discussion. First, it demonstrates the power of the community to come together around a singular, important, albeit painful, subject. It also demonstrates that even players who might be hurt by change (e.g., physicians who offer fewer expensive treatments and procedures) can come together to support the greater good of a program like Respecting Choices, or the PCCN.

How does palliative and EOL care fit into the PCCN concept? The PCCN can do the following:

- Bring families and others into the care process.
- Allow for broader discussion of the patient's health over a longer period of time.
- Allow for more spiritual and holistic interventions from familiar, communal resources and organizations.
- Promote the discussion of care preferences through an ongoing relationship with poly-chronic patients, so as to promote early decision making in EOL matters.
- Reduce the need for government intervention and mandates by promoting self-management, self-determination, and freedom of choice.

To implement a palliative program within your PCCN, you will need to refer back to the care strategies mapping sessions discussed earlier in this text. Using tools similar to those already used, such as swimlane maps and even simulations, and incorporating representatives of all the resources involved in palliative and EOL care, map the palliative and EOL care process flows, the tasks of proper care, the number and type of patient interactions and interventions, and the resources required for each process step. From this, you can begin to determine the resources from the communal pool that are available and capable of handling various specialized tasks. You can use a small simulation or flow-mapping software to experiment and tweak your care processes and resource allocations to match resource availability, patient preferences, care locations, and even legal requirements. (Arena software, from Rockwell Automation, allows you to build a quick simulation model using a Visio or other flowchart as its basis.) Using your newly found expertise in task optimization, develop workable and fully integrated programs that maximize the utilization of all available resources and optimize the cost and quality of care delivery.

Importantly, you will want to ensure that any and all resources utilized are properly trained in palliative and EOL care concepts, such that their support is made most effective. If you intend to use PCCN communal resources for these tasks, you may need additional training staff beyond the PCCN trainer if he/she is not an expert in palliative care or special training programs.

Lastly, you will want to consider the legal ramifications of your programs. Consult with the hospital's attorney(s) or independent counsel on any state regulations or "witches behind the trees" of your program and the involvement of communal resources. This is particularly important in the management of information related to patient wishes within the care circles. Ensure that your processes have been vetted by legal counsel to protect all participants from legal issues and opportunism.

PCCN Process Evolution and Palliative and EOL Care

In the previous text on dynamic capacity management, I spoke of "evolution" in the context of process change over time. Therein, I described how processes are altered over time, either through our own efforts or through changes to external variables. So, for instance, our efforts to reduce some process cycle time may result in a long-term change to the system as it evolves toward a more optimal state. Similarly, patient acuities in the emergency department (ED) will change over time, impacting key metrics like length of stay (LOS). If these changes negatively impact our system performance, the system will also need to change in order to maintain improvements or continue toward optimization. Evolution thus requires our processes to be under constant evaluation as the internal and external variables impact our systems.

Similarly, the poly-chronics in our PCCNs will change over time. Volumes of participating patients and physicians will change (hopefully growing due to the great successes we see), and patients' health will change as they improve, age, or deteriorate over time.

Thus the PCCN and the care circles will need to evolve as patients enter the EOL phase of their lives and need palliative services during specific phases of their disease progression. Care circles may evolve to include more clergy and a wider group of friends as patients near the end of life. Alternatively, care circles may begin to tighten as families of patients near their end of life find that they prefer a smaller and less-integrated group. End of life can also bring the need for privacy, intimacy, and greater or newfound spirituality, all of which should be respected.

Similarly, as patients enter into particularly difficult periods of their disease progressions, additional palliative resources may need to be brought forward into the care circles, such that the proper resources are involved in the PCCN and not left to siloed and unsupported activities.

This, in turn, requires three major activities of the PCCN management team:

- Constant updates to patient preferences and wishes
- Constant evaluation of the PCCN, its resource allocations, and organizational and operational structures
- Ongoing infrastructure alterations as the needs of the community evolve over time

The PCCN managers and primes must all be willing to allow for the changes to the care circles as the needs and focuses of the patients change over time. For instance, some patients who have not involved clergy in the care circle may suddenly have a spiritual need as their mortality becomes more evident through increased pain or suffering from disease progression. Likewise, nonhospital palliative services may require the alteration of care circle resource task requirements, or even changes to the structure of the care circle of a given patient. These alterations are part of the PCCN evolution and should be welcomed, not resisted. Otherwise, the PCCN will fail to serve the patients as desired, or silos of care may develop that exclude important elements of the PCCN's value.

The management team therefore must be willing to allow for the changes within the community to reflect in the resource allocations and infrastructure of the PCCN and its offerings, including "blowing up and starting from scratch" when the existing structure cannot meet communal requirements, or when the focus of the PCCN is altered significantly.

Evolution *will* happen in your community, particularly if your PCCN includes palliative and EOL care, so welcome it as much as you plan for it.

The Payor Role

Cost is a very touchy subject when it comes to EOL care. Discussions of medical expenses can seem insensitive and cold-blooded when the elderly, poor, and dying are involved. Yet payors do and will continue to play a large role in the financial implications of care during these difficult periods of life. Care should be taken into account for patient preferences as well as the patient's condition when analyzing and evaluating the costs of advanced treatments, palliative, and EOL care.

Though some, including famed lecturers at Dartmouth, have cited regional variances in care costs, the study of the cost of end-of-life care should be taken with a great deal of consideration of the patient condition in mind. Neuberg comments on Dartmouth's 2008 Atlas and its authors when he states the following:

> Wennberg et al. did not measure or adjust for severity, as they believe their model involves measures of provider efficiency and performance that minimize the chance that variations in the care can be explained by differences in the severity of patients' illnesses.
>
> They further state that "by looking at care delivered during fixed intervals of time before death, we can say with assurance that the prognosis of all the patients in the cohort is identical—all were dead after the interval of observation." From a clinical perspective, this retrospective logic misrepresents the prognostic and therapeutic uncertainty that we must contend with in real time. What matters in providing care are the apparent severity and treatability of illness at the time of patient evaluation, not at the time of death.
>
> Thus, the fairest way to assess treatment efficacy and efficiency is to assemble cohorts with

comparable disease burdens at time zero, and then track subsequent outcome and resource utilization in survivors and decedents. In contrast, looking back at fixed intervals before death identifies patients whose condition at time zero varies markedly, more so for longer intervals, and this alone could explain substantial variation in resource allocation. Furthermore, end-of-life spending does not reveal whether a provider's efforts effectively saved, extended, or improved any lives. For example, end-of-life costs cannot distinguish a patient who lives 24 months (on whatever treatment) from a sicker patient who would have lived 12 months on the same regimen, but instead survives 24 months with more aggressive care. In retrospect, care is viewed not a means to improve health, but as an accumulation of expenses that failed to prevent an inevitable death.

End-of-life spending would be a more straightforward indicator of provider performance if diseases progressed and presented in a uniform fashion, but this is not the case. In patients with fatal congestive heart failure (CHF), at least one third die unexpectedly, whereas most others experience progressive CHF requiring episodic hospital treatment before their demise. By the (Dartmouth Atlas) authors' method, if my practice randomly sees a greater proportion of inexpensive sudden deaths, we will be rated undeservedly as more efficient than others who see a higher rate of costly progressive CHF. However, if we prevent sudden deaths by implanting more defibrillators, we will see and treat more progressive CHF (because of the competing risks of these outcomes), and our efficiency rating will decline. If we offer such patients greater access to life-extending procedures like biventricular pacing or cardiac transplantation, our rating will plummet further, because they are sick enough that some will not survive beyond the measured interval after costly treatment, regardless of how appropriately or expeditiously it was provided.[15]

This tells us that the generalization of patient needs and care requirements cannot be treated lightly. If for no other reason than the complexity of their illnesses, poly-chronics are very different from one another, each requiring their own care strategy. So, just as one care strategy is only appropriate for one patient, so too one EOL ACP is appropriate for only one patient. While clinical decisions can be regimented to a certain degree, based on best practices, it would be folly to assume that EOL care can be equally as regimented. Patients will have their own wishes and desires for the end of their lives, and those wishes may change over time as their disease progresses (or doesn't), or other life-changing events occur. To assume that a patient's ACP will be the same before and after the death of a lifelong spouse would be as risky as saying that one's attitude about life will be the same before and after a diagnosis of terminal cancer.

Therefore, payors will need to develop flexibility in the acceptance of ACP and EOL planning and the decisions made by patients and their families. Respecting Choice is not just a name of the infamous Gunderson program, it should be a mantra for our attitude about EOL decisions. This should be especially true for government payors, since they will deal with more of the EOL patients than any other. Without flexibility and respect for choices, patients and their caregivers will push back on the reasonable use of the very delivery systems that can best control costs, quality, and system capacity. Government payors should therefore strive to stay away from regimentation of rules and payment structures for this very sensitive period of a citizen's life.

Government and EOL Planning

This of course brings us to the issue of government interventions in these decisions. As Michael Leavitt, former secretary of the Department of Health and Human Services puts it, "despite the mounting cost of Medicare, the treatment decisions of patients need to be left to these patients, their families, and the health professionals who provide the care rather than to the government ... My worry is that if too few of us make the decisions voluntarily, someday government officials, with their backs to the financial wall, will feel that they have no alternative but to begin making decisions about the care that people with advanced illness will and will not receive. It happens in other countries now."[16]

The heated discussions over "death panels" within ObamaCare demonstrate how passionately people feel about government intrusion in the most personal and private of decisions. But most would likely agree that, if given the choice, they would prefer to make EOL and ACP decisions themselves, with their own dignity, personal preferences, and health status in mind.

Government's role should instead be in the legal and cultural protection of the parties involved in the PCCN and the critical decisions of EOL and palliative care. The risk is not in the following of patient orders, but the legalities of those orders and the threats to those who follow them. For every well-intentioned care decision there is at least one trial lawyer quite willing to cash in on an unfortunate situation. Thus if it is to have a role, government should shield the PCCN and its resources from liability in the care of patients willing to participate, including those making critical decisions for how they want their lives to end. I firmly believe that responsible, informed people can make responsible decisions most of the time. There will always be those situations wherein families, patients, or lawyers prove unreasonable and obstinate. And for these scenarios, protections need to be granted to those genuinely trying to help the community and its patients.

Summary

The PCCN fits easily into the palliative, hospice, EOL, and ACP care models (and vice versa). Indeed, the care circle concept works well with the notion of a coordinated approach to care delivery for patients in the latter stages of earthly life. With proper training and education, each patient could and should direct their own EOL care in cooperation with their physicians and caregivers, close family, and clergy. With this as part of the PCCN's overall holistic strategy toward attaining higher quality and patient gratification at a lower cost, ACP and EOL planning and care will become integrated into the longitudinal care strategies for all patients, especially our poly-chronics.

Endnotes

1. www.nice.org.uk/nicemedia/pdf/csgspmanual.pdf, p. 24.
2. World Health Organization, "WHO Definition of Palliative Care," http://www.who.int/cancer/palliative/definition/en/ (accessed March 2010).
3. American Hospital Association, *FY 2002–2009 AHA Annual Survey Databases* (Chicago, IL: Health Forum, an American Hospital Association affiliate, 2010).
4. Cicely Saunders International, "About Palliative Care," http://www.cicelysaundersfoundation.org/about-palliative-care (accessed March 2010).
5. J. Hinton, "The Physical and Mental Distress of the Dying," *Quarterly Journal of Medicine* 32 (1963): 1–21.
6. J. Hinton, "The Progress of Awareness and Acceptance of Dying Assessed in Cancer Patients and Their Caring Relatives," *Palliative Medicine* 13, no. 1 (1999): 19–35.
7. A. Cartwright, "Changes in Life and Care in the Year before Death 1969–1987." *Journal of Public Health Medicine* 13, no. 2 (1991): 81–87.

8. Cicely Saunders International, "About Palliative Care," http://www.cicelysaundersfoundation.org/about-palliative-care (accessed March 2010).

9. Y. Zhao and W. Encinosa, "The Costs of End-of-Life Hospitalizations, 2007," AHRQ publications, November 2009, revised April 2010.

10. Ibid.

11. An excellent legal summary of the history of advanced care planning, POLST, and other tools can be found at the U.S. Health and Human Services website: C. Sabatino, "Advance Directives and Advance Care Planning: Legal and Policy Issues," Office of Disability, Aging and Long-Term Care Policy, Washington, DC, October 2007, http://aspe.hhs.gov/daltcp/reports/2007/adacplpi.pdf (accessed March 2010).

12. An overview of the Gunderson program can be found in B. Hammes, *Having Your Own Say: Getting the Right Care When It Matters Most*, Center for Health Transformation, 2012.

13. Ibid, p. 27.

14. Hammes, *Having Your Own Say,* 16.

15. G. Neuberg, "The Cost of End-of-Life Care: A New Efficiency Measure Falls Short of AHA/ACC Standards," *Circular of Cardiovascular Quality Outcomes* 2 (2009): 127–133.

16. Hammes, *Having Your Own Say,* xxv–xxviii.

Chapter 12

Final Thoughts

The vision and purpose of the poly-chronic care network (PCCN) is a new business and care model for the most difficult and costly patients in our system: poly-chronics. These patients need more than the traditional care models can provide, even though our care systems are staffed by dedicated and hard-working clinicians. The current systems are simply incapable of the kind of transformation required to salvage our healthcare system from future economic and capacity constraints. This is what the PCCN can bring forth.

Yet, while the idea is seen as great by everyone who hears of it, the "devil is in the details." As with any new care model or business concept, there will inevitably be glitches, hurdles, and troubles all along the way toward successful implementation. We've already discussed a few of these, and they and others deserve additional consideration. The main obstacles to success include the following:

- Reimbursement models. The fee-for-service (FFS) model has both benefits and disadvantages. But for the PCCN it carries an especially high price and many disadvantages. In order for the PCCN to thrive, something closer to a capitated model is needed to allow for both flexibility in care provision and needed constraints on utilization. Without a capitated model, many will worry for the "safety of their own oxen" and try to prevent any loss of reimbursement revenue. Yet, if the PCCN is established in an employed physician environment, reimbursement issues become infinitely easier to manage since the built-in incentives of FFS overutilization and revenue maintenance are eliminated, leaving us to chase much more meaningful and important metrics than volume.

■ However, since the poly-chronics are difficult and complex patients, a capitated model isn't easily developed either. Difficult questions remain, such as:

– How does one develop a single, annual payment for a patient with chronic obstructive pulmonary disease (COPD) as well as asthma and other heart problems?

– How do we alter the payment schemes as a patient progresses through the inevitable cycles of the disease and their condition deteriorates over time?

– Are we to mind the stages of disease progression and associate each with a capitated model?

■ How do we account for variations in the cost of resources across the country?

Furthermore, we know there are risks in the receipt and dispersion of funds to the various care providers. Yet, how will pricing remain competitive in a relatively uncompetitive marketplace with limited resources and expertise? And who sets the prices for each service, the sum of which should be the capitation amount?

Fortunately, the next book in the series will answer these questions. As the model takes hold we will begin to get a sense of the true costs of healthcare delivery in this new environment, and how these costs are reduced or altered over time. Furthermore, we intend to derive actual *activity-based costs* for a great number of poly-chronic care processes and tasks, so as to more precisely gauge the true cost of care provision.

Additionally, as we examine the longer-term outcomes of PCCN implementation, we will be able to evaluate the resource, infrastructure, and time requirements of various PCCN configurations, sizes, and scales. Through this we will learn how variances in cost and resource requirements can be mitigated and the total cost of delivery better managed.

■ Legalities. As mentioned before, for every caring and committed communal resource group there is a least one opportunistic trial lawyer waiting for a chance to cash in. PCCN patients, communal resources, supporting hospitals and physician practices, and the PCCN management team will therefore necessarily need to come to agreement on the limitations of their responsibilities and liabilities, and the protections necessary to ensure the ongoing cooperation of the community and the operations of the PCCN. Patients who opt in should of course be protected from mistreatment, abuse, and intentional harm. But short of that, patients will have to agree that the purpose of the PCCN is the support of the care that will enable them to have the opportunity for a higher quality of life. And this will include the understanding that the communal resources that will provide some of their care are as human as they are. Thus, the resources of the PCCN should be immune from potential litigation as they perform their acts of selfless generosity and kindness. Just as one would not think of suing a nun for her work in caring for the dying in the early days of U.S. hospitals, one should not imagine the need or desire to litigate against resources in a PCCN relationship. Mistakes will happen, as in any system. But communal resources are not, and should not be expected to be, perfect. And while perfection in quality care is a laudable goal, communal resources should not be quickly blamed for failure to achieve it. Theirs is to serve the community and do what they can with their God-given gifts, not to worry about legal attacks for their actions.

■ Thus, governments at various levels should strive to protect the communal resources and others involved in the PCCN from vindictive and unwarranted litigation while protecting patients from intentional harm and the most egregious and intentional violations of trust and confidence. This should not be a difficult balance to strike with reasonable and good-spirited people with common goals and passions.

■ Implementation and logistics. No, this isn't easy. The PCCN requires a lot of effort, synergies, passion, and time. It requires a well-considered strategy for roll-out within the physician and patient communities, an integration plan for the various communal groups and resources to be deployed, an ongoing training plan and regimen, specific training materials for each disease type or grouping, ongoing hospital management support and community outreach, and technology integration (to the degree required). And, of course, technology integration means technology rollout and ongoing training.

■ All this means that, unless you are stepping out in a very small way, you'll need some dedicated and passionate resources to get your PCCN started and running effectively. Yet even after you cross the initial hurdles, your work is not done. Whether you look internally or externally, ensure that your effort is staffed well for the job required, and commit the financial and support resources necessary to see the program succeed.

Once running smoothly, your PCCN will need ongoing "care and feeding." The training of new resources, retraining and updates of existing resources, patient placement and care circle creation and alteration, augmenting the resource pool, and the evolution of the PCCN and care circle infrastructures will require a very fluid management approach and constant management support (financial and otherwise). Without this, your PCCN will fall behind the needs of the community, and risk long-term failure.

■ Ebb and flow. Perhaps the most difficult part of the aforementioned ongoing "care and feeding" is the recognition that some of the resources will leave and new ones will be required. As in any organization in which volunteers are heavily utilized, and wherein there are few "sticks" with which to enforce work requirements and resource demands, the PCCN will require constant monitoring and the replacement of resources. Some will leave voluntarily, while others will need to be asked to leave because of failure of performance. As with any organization, you get the bad with the good, and only your ongoing training, motivation, and recruitment will ensure a supply of engaged resources and patients. Thus there will be an inevitable ebb and flow to the resources in your PCCN. Three to five years after it begins, the resource pool might be entirely different than it was one year into implementation. Resources and even entire groups will leave due to one reason or another. But, nearly always, others will lie in waiting for an opportunity to help their fellow man.

Indeed, this ebb and flow should be encouraged rather than discouraged. Changes in the composition of the PCCN will mean new and fresh enthusiasm, the "flushing out" of the tired, frustrated, or unenthused, and the constant introduction to new ideas for improvements. While certainly more work for the PCCN manager (or whatever title that role takes), turnover is both a harsh reality and a positive for the ongoing improvement and effectiveness of the PCCN.

■ Motivation. Since you don't have sticks to go with your carrots, your skill in motivating volunteers is important. You will have to motivate not only community resources but physicians and their office staff. It is inevitable that, even with the best of plans and designs, there will be errors, dropped tasks, missed handoffs, and other stumbles. Communication may break down despite the use of the social–clinical networking (SCN) platform and other technologies, and resources may struggle to find a comfort level that allows them to act on physician directives.

Yet, like a good coach working with a "building season" team, your inspiration and enthusiasm will carry the day. Regardless of what methods you use, enabling the PCCN with continuous energy and enthusiasm for the goals is critical to the long-term success. Supported by the SCN and other communication technologies, the PCCN manager and other PCCN management team members can inspire, cajole, and infuse passion into the entire community of care.

■ Finding the cost justifications. I add cost justifications to the list of potential challenges not because it is remarkably difficult, but because it is critical to the success of the program. Without a solid and sustainable justification for any and all expenditures, there is a low likelihood of long-term support from management and viability for the kind of growth and evolution that may be desired. As mentioned, justifications can come from a long list of potential benefits, from reduced unnecessary readmissions and emergency department (ED) visits to an increase in the percentage of task compliance to the general health and well-being of the entire community.

All these and perhaps other pitfalls await you. But, then again, you should expect that from the implementation of an entirely new business model for these complex patients, especially if you try to do it without external assistance. The value of the PCCN will, in the end, far outweigh the pain of the process.

Imagine

Imagine the PCCN in your community, working with and for your most difficult patients who are connected as never before. Imagine involving the community organizations and volunteers in your area in working with the physicians and patients to provide better care and population health outcomes. Picture friends and families directly and fully engaged and integrated into the care of loved ones; care provided through large integrated teams rather than siloed and frustrated clinicians; and the gratification of all participants increasing at the same time the cost and resource strain goes down. Imagine physicians corralling myriad communal resources into a sophisticated care strategy to help patients deal with their diseases, promoting personal responsibility and the gratification of the smallest successes, and increasing their own capacity to care for more patients without extra work. Imagine your community, its care providers, hospitals, and communal resources working together as one entity to significantly and permanently impact the Five Pillars of healthcare.

It's not so hard to envision if you follow the concepts, strategies, and guidelines suggested herein. It won't be easy, yet it is anything but impossible.

Closing Comment

I am sure that I haven't thought of everything. As this text goes to print, there will surely arise good reasons for a second edition and additional volumes in the series beyond what is already planned. Stories of successes and challenges, dramatic impacts and population health improvement outcomes, financial and reimbursement models, and new implementation ideas will hopefully erupt.

In the meantime, I sincerely hope to have added to the thought leadership in the industry by sharing a bold new concept that could help turn the corner on the cost, quality, capacity, access, and gratification of the care of poly-chronics.

God speed, and best wishes for a successful PCCN implementation.

Epilogue—The Latent Community

Kenji's mother-in-law had been the unwitting source of tremendous inspiration and creativity. Though she was released from the hospital after a few scary moments nearly a year ago, Kenji knew she would have few real resources now that she was home. Heck, she shouldn't have had to go to the ED in the first place … there should have been a way to prevent the entire incident from happening. Given her multiple conditions, and the limited time he and his wife had to personally care for her, Kenji suspected that she would have been readmitted soon after he discharge if something didn't change … something needed to "break the cycle." He knew that he had to find a way to get her more localized care than she was getting. Someone should have been able to intervene sooner, before her condition got to the point of "no return" and a trip to the doctor's office or the ED became inevitable. And maybe that someone should not have been her doctor's office. After all, he's a Physician not an onsite nursemaid! He wouldn't have had time to make a housecall even if he'd wanted to. And though Dr. Goodman had a Care Manager in his office to try to better manage patients like Nana, they couldn't be out in the community all the time checking on patients like her. All they could do was phone her periodically and hope she was telling the truth about how she felt, whether she was taking her meds, etc. Most of the time, Nana either didn't answer or simply fibbed, so as to avoid causing an issue. But Kenji also knew that neither he (personally) nor the hospital could afford another nurse, out in the community seeing patients, even if that nurse were shared amongst many patients.

Kenji's revelation came through an interaction with Meals on Wheels. They'd found Nana's name from the Case Managers at the hospital, and called Kenji's wife to ask about the service. Once Kenji realized the potential for onsite visits, the epiphany happened. There was an entire community out there waiting and wanting to help, if they could only be engaged. Like a small army awaiting orders from the Generals, there was a vast pool of volunteers, Nana's fellow church members, local civic groups, and social clubs like her husband had belonged to before he passed on, whose mantra was community service. All Kenji needed to do was coordinate them all.

In retrospect, the selling of the idea at this hospital and to the community Physicians was harder than the initial implementation. But this time, the hospital CFO was on board and extremely supportive. He liked the idea so much, the CFO made it Kenji's full time job and replaced him with not one but two new IEs in his old department!

The hospital had explored "remote monitoring" with the Physician's offices once before, but decided it was difficult to justify financially, and too difficult and expensive to manage logistically. All that technology sounds nice until the patient can't use the equipment or it malfunctions, or it's used incorrectly. Nana, as a good example, wasn't quite "sophisticated" enough for a "newfangled" device in her house. But Kenji's new idea, a "community of care," was different. Yes, they'd need a little software, and some dedicated resources. But the CFO was all too aware of the reimbursement issues associated with their high percentage of unnecessary readmissions, as well as all the unnecessary ED visits. States like Oregon were already starting to deny reimbursement for some ED visits, and the CFO feared that the State legislature would take up similar measures to save Medicaid dollars. As he considered all the "downstream" cost ramifications of the improper use of the hospital's capacity, from misallocations of resources to ED capacity to waits for an ICU bed, he quickly got on board with the Kenji's idea and became its biggest champion.

Kenji's idea quickly took shape, and, thanks to some visioning from the IT department and Case Management, the necessary social-clinical networking software was acquired and running within ninety days. Within a few weeks of starting, Kenji got support from the Lions Club, pastors of three large churches and their congregations, and several local community service agencies and volunteer groups. Once that happened, the hospital agreed to sponsor and house the necessary full-time staff. A retired nurse became a trainer for the community's many new resources, costing only a minimal amount.

Patients began to enroll, slowly at first, and then in increasing numbers as word spread among the Physicians in the community. Patient satisfaction scores began to rise, and comments from families and many communal resources were nearly universally positive.

Just a little over a year later, Nana was being seen twice, sometimes three times a week. And that didn't include weekend visits from Kenji's wife. She, as Nana's "primary community care resource," checked updates on her health and condition left by her "Care Circle" from work, knowing precisely when the community's resources would see her mother. She could monitor her progress, and periodically send out kudos to her new circle of caregivers. Of course, Nana's Physician was tickled to be able to get quick and easy-to-peruse updates on his patients, which helped him better manage his workload while seeing more patients than ever before. And, sure enough, the CFO was beginning to see tangible changes in the "frequent flyers" in the ED that so plagued his bottom line.

As Kenji left his new, fourth floor office (with a big window!), he smiled at his new title, "Director of Community Resource Services." As he headed towards the elevators past already darkened offices, he thought of the whirlwind the last year had been. What a change from his previous frustrations! There was still work to be done in the hospital, and lots of it. The ED was just beginning to see dramatic improvements from the work he'd started there years ago. But finally all the senior managers had "seen the light" of the value of Industrial Engineers in healthcare, and now continually looked to expand their ranks and promote them to strategic positions like Kenji's.

As he pressed the "down" button, he chuckled as the thought, "Now about that whole world peace thing."

Index

Page numbers followed by f indicate figure
Page numbers followed by t indicate table

advantages of, 63–64
discharge and care transitions
case, 187–189
example of use case, 184–187
in PCCN infrastructure, 176–177
as place for educational
materials, 182
as required technology, 14–15
using, 178
Social constraints, 70
Space, proximity of, 62
Specialists, physician, 157–158, 221
Standardized work, 90
Structured deployment, 7
Students, 2
Sub-PCCN, 23
Swimlane mapping, 76–78, 77f

T

Task allocations, engineering, 7
Tasks
allocation of, 139
classification of, 79–80
and resource consideration,
80–89
Technology, 63–64, 128
Technology infrastructure, 13–16. *see
also* Connectivity; Social-
clinical network (SCN)
about, 175
chronic disease management
system, 177–178, 192–193
costs of implementation, 195–197
health information exchange, 16,
177, 190–192
population modeling and
prediction, 15–16
resources and, 197–199
simulation, 15, 189–190

simulation software, 177
virtual monitoring, 15, 178,
193–194
Trainers, 11, 160–161, 204
Training
and marketing materials,
204–205
for successful PCCN, 126–129
Travel cost, 204
Tye, Joe, 117, 128, 131, 167, 203

U

UK National Health Service, 30
USA healthcare spending, 30–31
U.S. privacy regulations, PCCN and,
24–27

V

Variability, interdependencies and,
87
Variance
impact on capacity, 88–89
resource and capacity, 102–103
Variation, 81–82
Virtual monitoring (VM), 15, 160,
179, 193–194
VM. *see* Virtual monitoring (VM)
Volunteer organizations, 123
Volunteers, 6, 9, 166–167, 220,
249–250

Y

YMCA. *see* Y's
Youth, health and wellness issues
of, 129
Y's, 2, 6, 8, 51, 110
Yunus, Muhammad, 170